DECODING JINGDONG

www.royalcollins.com

DECODING JINGDONG

THE SECRET TECHNOLOGY BEHIND CHINA'S E-COMMERCE GIANT

JD R&D SYSTEM

Books Beyond Boundaries

ROYAL COLLINS

DECODING JINGDONG

JD Research and Development System

First English Edition 2020
By Royal Collins Publishing Group Inc.
BKM ROYALCOLLINS PUBLISHERS PRIVATE LIMITED
www.royalcollins.com

Original Edition © Publishing House of Electronics Industry
All rights reserved.

Copyright © Royal Collins Publishing Group INC.
Groupe Publication Royal Collins INC.
BKM ROYALCOLLINS PUBLISHERS PRIVATE LIMITED

Headquarters: 550-555 boul. René-Lévesque O Montréal (Québec) H2Z1B1 Canada
India office: 805 Hemkunt House, 8th Floor, Rajendra Place, New Delhi 110 008

ISBN: 978-1-4878-0062-8

*We are grateful B&R Book Program for the financial assistance
in the publication of this book.*

Contents

DECODING JINGDONG

Preface

A friend working for Jingdong ("JD") sent me a book manuscript on the road JD's technical team took in the past ten years and invited me to write a preface for this book.

As a consumer, I appreciate JD's two major characteristics: qualified products for online shopping and quick service. It took only ten years for JD to rise rapidly and became an e-commerce brand enjoying high popularity among millions of consumers. To build a large-scale service platform with high quality is no easy task, but to establish a trustworthy and dependable e-commerce ecology with scope of services covering the whole country is far more difficult. In reading this book, the readers may catch a glimpse of the efforts made by and persistence of JD's technology team in the last decade.

Being Constantly Persistent over a Decade

Behind the rapid growth of business, there were numerous traps as well as wrong paths in the course of technical advances. Failure or delay in the proper removal of one trap even may lead to bad quality of service, economic loss or brand damage. At every critical moment, the technical team tended to meet the challenge of bypassing these traps.

It's not easy to tackle these challenges. Except for skills and experience, devotion to this industry and team is also needed. Pursuit of the technical architecture is without bounds. A perfect architecture never exists. The technical team should have the spirit of "spending a decade grinding a sword" and be constantly persistent and focused over a decade to solve practical problems in the field of technology, one after another.

Technicians tend to be imperturbable and are rarely exposed to the spotlight, and unlike the products, no grand launch events will be convened for them, but they are real backroom heroes.

The Team Culture Advocating Trust and Inheritance

Behind the high-speed development of large service platforms, there must be a lot of organizational problems, difficulties, and contradictions. A perfect technical architecture does not exist; neither does an absolutely perfect technical organization. The organizational evolution of a technical team is also a process of dynamic development. There is always a solution to a problem if the team adheres to the faith of mutual trust and initiative inheritance.

The technical team always works very hard, but is accompanied by joys and sense of achievement. When a technical team can conquer itself, and building an atmosphere of trust and inheritance, its surrounding environment will be the Promised Land, with talented people joining.

I hope that JD's technical team will grow better and better, and cultivate more and more technical talent, develop more sophisticated technologies and create an even more elegant on-line shopping experiences for billions of customers.

Cofounder & Former CTO of Tencent
Tony Zhang (Zhang Zhidong)
October, 2014

Building the Most Influential Technical Team

Li Daxue

I joined JD in 2008, and witnessed the development history of JD's technical team from 30 people to 4,000 staff and how JD grew from a company specializing in business into a technology-driven company. In the following part, I will narrate what I saw, heard and felt these years based on specific examples.

JD R&D Organizational Structure

JD's technical team currently comprises more than 4,000 members and five research institutes based in Beijing, Shanghai, Shenzhen, Chengdu and Shenyang.

JD's system is complicated, covering the whole process and the whole value chain of the e-commerce business, from the front-end transaction system to the supply chain, storage, distribution, customer service and after-sale service. Except for the system of financial statements, JD has researched and developed all systems on its own. All businesses of JD are operated online. Liu Qiangdong, CEO of JD, only spends one or two months out of a year in China and most of the time abroad, but he can observe all production status or data via the information system. He never missed certain congested link of storage, for example.

JD's information system supports its rapid growth at a rate higher than the industry's average for several consecutive years—the market turnover of year 2013 surpassed RMB 100 billion, reaching RMB 125.5 billion. Within 10 years, JD attained a ten thousand-fold growth on the basis of its information system.

In the middle of year 2013, JD has basically consummated the "four carriages" strategy based on the business of "e-commerce," including e-commerce, logistics platform, technology platform and Internet-based finance. In the aspect of management improvement, organizing ability and organization collaboration, JD is carrying out more beneficial explorations and attempts. It is undergoing a transformation, from an e-commerce company of typical Chinese characteristics to the integrator of the industry chain. And the core of JD's strategy is still technology-driven development.

Adjustment of Organizational Structure: The R&D System is divided into 9 Modules and 4 Platforms

I think the optimization of organizational structure is comparatively important for controlling a team comprising 4,000 members. JD's technical team used to be functionally structured, consisting of Product Department, Research & Development (R&D) Department, Test Department and Operation & Maintenance Department. Nevertheless, when our product lines and projects as well as the number of employees increases, prioritizing may become intricate and more communications are required, thus creating a lot of difficulties for department collaboration.

JD made an adjustment to its technical team and divided the R&D system into 9 modules this year mainly based on the organizational form of accounts and business divisions.

The Cloud Platform and Operation & Maintenance Department, mainly in charge of low-level network services and solving top-level technical architecture-related problems, are platforms providing technical supports. Meanwhile, they also conduct researches on unified R&D tools including logs, supervisory control, workflow engine, etc. These tools can improve the efficiency of other R&D departments, and help them avoid repeating module development. This shows that, functions of these two departments are to provide infrastructures and unified tools and platforms.

The Marketing R&D Department focuses on the purchase and sales system which is primarily engaged in online marketing and acts as the leading drive of our company. We develop 3 major systems for the purchase and sales system. The first one is the transaction system designed to guarantee the stability of transactions and achieve improvement of the web conversion rate and optimize the user experience; the second one is the supply chain system aiming at connection with suppliers and forecast of the order quantity, and many relevant supply chain control measures are also taken in this system; the last one is the open platform which makes the whole supply chain system open to the third parties.

Operation R&D Department targets at the COO system and is responsible for Build to Order system, warehousing system, distribution system and customer service system.

Function R&D Department serves as an internal information management department within the function systems involving the administration, personnel and strategy, and our Finance Department is also included.

Marketing R&D Department, Operation R&D Department and Function R&D Department support all internal businesses and other departments are set up to serve these 3 research & development departments

Big Data Department provides a unified big data technical platform.

The data platform is based on Hadoop for collection, extraction, storage, processing and excavation of unified data, and development of value-added data products. Our search, recommendation system and open data service are all completed in this Department.

Mobile Department is responsible for construction of client applications and mobile innovation and it is a business unit undergoing rapid growth.

Research Institute is a collective term and we have a special department responsible for construction of our research institutes throughout the country.

Moreover, we have one more department like the General Management Department and it is referred to as the Technical Research, Development and Management Department. It is set up to build the management system, covering SQA, PMO, an IT service counter and monitoring and operation around the clock. We have arranged one phone number started with 400. In case of any system problems, the exterior or interior staff can dial this number to access to the processing flow. The operators will take over the problems firstly, and then hand over the problems to the research and development departments if they fail to solve. We put the research and development departments after operators because R&D personnel prefer to write codes rather than directly dealing with problems. Through filtration by the operation department, 80% of system problems are solved in the first procedure.

I think the whole structural adjustment is successful because it has greatly improved the customer satisfaction. The customers had to communicate with numerous departments in the past, but now they just need to contact one department. Target customers of every department are clearly determined, so the major duties of all departments focus on improvement of the customer satisfaction.

We have 9 departments, but in fact the whole R&D team is divided into 3 tiers and 4 platforms:

The first tier is technical platform is mainly based on the Cloud Platform and Operation & Maintenance Department for building a cloud-based technical architecture and supporting all applications on it.

The second tier consists of two segments, one of which is the Big Data Platform. We separate the data and cannot make every application process data. In case that all processes are processing data, the data will be disordered and separated, making it hard to share and circulate the data in the whole enterprise. The other one is the e-commerce open API platform. We build up e-commerce core platforms and provide services via API service approach. This matters a lot to the company with long value chain and complicated operation flows and systems.

The third tier is the Application Platform. With the support by the two tiers mentioned above, it becomes quite convenient to develop specific applications on this platform. Therefore, our Application Platform, website, mobile client application, internal ERP and external ISV development and application can call e-commerce core API, and the corresponding data will enter the big data platform at the same time. Furthermore, these applications can be run on the Application Platform.

At JD, we develop some good practices regarding the enterprise architecture. You can make comparisons and think over the benefits gained from reference to such a model for building our information system. In the past, when we needed to develop a demand, we had to start with the front-end web site, and went through the purchase & sale system, storage and distribution. Due to long value chain, a great deal of communications and coordination were required. Now opening of API makes it easy, and reduces the communication and coupling among various systems. As e-commerce business develops quickly, this model for development of application is more applicable for meeting the rapidly changing demands from business segment.

You may find the logic in these 4 platforms. The bottom tier is our technical architecture for solving the architecture-related problems. The data on it plays a role in data governance and API platform is designed for solving the service management problems. The developments are based on SOA, and chaos will occur when we use certain service, and a governance platform is required to eliminate such chaos. If the focus is kept on these three keys, applications on the Application Platform will be of full varieties and our system logic will be clearer.

IT Management 123: One Vision, Two Highlights and 3 Systems

The theories of MBA or EMBA come from the product lines and front-line workers. These management theories remain immature for today's IT field; thus, we are still probing specific theories for IT management.

First, there must be a vision. A team consisting of dozens of people deepens on personal practicing, a team with hundreds of people on the system and the team comprising thousands of people on a vision. With a vision, the team will be injected with the sense of mission, pride and achievement.

One of two highlights is the culture. When the team becomes stronger, culture and atmosphere are foremost.

Regarding the whole company, whether the senior executives such as Liu or heads of other business segments and whether the atmosphere respecting technology can be shaped up in the company shall be taken into consideration by our general technical leader. I want to create the environment where these experts are respected.

Inside the R&D departments, I propose 3 words: trust, sharing and growth.

Trust can be understood as delegation of powers, which can reduce the communication cost. A trusting atmosphere should be formed between the superior and subordinate or between peers. For instance, the R&D personnel may cause an accident and how will you judge on him? Did he cause the accident on purpose or for innovation? If you go against the procedure, punishment cannot be avoided. However, JD has a rule. We are tolerant of mistakes made due to innovation and no punishment will be imposed. Being tolerant of failures is helpful to form a positive atmosphere within the R&D system, and it is also based on the trust in our employees.

Sharing refers to sharing of the best practices. There must be someone being apt at certain fields in a team comprising 4,000 people. I will let them share such experience with others. We also advocate tolerance of failures and encourage learning lessons from mistakes and gaining experiences. Learning from best practices and mistakes is for sharing experiences and further improvement. Developers write codes every day and may produce certain codes they are proud of. Last year we initiated an activity in which the developers were asked to show their codes. No system was required for these codes and they could be what one has learned from work. This activity was held on Fridays in the afternoon and quite popular. In this way, our programmers may try to write excellent codes and want to imitate other's merits when learning from codes written by others. We have software similar to GitHub, through which the programmers can share their codes. Sharing is critical to the R&D personnel and can help them progress quickly.

As for growth, most of our R&D personnel are young and expect to learn more and improve themselves, so we create a culture of growth within the company and organize trainings for them. JD's technical personnel are subject to a hierarchy ranging from T1 to T6. The technicians at levels of T1 and T2 are fresh graduates or those who have graduated for two or three years but lack of experience. We arrange the technicians at levels of T3 and T4 to give lectures and trainings to them every day to help them grow better. We also engage some teachers from outside to give lectures. For example, a training course for UML was organized several years ago, and produced good effects. Our employees learned some structuring and thinking methods and mastered some tools. We began to provide training courses for R&D managers. Everyone attended with enthusiasm. They made progress, and our efficiency of development and research would be improved and there would be more innovative ideas.

The other one is structure. Many problems existing in the R&D management are related to structure.

When the team members expand by several thousand, special attentions must be paid to the structure. Speaking of the talent structure, it is an echelon-related issue. Talent echelon is of great importance. The lower tires were crowed with talents in the past, and those with levels of T3, T4 and T5 were rare. Thus, we tried to recruit talents via Weibo and received hundreds of CVs. Another effort is also made to improve the talent structure, that is, separation of management from the technology. Previously the technical personnel must be transferred to the management segment to raise their remuneration. Now we mark them off and grade the technicians, thus solving a lot of structure-related problems. The other one is our organizational structure whose adjustment has been mentioned above. It is marked off based on the customer direction and we also achieve great success.

In the end, I would like to talk about 3 systems.

The product system comes first. The experiences created by our company, whether consumer experience, third-party vendor experience, supplier experience or experience of internal business departments, are driven by products. We were exposed to a culture where product managers had the final say. In the past, products were determined by business departments which would tell how to create a product and how it look like, and the product managers noted down and directly requested our R&D personnel to produce. It was wrong. Furthermore, our executives tried to make something good, and may subjectively instruct the design of products based on personal likes and dislikes. This confined the product managers as well. Then the developers thought such design was too cumbersome and the other way was better, so the product manager was confined again. The product managers felt overwhelmed by these three confines like three huge mountains. We have the project managers call the shots rather than the management or the business departments. For instance, every purchase & sales department wants to set the rules for search sorting, but we have an internally established discipline—search rules only serve the conversion rate. The business departments provide suggestions only, so the product managers can be left with spaces to give play to their talent and be responsible for the ultimate user experience. After the product system is built up, we found a product committee and elected standing committee members.

The second one is the architectural system. The architecture is determined by architects instead of the management layer. Managers often consider that they are sharp at their expertise, but they have ceilings (limitations) as well. To have the architects call the shots, we found an architecture committee to determine JD's architecture. Planning, implementation and review of JD's technical architecture are the duties of this architecture committee.

The last one is the management system. This system falls into two aspects. The first aspect is project management. More power is delegated to project managers and a system in which project managers take responsibilities is built. Once a project is approved, the project managers will have strong power over many issues and are directly in charge of the project including schedule, quality, input and output. The Project Department is provided with bonuses and project managers have decision-making powers over the bonus allocation. The R&D personnel's participation in the project and assessment are also decided by the project managers. We have a project management platform on which we know very well about the status of all projects. Moreover, everyone and every task involved in projects can be listed according to personnel, projects and departments, and personnel performance is transparent. Therefore, governance of large teams depends on systems. The second aspect of management system is leadership system. JD's team consisting of 4,000 people covers 12 departments and every department comprises over 300 people. It is not easy job to manage over 300 people. Such difficulty originates from personnel control. It is beyond my capability to control more than 14 people. Both influence and leadership are necessary for personnel control. We are weak in leadership as many technical directors are transferred from experts who tend to apply professional computer languages. Their EQ is generally low, but the leadership system requires high EQ, especially during communications with business departments.

"Management 123" is what I gain from work as well as the concept implemented for our R&D system, and we achieve good effect.

A Vision for the Team: Being the Most Influential Technical Team in China

JD's previous vision is "to make shopping carefree and joyful", but this year it is changed into "to make life carefree and joyful". For a technical R&D team comprising 4,000 people, on the premise that the corporate vision is observed, we proposed a vision more suitable for JD's R&D personnel: "to be the most influential technical team in China". This slogan delighted our R&D personnel. They felt a sense of pride, achievement and mission and thought it relatively tallied with the wish of our engineers. JD inputs more in research and development every year. Among R&D teams in China, our inputs are relatively huge. If such input continues, our R&D personnel will be confident in doing better. Our technicians witnessing continuous improvement of their systems in the process of company development will feel a strong sense of pride.

In a team of 30 people, the leader may be able to practice what he preaches and set an example for others because everyone is watching you and following you, and you must pay attentions to the details. For a team consisting of 300 people, a system should be established or project management at least shall be organized. It is of great importance, or there will be great difficulty in controlling over 300 people. But when the team members reach 4,000,

I think bringing out a vision is necessary. Without the vision, 4,000 people will have varied targets and it is hard to unify them. I would like to highlight the vision of JD's R&D team here: "to be the most influential technical team in China"!

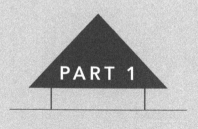

618

June 18 Online Shopping Festival can be taken as the coming-of-age cere-mony of Jingdong ("JD") and a yearly final examination for its research & development ("R&D") system and it provides an opportunity for the leap in the technical framework.

This Chapter will narrate how the team for "618 Battle" carried out expansion and upgrading of core network technology/order system/transac-tion system and how they passed those unforgettable sleepless nights.

- Sales Promotion Notes
- Great Optimization of the Data Center Network
- High-performance Transaction System
- Handling of Large Amount of Orders

CHAPTER 1

In the Heat of the Sun: Sales Promotion Notes

Diary for the Double 11 Event

For this chapter, we interviewed many technicians who were deeply involved in JD's big promotional events held on June 18 and November 11 (Singles' Day) over the years and listened to them tell some incredible stories. However, nearly all of them coincidently used the words "battleground" and "war" to describe their feelings at work in those days and these words could be the most appropriate words summarizing the technical development history of JD in the past decade.

Friday, November 8, 2013, 3 days before the Double 11 Event

"We cannot be defeated this time!" said Fei to us before we got off work before a weekend, speaking with knitted brows and a serious expression. He clenched his fist with one hand and took the orange I gave with the other. "Fruit given out again, *gelivable* (Chinese net slang for "awesome")!"

No one can deny that the Double 11 Event is of great importance. "For netizens, it is a carnival throughout the country; for us, it is a white-hot war. On that very day when all believe that we will sit in front of the computer as usual, we have become warriors wearing golden armor. We are facing powerful enemies in the dark; but we are backed by our dear customers. After the war is over, we are going to share the joy of harvest with them!"

Come on, you were lying in bed and sleeping on November 11 last year!" Xianjun interrupted and brought me back to the real world when I was immersed in happy memories. "Don't talk rot! I placed a huge order through JD at home that day!" I was not on duty on November 11 last year, but I would never forget the scene I saw when I went back to work the following day. Everyone was working hard and sticking to their posts, although they had worked all through the night.

Sunday, November 10, 2013, 1 day before the Double 11 Event

People were coming and going on the subway on the weekend. The most eye-catching were the ads of T-mall and JD on both sides of the subway. A bearded man and a suntanned woman are respectively expressing that "they can't wait for the Double 11 Event" in distinctive ways. When the subway door was opened, the crowd was so impatient that they abruptly pushed me into the subway. At the moment of entering the carriage, I felt a sense of achievement as if I snapped up the goods I desired.

At eight o'clock in the evening, the Victoria conference room was crowded. In this command post with Ma as the commander in chief, everyone was full of spirit and energy and had high morale. Fei was fully bent on breaking his previous record of staying at the battle line for 72 consecutive hours. Obviously, our current system was not the same as used in the past, thus he hardly had a chance to break the record.

Monday, November 11, the very day of the Double 11 Event

This day came. In the morning, I opened my eyes and suddenly found the date has turned into November 11.

I arrived at the office one hour earlier than usual but realized that everybody had already been there. "Long, keep an eye on the online log and the monitoring system," the mission had been assigned before I sat down. Our team members began to elaborately prepare for the war a half a month ago. Such preparations included code optimization, system adjustment and optimization, architecture upgrading, estimation of interface call volume, online log addresses, monitoring, and statistics. We formally ushered in the review on this day.

In November, Beijing had entered into an early winter, but the office was in a heat wave. With the background sounds made by the heaters, everyone was staring on the computer screen. Someone took off his glasses occasionally and wiped the lens with a shirt tail, and then raised his head to fix his eyes on the screen.

"The sales are mounting up again and again!" Youcun shouted out from time to time to remind us that it was a special day; Geng had run back and forth between his office table and the DBA office time after time, and after many runs, we finally saw smiles in his face. Tao encountered the greatest challenge from sales promotion. Various promotion and flash sales events tested not only the system's supporting strength, but also their psychological quality; Shichao was answering the phone without a break to make explanations to various questions, such as why the stock could not be synchronously updated; Honglai was engaged in solving different problems raised by sellers concerning the merchandise line.

At this moment, everyone was very, very, very busy.

Tuesday, November 12, 2013, the day after the Double 11 Event

In the wee hours after the end of the Double 11 Event, many colleagues published posts saying goodbye to the Double 11 Event. Various data such as new-high daily traffic peak, new-high daily order quantity, new-high daily distribution volume, and other data indicated that we had created another miracle.

POP (Platform Open Plan) Seller Client suffered no problems during the Double 11 Event; on November 11, new records were set for daily interface call volume in all system centers; both the seller center and the merchandise center achieved anticipated targets for the core interface call volume and stable and prompt responses were given when dealing with crucial stocks and prices. During the Double 11 Event, 96% of all sellers participated in the sale promotion, and nearly ten million in merchandise was involved in the sale promotion, and the call volume of all interfaces was substantially higher than usual. Various data showed that our system endured the huge test while JD's traffic surged.

Also, a lot of inspiring deeds sprang up on that very day. Xianjun volunteered to stay at the office for an all-night vigil; Fei carried on working overtime until midnight despite fever and the risk that we would be infected; Chen Chuan and Ouyang firmly chose work over a spouse when they were informed of a system alarm after getting off work.

I like a saying in one book very much, "Who you are determines who your companion will be! You believe in dreams and dreams will believe in you!" I am grateful that I am accompanied by such a team, and I'm sure that this year's Double 11 Event will not just be an end, but a new start.

During the next Double 11 and the next decade…May we be together forever and ever!

The War Regarding the Big Data Platform

During the Double 11 Event in 2013, one of the tasks assigned to the Data Department was to provide crucial analytical data of the Double 11 sales to backstage sellers, and provide every seller with real-time data of the cloud picture function. Above all, it was necessary to report the final sales data and traffic data to the Company at the top response speed. During this process, challenges appeared everywhere.

17:00-20:00, November 10
On the eve of Double 11, the staff were well prepared for the upcoming battle.

20:00-22:00, November 10
The page views went up quickly and doubled the views at ordinary times. The resource consumption of front-end display servers for sellers' real-time sales volume and real-time visits sharply increased and if such increases continued, the front-end real time reporting servers would not hang on for long. However, we immediately implemented the emergency plan, which was prepared before the Double 11. The colleagues in charge of real-time system carried out the switchover of a data push interface program immediately after those responsible for real-time display adopted the other display scheme in an orderly way. Afterwards, pressures on the real-time report display server declined and no data breakpoint occurred in the front-end display at any time, to wit, no impact was exerted on the tracking of real-time sales and views by the sellers.

22:00-24:00, November 10
The first user traffic peak appeared. The real-time data shows the Page Views (PV) got close to those on the June 18 Festival and doubled those on the Double 11 last year. We survived the first wave of peak!

0:00-4:00, November 11
The real-time system operated steadily and now it was the show time of Hadoop's task batch processing.

The order data was the most important for calculation of sale targets. After midnight, the process of online data extraction kicked off. 10 minutes later, but the colleague in charge of data warehouse found the speed of extracting data from the order lists was too slow, even slower than 1/5 of the usual speed. Here came the questions. We notified the Operation & Maintenance Department to ask the colleagues responsible for DBA and network for troubleshooting, and the colleagues in charge of SQL Server DBA at Victoria Double 11 command post found that there was something wrong in the data source network, so we urgently switched the data source with defects. Then we soon smoothly extracted the online production data and the Hadoop data warehouse operated normally, and the core targets for all previous data at 8 o'clock in the morning were completed.

8:0-12:00, November 11

The peak appearing in the daytime came again, but longer and more violent. The real-time system operated steadily, continually calculating the page views. The data tendency suggested that, undoubtedly, today's PV would exceed the industrial and average growth range.

12:00-20:00, November 11

The page views were still surging, and the colleague taking charge of the user view log server informed that the server was nearly overwhelmed, and additional 1/3 log server was urgently required. The fellows who were overseeing the real-time system and Hadoop batch processing service began to prepare for data access again. By 18:30, the new log server was prepared in the log system. By 19:00, the test of the new log systems was finished and we started to switch. Everyone was staring at the real-time statements, and observing any possible data exception caused by such switch. After 10 minutes, 20 minutes, viewing data increased steadily at the evening peak, marking the success of the switch.

20:00-24:00, November 11

Today, everyone was here to witness another sales and traffic peak of Jingdong. The large screen showed that the traffic was still rising. We surrounded the director of the large data platform with a discussion on the progress we made this year. The Hadoop Data Warehouse was developed from nothing; the real-time system remained more and more stable at critical moment; the data transmission tool developed from the first generation to second generation, and now can support transmission of several hundred GB of isomerous data every day; the scheduling system and monitoring system were improved; the team was increasingly expanded. The ecosystem of the whole data warehouse is thriving, and JD's big data blueprint in the future was also subject to rehearsal to a great extent today. It was almost midnight and we took a group photo in front of real-time statements to commemorate this unforgettable Double 11 Festival.

0:00-3:00, November 12

It was the most exciting moment for us since the sales volume and PV we achieved yesterday will be made known to us now.

It took only 80 minutes extracting the data on over 100 million order lists from production SQL Server to Hadoop.

With another 30 minutes, processing of viewing log data was completed on the Hadoop.

3:00-6:00, November 12

The Hadoop Data Warehouse began the calculation process and the core targets were achieved at the utmost speed. All demanders in the data could see the core targets achieved at JD's Double 11 Festival when they went to office at 9 o'clock a.m.

At this moment, the sun is rising, marking the start of a new day. In the first rays of the morning sun, the colleagues in charge of the data warehouse can finally go home and enjoy some sleep. While everyone is taking a rest, we are still working; and while everyone enjoys the fruits of victory, we have left. This is the Double 11 Festival on which colleagues in charge of the big data platform at JD's Data Department as well as every R&D person worked hard!

Pressure Resistance Battle for the Transaction System

After every great promotion event finishes, different problems will be detected when the upstream and downstream of transaction system are under high pressure. Currently, two big promotion events are held annually. Fellows in Song's transaction team take most seriously how to avoid re-occurrence of the problems which we encountered before on June 18, how to deal with new situations occurring on the Double 11 Festival, how to work out plans, and other problems.

Song recalls the bottlenecks encountered by the upstream of the transaction team's system on June 18 this year. We should close one server and open another server, and then restart the closed server. We had to keep doing this, or the shopping cart server would suffer bottlenecks immediately, thus users would be unable to place orders as usual after entering the shopping cart. On the eve of Double 11, Wang, the leader of the transaction group, signed the "soldier writ" and stated that the primary task was to optimize the performance of transaction system. For this purpose, Wang set up a virtual performance group and set out to adjust Nginx allocation, consolidate asynchronous calls to alleviate the pressures imposed on the shopping cart, optimize the user-and-merchandise interfaces, realize memory computing and conduct frequent rehearsals for various degradation schemes, standby nodes, asynchronous nodes, and Yizhuang equipment room, and regarded many tasks in the performance area to be completed routinely.

Prior to Double 11, we found in the process of testing that, the upstream of the system after optimization was outstanding, and the shopping cart and ordering system suffered no bottlenecks. The previous work done for the performance optimization had fully played their roles. Nevertheless, great challenges were posed to the downstream system, such as a huge backlog of order tasks, failure of circulation of order status for which the users had made payments, 3COD breakdown causing the consequence that the mode of pay on delivery could not be selected for SOP order, and other problems. If it was on Double 11, these problems may result in a terrible seller and user experience. Fortunately, through the previous rehearsals, Wang had a well-thought-out plan to lead his team to solve various problems existing in the system under high pressure.

Problems occurring in the downstream of the system are closely related to the system framework. Every time Lao Wang begins to explain the system architectures of order tasks and middleware, a huge and intricate architecture chart will be drawn up. He tends to tell himself that we must do subtraction in a bid to reduce the pressure on the downstream system; remove the redundant parts and transfer some logic relations out as the pressure of architectural adjustment is approaching.

Preparations for the War of JOS

In June, everyone entering and coming out of the Beichen Tower seemingly quicken their walking pace. The air conditioners equipped in the Tower have cooled down the indoor temperature to 22°C, but you can still feel the heat reaching 40°C blowing on your face.

We start to prepare for the war on the JOS Open Platform. The JOS Open Platform is a window gateway opened by JD as well as one of important bridges for normal call of rear-end service interfaces. The team in charge of JOS is acutely aware of this. Huang, who takes charge of opening API at the JOS platform believes that the loading moments of JOS system are closely linked to the 618 event. Every user-authorized login is the best feed-back for us; every put away of sellers stimulates every nerve of the team members; and a seller's stock removal is also testing the unremitting efforts made by the JOS team in recent months. The JOS team started to prepare several months before the 618 Great Promotion event held this year.

After the 618 event and the Double 11 Festival in 2013, the overall stability of the JOS gateway was sharply improved. However, to usher in the 618 Event in 2014, the JOS team still conducted overall analysis and evaluation on efficiency and performance of the gateway. They hold that JOS system required an all-round upgrading. Huang considered that primary tenet for the 618 Event is "stability is of top priority". But now after evaluation, the processing of rear-end service interfaces in JOS system are either too fast or slow, and this must be adjusted and refined.

The time required for processing of partial interfaces at the rear-end services of JOS Open Platform varies. Furthermore, capacity planning, release time and service quality of some systems are of various levels. Considering that the Open Platform is a window gateway, synchronism + container-managed thread life cycle of HTTP requests will spread the unavailability of single service to the platform, and the rear-end services ultimately cannot be accessed. Therefore, the process mode of requests from traditional containers must be changed. (provided that one service goes wrong and the limit time for service call is 3 seconds, if the maximum number of container threads of one application server is 600, then in the worst-case scenario, single server can only process 600/3 requires in 1 second, meaning that the normal rear-end services will be deemed to be unavailable as routing transit is not provided) The container thread pool is separated for connection, and the business processing is undertaken by the back-end business thread pool, which can also set some reservation and restrictive models, namely shared thread pool, on the basis of business priority to monopolize the limited thread pools. The JOS team has conducted "asynchronous model encapsulation + business channelization + business weighting thread pool". The asynchronous model design can shorten the response time of the system, and the weighting thread pool is designed for isolation of quality influence among services as well as the stability of services and platform, thus guaranteeing the stable operation of the system.

In the summary for the 618 Event this year, the total amount of interface calls during the 3 days before and after the 618 Event in the charge of JOS platform is nearly triple that of interface calls incurred on the Double 11 Event last year. The average response speed of the interfaces is 82% and

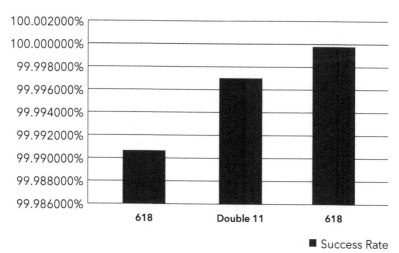

Average Success Rate of Interface Call

Comparison of the Average Success Rate of Interface Calls among the 618 Event of 2014 (right), the 618 Event of 2013 (left) and the Double 11 Event (Middle)

25.6% greater than that of the 618 Event and the Double 11 Event held last year respectively.

An Unexpected Journey of the Qinglong System

Chengdu 16th Floor Conference Room, June 19, 2014

In the command center, except for those on-duty colleagues who are still sticking to their posts for monitoring after working overnight, the monitoring charts concerning various production systems placed on walls and tables are eye-catching as well—traffic monitoring, server performance monitoring, interface performance monitoring and so forth. Various monitoring systems are provided. As monitoring cameras are everywhere, if any abnormality suddenly occurs anywhere, the head of corresponding systems will make a response at once. The Qinglong System was exposed to the maximum loads on June 19, 2014. The orders which came flooding in were subject to distribution one day later. After 5 o'clock a.m., the system visits surged sharply and we placed our priority to loads of database and backlogs of Worker tasks in this period. By 8 o'clock a.m., the visitor volume began to drop and the system's performance and indicators returned to normal, and everyone felt released. To succeed in this year's 618 great promotion event, we started to prepare several months earlier. We embraced both accidents and surprises in the whole process, but more importantly, it was a journey full of adrenalin.

After the 618 Event and the Double 11 Event in 2013, Qinglong System has been steadily operating for a long time. To be well prepared for the 618 Event this year, we decided to raise the security level of the database. On the early morning hours of April 5, 2014, we started to change the database's passwords. There were dozens of applications in the Qinglong

System, and a document of operating steps was prepared according to the System's sequential dependency. Following these steps, everything proceeded smoothly and the System ran normally before the business peaks in the morning. When everyone considered that the System would maintain stable operation all the time, an alarm was reported. Then we immediately put our staff back into the alarm and all problems were finally solved till the afternoon. There was something wrong in the operating steps for switch, resulting in greater dependent visitor volumes among various systems than usual. Access exception would lead to retries in a vicious circle until the system's maximum loads were exceeded.

After detecting this problem, we rethought it that if our systems are strongly capable of self-protection or any degradation scheme is available for the system or we have prepared complete emergency plans, this problem will not endanger the normal operations of our systems so easily. Since both the IPO and the 618 Event are around the corner and the alarm has been sounded, we must take actions. A saying can accurately describe the situation at that time, which is "Heaven helps those who help themselves." Based on this set of systems which we developed by ourselves and we are very familiar with, we worked out a series of assumptions on possible problems for the Qinglong Waybills.

1. The problem concerning MemCache: in case of any performance-related problems, it will become inconvenient to extend the MemCache and no maintenance team is specially organized for it;
2. The problem concerning dependence on the bottom basic information services: in case that such basic information is unavailable, partial services of waybills will be indirectly affected;
3. In case that the RAC production base crashes or suffers performance problems, its performance will be significantly impacted, thus influencing other upstream business systems indirectly.

Regarding these risk points, we carried out several rounds of intra-group brainstorming, and finally worked out a practical and feasible solution.

The initial research and development was completed in a short period, and the deliverable for the first stage was smoothly launched at the beginning of May 2014. Subsequently, we kicked off R & D and modification for the second stage. At this stage, the crucial time was limited with wide modification coverage. From the middle of May 2014, a new application version was released online. After this release, we specially analyzed performance of the database and found that, with additional full-capacity caches, the load on the database did not descend, but rose instead. Through analysis, we drew a conclusion that it resulted from the caches and refreshing of transaction running lists. In the end, a strategy adjustment was carried out for the data-caching mechanism with large business volumes and less page views. Upon release of the new version, the database load was significantly dropped and the cache hit ratio sharply increased. In the process of the system optimization, we drew up a practical and feasible system emergency plan to support the optimization and improvement. After all optimized points were put online, we affirmed through evaluation that the system could accommodate the orders even the latter doubled.

Extraordinary Year 2014

"Year 2014 is destined to be an extraordinary year for JD", said Li Daxue during the 618 Battle this year, "JD's Technical R&D team can gain adequate experiences through the 618 Events every year. Our systems become increasingly refined with years' development, making greater achievements. It is lucky for technicians to participate in the 618 Battle. If you ask me what attitude and way a computer engineer should adopt for working and learning, I may give you a plain suggestion which can be a good answer, that is, participating in the 618 Event, finding and solving problems. Don't bypass problems, and try to do more practical things, which may be none of your business. You won't lose anything." This suggestion is seemingly simple, but in fact, it is not easy making it. However, our R&D system really made it on June 18, 2014.

Authors: Ma Pei, Xu Lilong, Zhang Kan, Li Gang, and Wang Xianke

CHAPTER 2

The Matrix: Optimization of the Data Center Network

The 618 Event in the Honeymoon Period of the IPO

The 618 Event in 2014 has an unusual meaning for JD.

On May 22, 2014, JD.com was listed through the NASDAQ stock exchange. Originally, the 618 Event provided an opportunity for yearly self-testing and continuous enhancement for JD. However, the 618 Event launched this year is the first piece of answer sheet delivered to the market and investors apart from the IPO, and the technical system in JD's R&D system became an important link to accomplish it.

JD was still faced with various challenges in the honeymoon period of the IPO. First, pressures from all sectors of the society. Unlike in previous years, JD really required a perfect 618 Grand Ceremony to consolidate its position in the industry and boost the confidence of investors. The second challenge is integration with Yixun and WeChat. JD has rapidly entered a strategic partnership with Tencent before the IPO. JD must put the fruits of strategic cooperation into service, and convert resources and popularity into earnings. The last challenge is posed by the pressure caused by the high-speed development of its businesses. JD's sales have undergone growth at a speed higher than the industry's average speed, which is directly embodied in the doubling of its page views, turnover and website traffic. JD's R&D system should accomplish quick upgrade and continuous optimization of the architecture and systems while high-speed growth of businesses is achieved.

Challenges and pressures exist objectively, and will not be subject to essential changes due to the IPO, but everyone in JD recognized the significance of the 618 Event this year and ardent expectations inside and outside of the company. Therefore, JD's R&D system puts special attention and energies into the preparation made for the 618 Event.

The 618 Event is launched once a year, but upon completion of the 618 Event in 2013, JD's R&D system kicked off preparatory work for the 618 Event of 2014.

Core Services

The author serves the Infrastructure Division subordinating to the Operation & Maintenance of JD's R&D Center, and the Division is mainly responsible for operation of the data center-oriented system and network foundation platform.

JD's data center network includes 3 core services: CDW, load balancing, and fundamental network, which bear almost all businesses and traffic of JD and are the most basic critical network services, and directly concern the service ability and quality of the business system. As the foundation platforms support other business systems, they are subjected to more restrictions and limits in the areas of construction cycle, scheme optimization, and infrastructure upgrade. With the explosive growth of the business, the infrastructure plays a greater role in meeting the demands of rapid growth of businesses, thus many problems are caused in aspects of architecture availability and expandability, thus affecting the long-term and sustainable development of infrastructure services. With further improvement of the business systems and accelerating expansion of the data center scale, the negative impacts of these leftover problems are more sharpened and even result in a dramatic decline of the quality and availability of business application services.

Except for old wounds left over for historical reasons, at the same time new demands are created with advances in Internet technology. The technological evolution of the front-end applications, wide application of distributed systems, and promotion of new technologies, such as cloud computing and SDN, bring unprecedented challenges to the infrastructure. These three network services are faced with seemingly different problems.

CDN
- JD began self-development of CDN service in 2009
- Bear 90% of Internet traffic
- Some performance and structure-related problems need solutions.

Load Balancing
- During the Double 11 Event in 2013, JD primarily applied commercial products for the load balancing service
- With business expansion, the commercial products' load balancing exposed some prominent problems: overload, increase of breakdown, difficulty in enlargement

Fundamental Network
- During Double 11 Event in 2013, Data Center's TOR uplink bandwidth congestion problem became sharpened
- A great number of trans-computer room service call and data transmission demands raise more strict requirements against the special bandwidth and reliability of POD room and DC room.
- Lack of racks

Major Problems Confronted by CDN, Load Balancing and Fundamental Network

Problems confronted by CDN

In 2009, Gavin, an old head of the Operation & Maintenance Department, set up the first version of JD's CDN service based on Squid through self-study by finding data online, repeated experiments, and environmental testing, although he hardly had any experience regarding CDN. Driven by curiosity, I asked Gavin for the reasons why he decided to build CDN by himself. He told that multiple serious breakdowns of commercial CDN services used then drove him to do it independently.

Without external support, several members of CDN conducted self-study and self-development. CDN service was gradually improved and refined in the process of ongoing explorations, and JD's CDN scale became more important with the rapid rise of the business and traffic. In the first half of 2013, JD's CDN accomplished the transfer of all nodes from Squid to ATS. There are dozens of CDN nodes in China, bearing 90% of the total Internet traffic. The peak traffic on June 18, 2013 even surpassed 100G.

I believe that many enterprises have undergone the process of developing from nothing and such experiences are extremely valuable to either enterprises or individuals. At present, with highly advanced information, we can obtain rich theoretical knowledge, technical proposals and application cases through a variety of channels, but in face of various demands and options, long-term practices and accumulations in the professional fields are needed for accurate satisfaction of core demands, targeting the most suitable choice and determining direction and strategies for the long-term development.

However, starting from 2013, some problems of CDN products were gradually found, such as deficiencies in cluster performance, system structure defects, poor extensibility and other problems. Hardware upgrading, software changes, and bandwidth increase are far from being solutions to these problems. Moreover, in the past, considering cost and demands, the data centers and networks provided by second-tier operators were mainly applied to CDN nodes. Although the machine room environment and level of services are much better than those of the first-tier operators, owing to the special situation in China's telecom industry, the quality of network provided by second-tier operators was relatively poor, which makes a fatal impact on the service quality of JD.com.

Problems Confronted by Load Balance

JD has been using business equipment since it started to use the load balance service. As there are objective requirements for business and the enterprise has certain purchasing capacity but is incapable of independently developing the load balance products, using commercial load balance products seems to be a spontaneous choice.

In JD's business scenarios, all businesses for the public network basically provide services through load balance, and the business for the data centers also applies the load balance technology at the same time for the purpose of meeting load demands or fault tolerance, and some network services such as NAT are also deployed for the load balance equipment. With continuous expansion of business and network scale, the pressure on load balance becomes greater and greater. As time goes on, the commercial load balance equipment with different brands, models, and large scale appear in the network.

Finally, various problems begin to appear in the load balance service due to performance and structure-related problems. Both the old equipment and new type of equipment suffer an insufficiency of stand-alone performance, and we must keep increasing the amount of equipment or select models with higher performance in order to alleviate the equipment pressure. As the two-in-one Active-Standby structure was adopted for the commercial load balance products, if every set of equipment is increased, business separation should be carried out on the original equipment. This is a painful and inelegant process, and management and maintenance are costly, risky, and lack elasticity.

In fact, there are many Internet peers using open-source load balance software such as LVS now and a lot of relatively mature solutions are formed. We refer them as software load balance to distinguish them from commercial products, but software load balance demands certain capability of development and optimization, or its service ability cannot replace commercial products. JD has been accumulating power in software load balance, and is awaiting a suitable tipping point.

Problems Confronted by Fundamental Network

The fundamental network possesses 3 core functions, which are also referred to as services.

1) The network access service of host equipment such as servers, which mainly affects the efficiently accessed bandwidth and availability of the host equipment network. After the year 2010, the physically accessed bandwidth for the data center's Ethernet basically reached 1000Mbps, but the bandwidth convergence on the up links including TOR or convergence device lead the average available bandwidth of host equipment to be far lower than 1000M. With vigorous growth of host equipment's traffic in recent years, the problem of shortage of access bandwidth is increasingly highlighted.

2) Internet access service provided by the data center, which mainly affects the capacity and quality of Internet services provided by the data center. With wide application of the technical architectures such as large cluster, distributed application and big data application, the Internet traffic is still subject to sustainable growth at a relatively high speed, but the increase of east-west traffic exchanged within the data center still far exceeds the increase of south-north traffic. The growth of east-west traffic and south-north traffic poses great challenge against the host access and Internet access.

3) The interconnected service between data centers, has primary impacts

on the network's supporting capacity of trans-data-center data scheduling and distributed application and the network quality optimization ability. The currently popular concept of the data center cloud can best explain this service. The fuzziness of data center's bound and platformization of the network service are comprehensive demands from upper applications and development of the network. Special high-bandwidth lines and transmission systems based on DWDM are the only way for goal achievement. The network architecture with multiple data centers is the core guarantee which decides the service performance and expansibility.

JD made little investment in the fundamental network at the beginning. During rapid growth of business, firstly we should meet the demands of expansion of equipment scale and neglected the areas of network capacity, reliability and expansibility, but the infrastructure located at the bottom layer of IT service system, which underwent a long construction cycle and slow iteration, so the resources and performance soon went wrong. For instance, some old networks were accessed with a convergence ratio of 10:1, and the structure of HSRP+STP was still applied when the network devices were replaced after 2010, thus resulting in a disguised decline of network bandwidth and resource utilization rate. With the aging of equipment and expansion of equipment scale, bandwidth congestion and partial failure occurred frequently. The network stabilization of second-tier operators affects not only the CDN service, but also the public network services in all data centers. The internal network structure of data centers also reduces the stability of the network service and reliability of upgrading and recon-struction due to the early design flaws. Excessive reliance on the network by many core business applications leads the fundamental network to become a malignant tumor and puts us in dilemma.

After experiencing the 618 Event in 2012, we have realized that, finding the solutions to the above-mentioned problems concerning CDN, load balance, and fundamental network is a matter of great urgency.

Upgrading and Improvement

Identification of Core Problems and Setting of Development Objectives

Through deliberate pondering and summary, we dodge a lot of interference caused by emergency and abstract various problems in front of us into five major core problems: performance, capacity, expansibility, reliability and monitoring.

These five problems act on each other and act in coordination with each

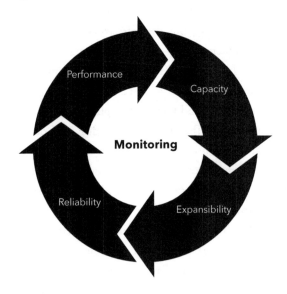

Five Core Problems Existing in Sustainable Development of Fundamental Network Service

other. Performance can influence the capacity, and capacity planning depends on favorable expansibility. Furthermore, without sufficient reliability assurance, the design and framework, no matter how perfect they are, will lose the most elementary value and significance. But all this demands analysis and confirmation through the monitoring system. Based on accurate data, controlling the running status of service and conducting reversed corrections of the framework and strategy according to the data and results constitute a process of service visualization.

Based on the above plan, JD took a series of quite effective measures in the data center's fundamental network service.

Improvement of CDN

In the first half of 2013, JD's CDN was transformed into the structure of HAProxy + ATS.

Subsequently, to begin with, HAProxy's stand-alone performance was doubled. On this basis, multiple 1000-M network cards of HAProxy were upgraded to single 10-G network cards. In this case, except for the network cards, the service ability of a single HAProxy was significantly improved when other hardware configurations remained unchanged, and it would be difficult for commercial products.

Secondly, the load balance framework was upgraded from the

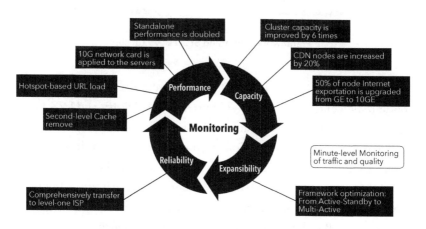

Improvement of CDN Service to Support the 618 Event

Active-Standby mode to the Multi-Active mode. Such upgrading was realized by increasing a three-tier switch in the cluster. The switch was used to accomplish ECMP work based on the flow forwarding, thus the maximum capacity of load cluster directly produced a several-fold increase, and the cluster's capacity was continuously enhanced by three-tier switches such as 16-Way ECMP, 32-Way ECMP, and others.

Here, we need to mention Si Xing, the core leader of the above-mentioned

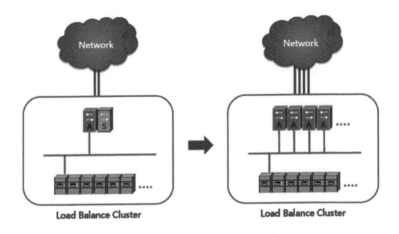

Framework Upgrading of JD's LVS Cluster

essential changes. After joining JD, Si Xing led a deep development and optimization of related products of Linux kernel, HAProxy, and LVS. Long-term accumulation and demands of JD reacted with Si Xing's ability of materializing ideas like a chemical reaction. In my opinion, it is Si Xing's work achievements that make the perceptive realize the importance of development, and apply the word "development," which was a front-end business oriented to operations & maintenance and any fields requiring development. But this is a new topic, so we must stop here.

Upon completion of two core optimization works as mentioned above, in the last year, the capability of a single-node actual deployment at JD's CDN was improved by 6 times, the number of nodes of CDN throughout the network was increased by 20%, upgrading of Internet access (from 1G to 10G) and framework upgrading were conducted over more than 50% of CDN, and the proportion of CDN nodes provided by tire-one operators was increased. Meanwhile, upgrading of certain functions of CDN was also realized for certain business demands, such as second-level cache removal, hot-spot URL load, etc. Finally, minute-level monitoring was implemented on CDN node traffic and quality, and data analysis based on the logs was conducted as well.

Improvement of Load Balance

JD is using various software load balance products of which LVS, of which

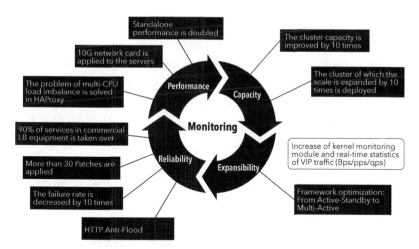

Improvement of Load Balance to Support the 618 Event

HAProxy, and Nginx are the most common. In fact, after joining JD, the first and the most important task undertaken by Si Xing was to determine the structure of load cluster as LVS + HAProxy. Apollo and I worked with Si Xing together. Through structure optimization, problem solving and development, the flow-based ECMP + LVS + HAProxy structure was finally determined. The optimization in this part was basically similar to the optimization of CDN's software loan balance.

Compared with the commercial load balance products, the software load cluster possesses the following advantages:

1. The performance and capacity are increased by several or dozens of times;
2. The expansibility is excellent and, smooth and level capacity expansion is available as required;
3. The reliability is good, and a local error will not result in service interruption;
4. Newly added business and management requirements can be rapidly developed, and maintainability and visualization are significantly improved;
5. The cost of equal performance is sharply reduced and the ability of continuous services are greatly improved.

Without doubt, the increase in equipment amounts, power consumption, complex rate of structure, and cost of management and maintenance is apparent, but cannot be compared with the gains.

In the last year, the standalone performance of the software load balance was doubled, the cluster capacity was improved by 10 times, 90% of commercial load balance equipment was replaced, nearly 90% of the total business was gradually transferred to the software load products, the cluster scale was expanded by around 10 times and the service downtime sharply declined. In the process of development and utilization, more than 30 patches were developed for the elimination of defects, performance improvement and promotion of functions, and a kernel monitoring module was added to conduct Bps/pps/qps traffic monitoring and business granule-oriented monitoring over VIP. Moreover, those relatively complicated problems such as multi-CUP load imbalance of HAProxy, failure in VIP host-standby switch caused by defects of Gratuitous-ARP in the specific version of Keepalived were solved and first-phase function of HTTP Anti-flood was put into service prior to the 618 Event in 2014.

Si Xing and the system development team were critical factors in accomplishing the these works. In my opinion, they were the tipping points of qualitative changes in JD's fundamental network application. But we must say that, if a qualified product is the seed, then a well-organized operation and maintenance should be the soil which the seed depends on for existence. Qualified products and design are for the purpose of meeting demands and solving problems, but the product design which leaves the application scenarios and deviates from the real demand will result in blind actions and idle theorizing. In addition, products, no matter how good they are, demand qualified operation & maintenance to assure sustainable and favorable development. The infrastructure-related services lay special emphasis on lasting vitality and stability of the products, and only an open and inclusive technical environment can breed qualified products and services.

Improvement of Fundamental Network

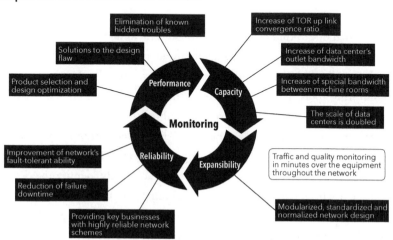

Improvement of Fundamental Network Service to Support the 618 Event

JD's data center fundamental network confronts the most prominent problem among all known problems and has influence on all upper services and applications. For a long time, bandwidth congestion was considered to be the sole cause of service quality reduction and occurrence of failures in many applications. In certain early network environments, the access network convergence ratio (10:1) will give others a handle, and the greater problem is that network monitoring lags far behind the development of network scale, so the coverage area and accuracy of monitoring are insufficient to reflect the quality and operation status of network services. Lack of such a function results in a situation where the business and network pass the buck to and become entangled with each other. Furthermore, poor performance and reliability of early network structure lead to some accidents and complicated operations which were originally insignificant, but had a negative impact on services later, thus hindering the network optimization.

To solve the above-mentioned problems, JD's network team endeavored to solve the problems in two directions.

First, finding solutions to urgent problems from customer feedback

When confronting the problems from customer feedback, a deep analysis was carried out to find essential reasons, and then identify the most urgent and optimal problems concerning the fundamental network. Simultaneously, we should independently design and develop SNMP-based network monitoring tools, realize minute-level traffic monitoring on the network equipment and all kernel, convergence, three-tier equipment, all uplink interfaces connecting switches and down-link interfaces of early network with great convergence ratio connecting switches are covered. Therefore, in case of customer feedback problems, we can accurately identify the degree of influence from fixer network when the business problems occur. Through a long spell of accumulation, on the one hand, the network team has won over the customer's trust; and on the other hand, some network problems to which the solutions should be prioritized are also detected. Then, around the Double 11 Event held in 2013, the equipment which suffered the most congested bandwidth was subject to expansion of bandwidth capacity, thus alleviating the influence of the problems and buying time for optimization and transformation of framework.

Second, finding the fundamental solutions to the problems in design of network architecture

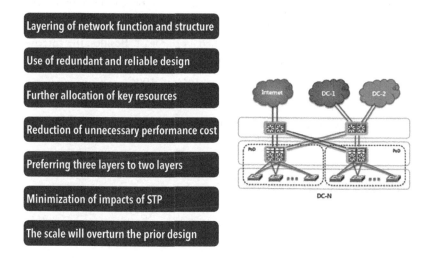

Layering of network function and structure

Use of redundant and reliable design

Further allocation of key resources

Reduction of unnecessary performance cost

Preferring three layers to two layers

Minimization of impacts of STP

The scale will overturn the prior design

Network Structure Summarized and Optimized Based on Experience in Network Operation & Maintenance

The most significant change is the layering of network functions and structure. The network functions fall into 3 parts: the first is access switched network with PoD as the unit, which consists of a kernel and access switch for the purpose of meeting the servers' access demands; the second is the public boundary network which enables the access of the data center's equipment to the Internet; the third is the private boundary network based on DWDM transmission system for interconnection of data centers. Such functional segregation and structural adjustment directly yield a narrowing of the network's failure domain, thus empowering various function networks to perform their own functions and be mutually uncorrelated and materializing normalization and standardization of network framework design as well as favorable expansibility and reliability.

Secondly, optimize the network resources and functional configuration, and realize the redundancy and one-shot move within the allowable cost range. On the eve of the 618 Event of 2014, all newly built data centers and newly transformed networks of JD were accessible to the network with 1:1 convergence ratio, function networks were segregated and redundancy of key accessories and equipment reached 1+1 at least. Besides, the Internet outlet bandwidth was comprehensively upgraded from 1000M to 10G, and point-to-point special bandwidth from 10G to 100G; tier-two operators were all replaced by tier-one operators for the Internet and overall performance, capacity, expansibility, and reliability of network were essentially improved.

Improvement of Network Services

In the process of ongoing services and optimization, the network team has accumulated a rich experience, and formed the methodology and principles suitable for its own business.

No matter how adequate and just the reasons are, interests and demands of users cannot be sacrificed, and the essence of services should meet requirements of the user and business. The user demands seem to conflict with the long-term planning and development of the network services sometimes, but in fact, the demands and development can be unified. The substantive issues behind the demands must be recognized to avoid palliatives. It is necessary to convert the user's superficial needs into essential ones, guide the development direction of network services by means of understanding and mastering the user needs, and provide rational guides on the user needs. The network service belongs to the underlying infrastructure of the IT service, with a long construction cycle, significant influence and high interconnection, so scientific and long-term planning and design are required to avoid the far-reaching influence of short-term hardships. Lastly, the framework design should not dodge difficulties and problems, and the root causes must be identified and thoroughly solved. The framework evading problems will result in continuous adverse effects and disasters.

Although JD's order quantity and sales amount hit another historical

Urgent demands of the users must be met on a prioritized basis

Balance short-term demands and long-term objectives

Comprise cannot be made on the problems for framework design

Key Principles of Network Service

record on the 618 Event in 2014, our R&D command post performed calmly and skillfully, and systems provided support steadily through the optimization of core services. Now we have kicked off a new round of planning to move on to and prepare for the upcoming great promotions by the end of the year.

Author: Wang Dayong

CHAPTER 3

Battleship: High-Performance Transaction System

Ten Principles for the Design of a Mass-traffic and Stable Transaction System

The transaction team was facing the same problems confronted by the noted ancient Chinese flood controller, Yu the Great, thousands of years ago. Unstable online mass traffic is like the flood and various subsystems supporting the business can be compared to rolling villages and dams. Through years of 618 Events and Double 11 Festivals, the team has summarized ten principles, which have successfully resisted multiple traffic shocks.

The first principle: divide the system based on business types. For example, JD divides its system into various parts of home page, channel page, shopping cart, transaction and payment, and different domain names are separately deployed.

The second principle: switch of backup for disaster recovery. The online transaction system sets high requirements for stability at ordinary times, but if you intend to achieve high stability, do not put all your eggs in one basket.

The third principle: horizontal extension and split. For the online transaction system, the visitor volume at ordinary times is normal, but the traffic flooding into the whole system will be raised by several times, dozens of times or even hundreds of times during 618 Events and various limited-time promotional activities. When the peak is reached, how can we cope with such situation? The most elementary method is traffic shunt.

The forth principle: limit of traffic beyond expectations. For the online mass-traffic system, the best plan is to shunt the traffic and the alternative is to limit the traffic. If the alternative still does not work, the traffic we deem malicious will be blocked; the last plan is to protect the system. The traffic is overwhelming sometimes when the traffic brought by normal users may be as much as to prevail over the system, then we will pick out some service points to protect the system and guarantee the normal operation of most users and enable them to place orders as usual and take a joyful shopping journey.

The fifth principle: to protect system through degradation.

The sixth principle: to improve performance through reading-writing splitting.

The seventh principle: asynchronization

The eighth principle: separation of dynamic and static traffic

The ninth principle: to detect bottlenecks through online pressure tests

The tenth principle: pre-arranged planning. In fact, occurrence of failure is not troublesome, and the most terrible thing is that you are at a loss what to do when there is something wrong, so pre-arranged planning is necessary.

In the following part, I will describe these ten principles in details. A practical case will be taken to illustrate flexible application of these ten principles in the actual scenarios.

System Splitting

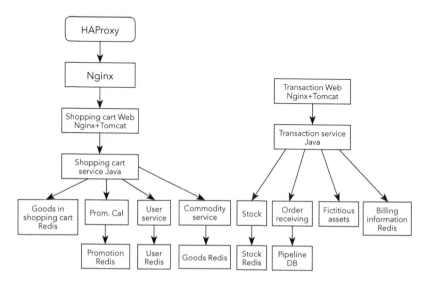

System Architecture Chart of JD's Transaction System

First, we split the system according to the business logic as follows:

- **Website system:** home page, list, channel, single item, search
- **Transaction system:** price, shopping cart, settlement, payment, order center
- **Basic service:** promotion, stock, merchandise, user
- **Order system:** pipeline, OFW, order middleware, production system

In this way, the data and traffic are first split.

Switch of Backup for Disaster Recovery

Switch of backup for disaster recovery falls into two scenarios, which include a multi-machine room deployment scenario and a scenario in the same machine room.

Switch of Backup for Disaster Recovery in the multi-machine room scenario

JD's online transaction systems are basically deployed in 3 machine rooms, two of which are principal, i.e. Machine Room I and Machine Room II. Multi-machine room deployment will encounter two problems: wide-area failures within the machine room and abnormal entrance traffic. To solve these two problems, an automatic switch between machine rooms must be available. The current speed of the machine room switch is relatively fast, with a round of switch basically taking less than 5 minutes.

Two strategies are applicable for a switch of backup for disaster recovery in case of multi-machine room deployment: switch of the entrance traffic and a direct routing switch.

Strategy of the entrance traffic switch: the operations department switched the entrance traffic by transferring the traffic to another machine room for analysis. Its advantage is the regional feature, which empowers an individual switch of the three northeast provinces of China or a priority switch of those regions of greater importance. However, this process is slow, and many systems are involved. For instance, there are a lot of things awaiting the switch behind the shopping cart in the transaction system.

Direct routing switch strategy: this strategy is applied to cope with wide-area failures in machine rooms. In fact, wide-area failures seldom occur. In this case, with only several seconds, it is quite efficient to use AHbroad.

When any online problems occur, both strategies will be implemented simultaneously no matter what the causes are. Thus, we think the two-pronged approach is feasible for large-scale failures.

Switch in the scenario inside the machine room

This strategy is to switch the applications layer by layer through the call of the Client End.

For a switch of the Java application layer, we use the independently developed bottom framework, which enables the callers to select server types and is very fast. Another one is the switch of interior domain name, which is relatively slow.

Regarding the cache switch, JD applies a great number of Redis. We have transformed the Redis Client End to achieve a quick switch between various levels of the End Switch of databases is also available for the selection of client ends. Some systems also allow self-service selection of client ends and other systems can make use of the database's switch mechanism.

Routing handover is not cumbersome, while how to guarantee consistency of data is the real problem. For example, inconsistency of data is fatal to stock management and similar critical businesses. We may take the iPhone as an example. If the price drops to RMB 10 per iPhone, binge buying will happen. At this time, in case we intend to switch the machine room, it is difficult to determine the quantity of decreased stock. If the quantity is mistakenly determined, it is apt to witness short-supply or over-supply.

Consistency of data can be realized by the following methods. The first method is an automatic switch of procedures. The advantage is that a commercial switch is very feasible and quick. It takes less than one minute to switch from Machine Room I to Machine Room II. Moreover, data import or export is not needed, because the data is subject to dual writing. We have adopted asynchronous dual writing. The data dealt with by asynchronous dual writing may have relatively poor data consistency, but has a good performance. We need to input 6 or 7 clusters for the online shopping cart, and synchronization dual writing cannot stand such workload.

The second method adopted for data consistency is to replicate the data saved at the bottom layer. The advantage is good data consistency. For example, Redis works out a set of complicated systems, and the databases of Microsoft and Oracle have their own matured data replication link. Its shortage is the inflexibility of an initiative handover. For example, in case any problem occurs in the process from the master node to slave node or from slave node to slave node, it will be particularly difficult to achieve data consistency. The inventory system must use data replication because the requirement of high data consistency.

Clusters of Backup for Disaster Recovery

Let's talk about the strategy of a clustered backup for disaster recovery in idle state. We have some standby machine rooms where many applied machines are placed and no traffic is produced at ordinary times. However, we cannot put the whole transaction system on that, as we will encounter two related problems, management cost and heat cache.

Cluster management is cumbersome after the business is put into operation. Because we have a great number of machines, JD sets a hard-and-fast rule that every machine should receive inspection and backup after the transaction is released. To avoid network-related problems, a manual switch is necessary, thus causing high costs due to release management. In addition, the cluster of backup for disaster recovery in idle state will cause a problem concerning heat cache. The transaction system will use lots of caches. If the online heat cache is switched to a system without traffic, each switching operation will generate large instantaneous traffic. This problem should be taken into consideration as well.

The second strategy is to create a clustered backup for disaster recovery with minor traffic. For example, relatively minor traffic is properly allocated to the cluster of backup for disaster recovery at Machine Room II. As the traffic from the three northeast provinces is low, we can switch such traffic to Machine Room II. But this will not be free of problems because the accident risks will be increased and management cost is higher due to cross-machine room register.

Lastly, let's turn to the cluster switchover strategy. For the transaction clusters, the switchover strategies are optional. The traffic can be switched in whole or in part. For example, if any problems occur in the merchandise system, we may switch partial traffic of numerous online clusters in a bid to alleviate great pressure. This is also a feasible strategy.

Traffic Limiting

On the Internet, there are malicious users as well as robots, say competitors' robots, apart from normal users, so we must limit the traffic, but we must be prudent doing this. Strategies for traffic limiting can be implemented at 4 levels.

The first level is traffic limiting at the Nginx layer. In addition to a set of self-developed traffic limiting strategies based on the original Nginx module, we also have many rules for traffic limiting.

The second level is traffic limiting at the Web application layer. The rules are identical to those for the first layer, but this layer can be only subject to individual traffic limiting since the Web application layer is mainly responsible for presentation logic and its logic is particularly clear.

The third level is traffic limiting in the business application system. The risk of traffic limiting is significant, so we do not expect to limit the traffic. If the traffic of the business system is limited, great influence will be imposed on the user experience. For example, if the inventory we mentioned before is subjected to traffic limiting, loss of user traffic will result, especially the traffic brought by new users. Therefore, traffic limiting cannot be easily carried out for the business application system, but appending caches is allowed, including local, hot-spot, and remote caches. Sufficient caches can solve performance-related problems.

The criteria for traffic limiting are set based on the pressure test. For example, in case of calling an inventory system, how many calling times would be proper for every second? Neither too high nor too low is applicable, so we conduct repeated online pressure testing and monitoring, and finally determine a relatively reasonable value.

The fourth level is traffic limiting of the database. Only the frequency per minute or per second of data writing is limited, and the remaining requests are either rejected or put into the array for queuing.

Shunt

At the beginning, JD combined the second kill system with the transaction system, but we separated them later. As for the second kill system, the first step is a completely independent deployment of data. When the system seizes up every time, the primary cause is data writing. As for data writing, no matter how great the splitting or the cluster expansion is, it will definitely fall into one machine. Take the inventory as an example, for it will point to certain Redis, and it is difficult to solve this problem. Therefore, the data must be subject to complete physical deployment. The second kill system is featured by its relatively concentrated hot data, and after second kill is completed, only a few products will be left, so we put the inventory and promotion-related data for single merchandise into an individual cluster to improve the performance, and the best of all is that no impact is exerted on normal users who intend to place orders through the master transaction system.

Application deployment customized strategy is also closely related to the business. When JD's shopping cart is opened, the inventory status and the merchandise information will be shown without interference within the shopping experience. In case there is something wrong with the service, the inventory status still can be seen, and order placing will not be affected. We assign the shopping cart's inventory status and freight insurance to the individually deployed user cluster through major nodes. Even the problems may occur in the whole cluster, only online users will be subject to significant influence, and no influence will be imposed on the order quantity. Furthermore, the complexity of primary business model is also reduced.

Degradation

Degradation should be our last resort. The online systems are very complicated and dependent on too many things including software and hardware, so the first action we should take is to degrade the system level. What does degradation of system level mean? Let me take an example to illustrate this issue. If the page showing a successful operation crashes, the user will jump to the order center when clicking the "submit" button and the order will still be displayed in the order center and the payment button is available; if the order center also crashes, then it will directly jump to the page showing order details.

The second one is degradation of the business function module. For example, for the real-time price module, the degradation can be realized without timeliness and this will be illustrated on the basis of the case of real-time price later in this book. Another one is the degradation of page level. For instance, if there are many dynamic things shown on the home page, then a great number of services should be called to figure out the results. We have prepared a static page. In case the dynamic page crashes, the static page will be launched. The available information in front of the users is less than that of the dynamic page, but at least there is something to see and they will not leave immediately.

The third one is shielding of non-critical business. The aforementioned state of shopping cart does not belong to the critical information and thus will not be displayed after the degradation.

The last one is the degradation of remote services to local caches. For example, in case of freight calculation by POP sellers, generally sellers will provide us with a freight calculation template specifying the freight charged for certain merchandise. But as our system is linked with POP sellers, when any problem occurs, we will fetch a default from local caches for temporary use.

Reading-writing Splitting

The first principle is the reading-writing splitting of the integrated system.

The second principle is whether the writing performance can be integrated after the reading-writing splitting. It is easy to improve the reading performance through memory cache and remote cache. The hot data is generally saved in the memory cache. For example, if the quantity of orders during the 618 Event reaches 5 million and one order includes 10 items of merchandise, then the total amount comes to 50 million which can be accommodated by our memory storage.

Third, improvement of the writing performance. One way to improve the writing performance is to fetch the data through JD's data message queued services, and write based on such data with Redis; the other alternative is to conduct data fragments. For instance, use Redis and other databases to build sharding in order to expand the cluster and write the hot data.

Fourth, dynamic-static separation. It is a method that everyone is capable of. The static and dynamic pages are separated, avoiding CDN from mixing with the dynamic pages. As for the structural deployment of transactions, the only thing we must do is put the static page of the shopping cart on the headmost master node.

Online Pressure Testing

Online pressure test falls into 3 aspects.

The first aspect is the online pressure test of reading logic, which can be realized easily, because the users' data will not be destroyed. In the worst scenario, the system will be exposed to problems, but the system can recover soon because it is controllable.

The second aspect is the online pressure test of writing logic, which is the most difficult. JD now has lots of important writing logic for online pressure test. We also arrange online pressure tests for that writing logic which is not suitable for degradation, such as inventory and order placing, behind which there are a lot of tools data requiring online data cleaning.

The third aspect is the coverage. Addition of links and business flows mainly depends on common understanding of online businesses and what order magnitude will impact the business cycle and flow direction of the primary business process; attention should be paid to analysis on the online log and observe those requests with large call volume. In the process of pressure flow, we should focus on the indexes of both software and hardware. The indexes of hardware include CPU, memory, hard disk, and network. All systems are different. Some are CPU-intensive, some are added with excessive heat caches, some emphasize the number of network connections, and others pay attention to both interface traffic and export traffic. Indexes of software involve throughput capacity, concurrency amount. and duration of service response. The whole transaction system has become completely service-oriented, and the response time of service-oriented service end and client end should be measured in the process of pressure testing to find the system's actual bottlenecks. For example, when the time of service end is short and client end is long, we can check if there is any problem in the network link between the client end and service end including the bottom framework.

Pre-arranged Plan

Occurrence of online problems will not result in panic, but lack of pre-arranged plans will. We prepared more than a thousand plans for the 618 Event, and over one hundred plans were implemented.

The primary role of pre-arranged plans is to find problems. We set up monitoring platform and logging platform to monitor software, hardware and business. Artificial monitoring is also available.

The second role is to identify problems. In case of any problem, its cause and location must be analyzed and identified with the help of monitoring data and log.

The third role is to solve problems. The methods have been mentioned above, such as turning on the routing switch for shunt, or degrading if the problem is not identified.

To carry out online exercise is above all after the plans are prepared. Without online exercise, the corresponding plans may be invalid in case that any problem occurs. Furthermore, pressure tests are necessary because every pressure test will form an event suitable for plan exercise. We will find out more bottlenecks for the system through every pressure test; when the system is in a bad state, those pre-prepared plans will be useful.

Application Examples: Real-time Price System

The principles are rigid and similarly expressed by Internet-related enterprises. How can we apply these principles to the field of e-commerce? In the following part, we will take JD's real-time price system as a real-life case for analysis.

In the above screenshot, we specially mark the price in an attempt to

The Page for DELL Display

make illustrations. How is this price obtained? Every merchandise is set with a basic price and it is subject to promotion, so its final price is obtained by taking into consideration both the basic price and promotion.

It seems to be an easy service, but, in fact it needs supports of a great number of systems. First, let's take a look at the simplified structure chart of real-time system.

We frequently use Nginx+Redis+SSDB. Nginx has two functions

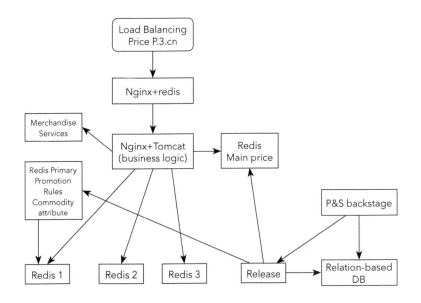

Simplified Structure Chart of Real-Time System

including business routing and simple handling of business.

In terms of business process, P.3.cn on the public network is our user analysis. The first node Nginx+Redis is a group of online clusters and the calculated prices have been stored in Redis. Redis and Nginx are deployed to the same machine which can be expanded at any time, so Redis can save all price information, or it will be hard to use the expansion. This layer is followed by the business logic layer developed by Nginx and the other one is Redis node of primary price. What is the use of this layer? On the one hand, in case of promotions, we invalidate the prices and then calculate the price again; on the other hand, non-popular commodities also require reverse source even they are not cached. The following business logic layers are called by the reverse sources and then the business logic layers will calculate the price and put the prince into Redis host, and lastly the Redis host cloud will synchronize the data to the clusters horizontally expanded by Nginx+Redis.

The sales & purchase system writes these prices into relational data bases and we specially develop an asynchronous release procedure by which such prices can be extracted from the relational data bases, and then we write the promotion information and put it into the promotion-related master Redis clusters and put the price information after calculation into Redis master framework clusters for synchronization. Since the promotion information is so important that we assign 4 Redis clusters to save the promotion information. The first one is the master cluster, and the second one is the slave cluster under the master one for synchronization and the remaining two clusters are also slave ones. The master cluster can be synchronized to the second slave cluster, and then to the third slave cluster in a bid to prevent breakdown of Redis. As we have 3 clusters to define online traffic, we can leisurely switch the backups for disaster recovery. Targeted reproduction by the third and second slave clusters can reduce pressure of the reproduction of Redis clusters. This is the closed loop of a rear business.

The real-time price system is applied with the following principles.

The first one is the principle of horizontal scalability partition. The greatest strength of this real-time price system is statelessness. All data is exactly alike and is convenient to use. The bottleneck lies in the data load capacity of the master Redis. If the master Redis carries excessive data fragments, it will be difficult to assure the consistency of separated data and the performance.

The second principle is traffic limiting. Many limiting rules and limiting data are added to Nginx nodes. The overall system receives online pressure tests in the end, and we found that the bottleneck of the whole system to be the call of reverse sources because calculation of the relevant business logic is too complicated. Both the promotion information and merchandise information should be obtained, and a great number of services are required for logical calculus, thus causing difficulty in call of reverse sources.

The third principle is degradation. We will conduct degradation aiming at the reverse source bottleneck. The price information seen before entering the shopping cart is allowed to be inconsistent, but the information displayed in the shopping cart should prevail because the shopping cart cannot be degraded. This is applicable to most commodities.

The fourth principle is reading-writing separation. The reading-writing logic as stated above is comprised by the enclosed loops of the reading-writing business logic. The problem occurring in the rear systems will not affect the previous systems.

Author: Wang Xiaozhong

CHAPTER 4

The Perfect Storm – Mass Order Processing

Importance of OFC

The 618 Event of 2014 seemed to be different from any shop celebration and promotion days in the past due to the challenges posed by ongoing swift development of e-commerce in China on JD's technical systems, and more importantly, the dazzling rays of light given out by its entry into NASDAQ "Palace" on May 22, 2014. Will such rays of light keep shining? The 618 Campaign would be a convincing answer sheet. Of course, we finally provided a satisfactory result. The home page of JD Mall will jump into your sight when you type www.jd.com in the browser and enter. Then you can select the merchandise you like according to your needs and add selected merchandise to the shopping cart. After the order is submitted, you can enjoy JD's speedy logistics experience and a simple and joyful shopping journey ends then. In fact, after submission of the order, multiple links and processing of various systems are required before the mission is accomplished. OFC (Order Fulfillment Center), is one of the necessary links for the order and connects the process of order placing and production for the orders in warehouses. In this chapter, we will unveil this department.

After the 618 Campaign of 2014, JD's technical team shared its experience and exploration in the field of technology concerning how to cope with the mall celebration day and promotional campaigns launched in the past. One of the chapters entitled "Key Technical Links of OFC for E-commerce Mass Order Processing" (see details in the first issue of JD Technology Open Day, http://dwz.cn/v3qc0) is discussing assignments undertaken by this department.

The duty of this department, as described by Peng Qing, is to transfer the orders placed by users into production orders of terminal systems, and deliver them to corresponding terminal systems as required. It is just like we cook the raw food materials according to the customers' different tastes (different systems) and deliver the food to the customers (terminal systems) on schedule. The whole process includes order division, transfer and release. In fact, the orders placed via website (also known as original orders) cannot directly go into production in the warehouse and require processing of OFC before these orders are delivered to various production systems. This link should process mass data and time is needed.

The modes of distribution provided by JD such as 211 and 311 are well known. The users may choose different delivery time and the express packages must be delivered to users by the time specified by users. However, if the downstream production system delays in receipt of the order data, the subsequent time of delivery will be affected and the customer experience is thus comprised. Now as for the order release, we set up nearly 150 warehouses and almost 20 external order processing servers throughout the country. As different systems vary in processing capability and responsiveness, we must accordingly allocate for the traffic regulation. If one of the systems is exposed to a problem, the order release will be influenced.

Formation of OFC

Since JD's website was launched in 2003, the rapid countrywide development of e-commerce was ushered in and JD's businesses were also increased, leading to increase of corresponding business systems. Until 2011, a small team was built along with increase of systems and business needs and it took charge of data transmission between different systems, transferring the order data to warehouses and transmitting over twenty businesses data concerning purchase orders, suppliers, etc. to the corresponding business system. OFC thus took shape.

At the incipient stage, imperfect systems imposed a variety of problems on the process of data transmission and the orders were always blocked at this link, while this transmission link must assure correctness and completeness of data transmission. Thus, we must understand the business of upstream and downstream systems and the process of data processing, thus we could figure out causes of problems and how to solve these problems. However, new demands for the upstream and downstream systems should be continuously released, so we had to know how to deal with the businesses of upstream and downstream systems every day to guarantee that no problems arise in our link.

That period was tough for our team. They immersed in thousands of work orders every day and overtime work was so frequent that one colleague even dreamt of dealing with the problematic orders. Due to problems existing in the division of business fields and unclear system boundary, a lot of baffling problems emerged and our fellows underwent a quite tough and tiring period until Peng Qing joined. Peng was not tall and wore thick fully-framed glasses. His student-like hairstyle presented us a cordial feeling.

Peng Qing divided this business segment thanks to his years of working experience and understanding of systems, and transmission of the data from non-customer work orders was handed over to corresponding systems. The fellows then were freed for customer order processing.

By the end of 2011, Peng led us to grow into a team comprising over twenty members. To further expand the businesses in respect to customer orders, we took over the order division system and order transfer system of our own accord. These two senior systems were developed by .Net, but it became very difficult to modify the systems since we lacked experienced tutors due to departure of some senior colleagues, relevant documents were incomplete and very few persons understood the interior businesses. At this time, the problem orders resulted from the system problems reached up to a hundred, in other words, the workload concerning operation and maintenance was impressive. In this case, no one objected to our undertaking of these two systems.

Technical Reform

From .Net to Java

After the systems are taken over, the first thing was to rewrite them. In consideration of the Company's technical development strategies at that time and Java's popularity, we selected Java. In the process of rewriting, the existing businesses must be combed and thus we should communicate with the previous colleagues who were in charge of the systems in order to confirm the business process and details of technical processing. With over one month, we completed rewriting of the systems and the next step was to launch the systems.

We began to split the traffic bit by bit and took control via switch. The traffic was separated in provinces, cities, towns and towns. By December

2012, the systems went launched finally and the previous .Net systems were gradually abandoned. By then, OFC was divided into 3 segments, i.e. order splitting, order transfer and order release & return as mentioned above.

Relevant explanations are given as follows:

1. Order division: as you may have it in mind, orders placed by our customers are divided based on types of warehouses, such as large appliances warehouse, warehouse for general commodities etc. Certainly, it is an initial and basic understanding of order division and we will explain how we split the orders today.

2. Order transfer: transfer orders to the downstream systems based on the orders which have been split and attributes like inventory.

3. Release and return of order: for the orders after transfer, the service links such as packaging related with the warehouse are called for release and return of orders. When the merchandises listed on the order are successfully delivered to customers, the order-related data should be returned. We will make further explanations in the following chapters.

211 Order Fulfillment Rate Improvement Project

After system is rewritten, the systems could operate normally and the next task was to comb and optimize the system in a bid to better support the growth of business demands and expansion of technology. Of course, sometimes the system improvement resulted from failure of exterior business in adaption and this conformed to the essence of reform. User experience is prioritized by everyone working in JD. Even Lao Liu (Liu Qiangdong) often placed orders on the website, and he found some problems this time. He placed an order and waited so long before receiving the order. Through investigation, he found that it took over two hours transferring the order to our warehouse.

Then Lao Liu initiated a program called "Improvement of 211 Order Fulfillment Rate," which targeted at upgrading and transformation of 11

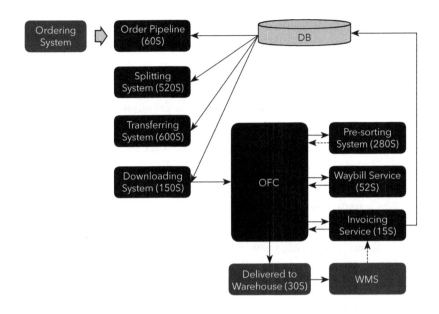

Overall Design Sketch of the System before Transformation

systems including order transaction system, order pipeline system, splitting system, transferring system, order task system, OFC-related system, presorting system, waybill system, VAT qualification system, invoicing system and WMS system, four of which needed to be completely transformed, three of which needed to be greatly transformed and the remaining four systems should be subject to slight transformation. Furthermore, the order-related businesses had a lot of points and involved in complicated logic, so they could not be comprehensively tested in the testing environment. This would affect not only normal production of orders, but also finance-related businesses. This project was of great importance. It aimed at shortening the time spent from the order being placed till the order being delivered to the warehouse to five minutes with 2-month efforts. Everyone began to work: six days for discussion on demands, five days for designing schemes, 15 days for development, 20 days for functional test, 44 days for performance test, 26 days for deployment and debugging. The working hours totaled 5066 and the project target was finally achieved. Meanwhile, the service performance and index of all links for order release were standardized and the process of order release tended to be stabled and smoothened. The techniques were sharpened as well. Zookeeper distributed configuration, CXF Timeout setting, Log4j multi-Tomcat sample configuration, Oracle database partition plans were adopted, and Oracle Exadata and MySQL were applied to the databases. In this process, the communications with Oracle technical team were carried out 10 times, and the database design, performance optimization, and historical data transition were all improved. More importantly, the team was trained and gained greater confidence in fulfilling arduous tasks. The overall design sketch of system is shown as follows.

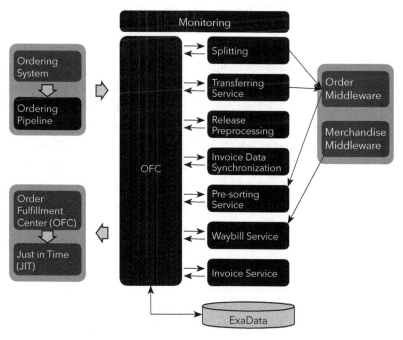

Overall Design Sketch of the System after Transformation

Several talents combed the businesses of splitting system and found that some businesses were disordered and the business areas were not clearly classified. In the splitting system, except for splitting according to the commodity attributes, the information of amount, special offers, and freight needed to be separately dealt with. These talents subtly found that it was unreasonable to design the system in this way, and then picked out the processing logic of amount information and developed an exclusive service, called the Ordering Charging System (OCS), and call of this system was required. Meanwhile, we carried out persistent storage for the data about OCS results. The system was designed in this way so that the business processing logic which was disordered before service splitting was solved and OCS data filled up the blank of data in this area and became the basic data sources for using other systems and processing the business logic. Up to now, over twenty systems are using OCS data, so its importance is evident without saying.

SOP Commodity Consolidation Project

In 2013, the company-level SOP commodity consolidation project was to be initiated, i.e. the commodities sold by JD and the commodities from POP sellers were consolidated in the customer's shopping cart (SOP). Customers only needed to submit once when making payment (in the past, they had to submit separately, such as Taobao, in which the commodities sold by different sellers should be submitted separately). To improve the user experience, the divided sub-orders after submission would be displayed and our team was required to deliver a splitting service for the transaction team. It was a major test. Order placement was then sped up. TP99 took only tens of milliseconds, but our current services required tens of seconds. The gap was significant. To accomplish this project smoothly, we needed to not only satisfy the routine business demands, but also set a new branch serving modification for this project. Meanwhile, the codes associated with new demands must be synchronized to these two branches, comprising a quite arduous undertaking. After development-related problems were solved, the attentions should be paid to improvement of performance. For example, prioritize processing should be conducted in the memory for the best; minimize the dependence on external services; asynchronize those non-synchronized operations; degrade certain services, and degrade via switch if necessary to assure the overall performance. And we requested the performance test team to conduct performance test over our service. We then optimized at the code level and successfully accomplish the project on schedule. At the same time, we were maintaining three splitting service codes at the same level. The old ordering operation corresponded to the old splitting service mentioned above, and the new ordering operation corresponded to new splitting service and the pre-splitting we developed for the transaction system.

However, at this moment, what nagged us the most was not maintenance of these systems, but service timeout for an order due to poor network, thus resulting in retry of service (in fact the order had been successfully submitted). This may cause our users to submit orders for twice or several times falsely. For instance, a customer placed an original order and needed it to be split into two, but many orders may be generated due to the abovementioned reason; if customers selected delivery on cash, they would be confused and our delivery cost was increased; and if they selected on-line payment, the Company would suffer loss. At the beginning, there was no effective solutions, so we had to control by monitoring and we artificially locked them after detecting such orders. In this way, operation and maintenance pressure was boosted and it was hard to avoid mistakes in the process of manual processing. As we would obtain order numbers before submitting sub-orders, the order numbers we obtained every time were new ones. This would make us unable to avoid repeated order numbers when calling this service. Later, Haibo came up with a scheme to avoid such problem. He suggested us to type the order number information into the anti-repetition base before calling this service; when there were new orders, we could search the anti-repetition database firstly; and if any order information was targeted, indicating that the same order had been submitted before, then we submit the data with the same order number in the base to save order numbers. If nothing was found in the base, we would insert such order number into the base and call the service at the same time. The problem was efficiently solved. After optimized processing of the submission process, the systems were finally stabilized.

Upgrade of Transfer Architecture

The transfer system was also greatly adjusted. In order to further guarantee that the orders could be promptly and accurately transferred to the downstream warehouse system, the transfer team conducted a series of improvements in terms of the business and technical architecture: asynchronize the business and data processing, i.e. the business and data available for asynchronous processing were put into a distributed queue and processed by corresponding modules; simply and rapidly circulate the primary process and business; parallelize the data processing, and divide the data into several business units which were subject to parallel processing; apply cashes and updating mechanism to the hot data with few changes and slack real-time requirements so as to improve the performance; and protect the subsequent systems from being overwhelmed by the flood peak in case of the business flood peak.

The business process was also optimized. As the build-to-order process was involved, the speed of change in demand was very high, and the existing processes must be continuously combed, unnecessary processes should be removed and the concerns about unnecessary business process and branch were reduced when there were demands. Meanwhile, the current dispersed business was subject to continuing abstraction and transformation to facilitate business expansion.

After such optimization and improvement, undoubtedly we would be exposed to tremendous risk when the systems were launched every time.

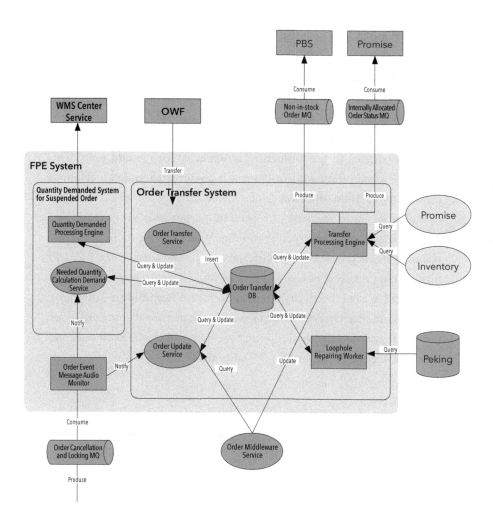

Overall Flow Chart of Transfer System

How to avoid the risks? The solutions were to split the traffic, provide configurability and prioritize the operating tools. Those newly launched projects may be exposed to high risks, some functions for external interaction may be easily omitted and on-line problems could not be timely switched. Thus, release of new businesses should be split and controlled through the flexible and convenient configuration center at any time. Priority must be given to abnormal situations and corresponding operating tools should be developed for emergency circumstances. In particular, a fluke mind believing that small probability events never happen could not be held.

The head of transfer team, Manager Tie (everyone called him like this), has been engaged in the business of e-commerce for ten-odd years. This man, who comes from western Hunan, is always strict and conscientious to work, but enthusiastic towards life; before marriage, he was crazy about computer games or obsessed with badminton, but after his daughter was born, this girl became everything for him. When talking about the future planning and development of transfer system, he said confidently, "We will highlight optimization of cost and process while the customer experience is guaranteed in a bid to reduce the cost in the future. Regarding the inventory allocation, the current rule will be broken on the premise that the orders are fulfilled to improve the inventory turnover rate and the in-stock rate, and provide earlier receiving time for our customers."

Love for Operations & Maintenance

At the beginning, when we just took over the customer order system, thousands of tickets (order events) awaited us every day, but now we only need to deal with dozens of them. Such a sharp reduction not only suggests that our system is becoming healthier and the business is increasingly standardized, but also reflects that our operation & maintenance process and institution are increasingly advancing. These results cannot be achieved without Wenjie who is proficient in analysis and summary. Born in the 1980s, he comes from Shandong Province and is primarily in charge of optimization of operation process and the coordination-associated works in the team. He can solve nearly any problem with respect to operation and maintenance. OFC is the important channel and hub to connect our users and terminal warehouses throughout the country, thus any system fault may cause errors in delivery of orders to the terminal warehouses on schedule and the consequences would be disastrous. Therefore, for each additional warehouse, the team must deploy and debug this warehouse's terminal systems until the testing of production system is completed. We call it the warehouse opening process. With development and expansion of the Company and perfection of order processing, the number of existing warehouses across the country has surpassed 150 attributed to efforts made in a long period by Wenjie and his team. Support of audits is also an assignment that cannot be neglected. We will introduce new businesses to colleagues and explain reasons of differentiated orders to them. Meanwhile, we also take charge of learning and promotion of new businesses, guide new members to quickly understand the business knowledge and be familiar with the business system. When the business and system are increasingly improved, we are also trying and popularizing intelligent operation, maintenance and support continuously, and believe that unattended operations and maintenance of systems will be materialized in the near future.

From the 618 Campaign to the Double 11 Festival

Since 2012, more promotional campaigns for mall celebration were launched, accompanied by sharp increase of order quantity which posed increasingly greater challenges to our systems. Processing of orders became more and more complicated and more and more procedures for business processing appeared, thus causing inconsistency of data. Consequently, it is very essential to maintain consistency of data in processing the mass orders. Integral control of systems applies the process control center instead of stepped control. Owing to direct independence on the databases in the past, the databases would finally become the bottleneck for order processing and it is hard to guarantee the consistency of data. The mode of process control center could sharply decrease the probability of occurrence of data inconsistency, and the workflow and state machine can be relied on for materialization of centralized control for the convenience of operation and prompt detection and determination of solutions to the defective orders.

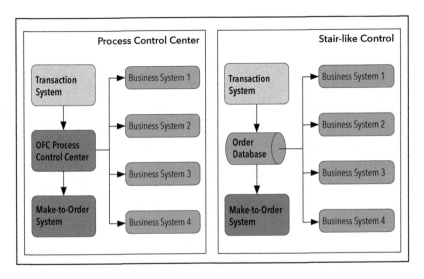

Process Control Center and Stair-like Control

Support of Mass Order Processing

No matter how perfect the systems are, a single system always has bottle-necks, so the key to support the climbing order quantity is to improve the expansion capability of systems. In the first place, every layer of the core system should be endowed with the expansion capability to expand with the example or cluster as unit. Secondly, the whole system must have the expansion capability and is capable of vertically splitting the businesses based on their practical features or conveniently adding a cluster having integrated functions by means of distributed deployment, thus rapidly improving the processing capacity. This can save costs compared with the practice of only preparing standby systems.

All core OFC order processing systems have been equipped with the horizontal expansion capability and some systems have received distributed-deployment improvement. Prior to the 618 Campaign in 2014, this expansion capability possessed by the systems empowered expansion of processing capability in very short period, thus ensuring the promotional campaign could be held successfully. Our final aim is to ensure that all core systems receive distributed deployment.

Solution to Data Inconsistency

In the early stage, order handling processes were spread among multiple application systems, causing varied data sources and lack of a uniform state machine control and accordingly, problems about data inconsistency occurred time to time. However, at the same time, it is impossible to manage all processes with a single system because the work for maintenance and management require enormous and complicated efforts. The solution is, to figure out a master process and the state machine for order processing and then cause this master process to be in charge of dispatch of the whole process and data pushing. This master process may cross large business domains such as logistics domain and capital domain, and every domain may have workflow which should not be in conflict with the master process. Identifying the master process system has other advantages: firstly, the emphasis can be only placed on establishment of the systems relating to the master process to make for a stable system cluster, and less costs are invested in the systems irrelevant to the master process, thus ensuring better progress in the business and reducing the cost for the whole construction; secondly, the master process can effectively guarantee execution of the production plans; thirdly, the master process system can regulate the system traffic, effectively smooth the business peak and maintain stable operation of the major systems relating to the master process.

Supporting the Operation Work

Supports for the operation work comprise emergency rescue, prevention and "upgrade of governance + prevention." In the early phase, the system architecture mainly supported the realization of business functions and was not designed for the operation. Online systems would influence businesses due to various incidents, which exhausted the system team. Later, the philosophy and principle designed for operation were established, which required considering possibility of monitoring and operating in the process of design and highlighted availability, stability and robustness of design. The specific methodology was also set up in the process of practice.

Firstly, sort the systems, identify the core systems and furnish these core systems with high availability and reliability, and ensure that these systems are less problematic and able to automatically recover in case of any failure.

Second, ensure that problems can be quickly identified after any problem occurs to the system, or the early warning can be given before the problem occurs. To this end, it is necessary to monitor the data backlog tendency as well as the throughput capability in case that there are backlogs. Such monitoring must be without delay, and we developed a distributed monitoring system which can swiftly reflect the situation of every example and collect the overall operation data for the distributed systems.

Third, ensure that problems can be rapidly identified and solved. For this purpose, we designed a consolidated analysis tool integrated with system processing capability, data backlog, data processing, log and system load.

Fourth, in case that certain system fails, other systems may be affected. System management is imperative. Currently, we have set up SOA management platform (under optimization), targeting at untangling the genetic connection among various systems and perfecting SLA system; in case of any failure, the affected system(s) can be timely identified and quick emergency response can be made.

The Start of Mass Data

General Guidelines

The order processing system is essentially different from the transaction system. The transaction system directly faces customers, so it requires high system availability and performance, especially the system's performance under the circumstance of high concurrency. Therefore, the emphasis of transaction system lies in solving problems with respect to these two areas. However, the order processing system is on the contrary. A short period of

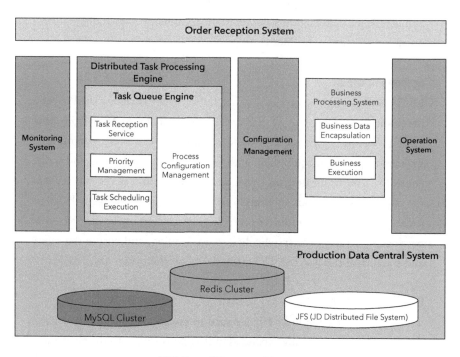

OFC Overall Structure Diagram

system unavailability or delay in response will not have direct impacts on our customers, that is, what we care about is the average value rather than the peak value at any time. The key point for architecture design of order processing system lies in how to process mass data and assurance of data consistency. In recent years, JD makes ongoing efforts in expanding its business domain, leading to rapid increase of order quantity, so we must ensure improvement of the system's throughput capability. Concurrently, multitudinous systems are involved and varied business handling methods and processes are applied by different systems, resulting in significant difference in performance indexes, thus SLA indexes must be prudently defined for various systems. Since more and more complicated order businesses will cause the systems to generate more and more business processes, we need to identify the primary and secondary business processes and their priority, and work out flexible and diversified degradation schemes in the meanwhile to guarantee normal operation of primary businesses.

System Protection

OFC needs to call many order systems, but different systems varied in their processing capability. Not all systems have to bear the pressure from peak value processing. This requires us to control and call these systems in a targeted manner and equip them with functions of peak clipping and traffic control to directly protect upstream and downstream systems and prevent the caller's systems from suffering a snow-slide-type breakdown. Furthermore, the capacity monitoring must be uniform; it is necessary to avoid overloading, control the systems before overloading, and ensure the safety and stability of the systems. The quick denial mechanism is also available.

Distributed System

The expansion-related links are designed to ensure that every fragment of the system can horizontally expand as well as expansion with the cluster as a unit, thus realizing the distributed task queue. The order quantity that each

Group is able to process is under control, and in case any bottleneck occurs anywhere, we can deploy one or one set of Group at any time. As shown in the following diagram, different Groups can be deployed separately or as a whole. In case of any problem occurring in any link, separate deployment can be adopted, and replica deployment is applicable when the overall traffic is large.

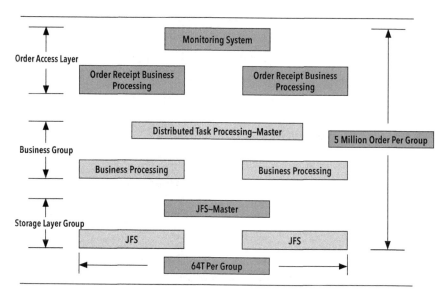

Distributed System Architecture

The distributed task processing structure diagram is shown as follows. Because of the distributed task processing engine, we can fetch tasks from the Distributed Task Queue at the lower left (Redis Cache), and the engine will dispatch corresponding services one by one and then return the results to the corresponding services for business processing, meanwhile, the results we need will be returned and the transaction snapshot data is really converted into production documents. Finally, the data will be pushed to the Client system such as warehouse system or POP seller's system.

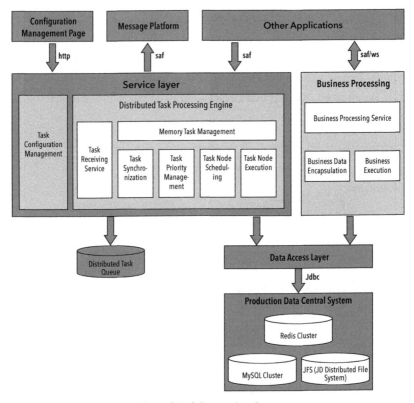

Distributed Task Processing Structure

The distributed task queue design may be illustrated by the following diagram. We firstly fragment the tasks and define each task as one fragment, and then process the tasks in the task performers, each of which have many threads used to process and call different services, and finally return the results. There will be an abnormal task queue covering the failing tasks, and then the processing flow for abnormalities will be performed. Perhaps you will wonder that if the system breaks down, the data of task will lose and what should be done if the task has not completed. In fact, if our initial order data is saved, the task can be performed again, slowly maybe, but the data consistency will never be caused.

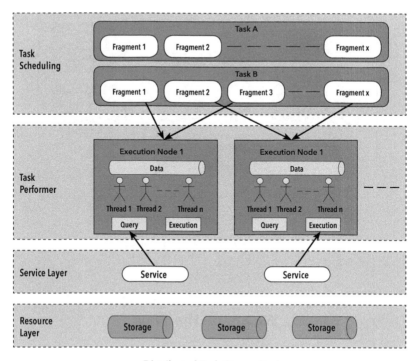

Distributed Task Queue Design

Our distributed task queue employs the mechanism of workflow, supporting flexible process configuration. The distributed configuration is primarily carried out through Zookeeper and the business processing links can be added at any time. Meanwhile, the throughput capacity of the systems can be automatically adjusted. When any link suffers a problem, auto reduction of speed will be activated. After the problem is solved, we will conduct auto increase of speed to assure the system's throughput capacity; we may prioritize production and processing of prior orders through configuration.

The system deployment is shown as follows:

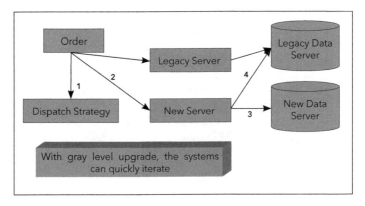

System Deployment Diagram

We are on the Way

Our team grew from a small one of five or six in the early June of 2011 into a team of thirty members today. At the beginning, we were only assigned to the non-customer-order-related business systems and now we are taking charge of the Company's 0-level core order system. OFC's scope of business stretches over more than a half of the life cycle of the whole make-to-order process. Yes, it is the ordinary staff who never bewildered in turmoil and never forget their missions in mirth, and who are common people seen by appearance but long for advances that adhere to the front line of order systems without hesitation. Looking back to the road we have taken, we are so calm and poised; looking forward to the future, we are still passionate and will give sunshine smile. In this great era, in this great nation, there is a group of great people doing something great: to make shopping simple and joyful, and that's who we are.

Group Photo of OFC Development Team and Testing Team

Author: Peng Qing

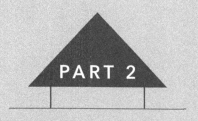

Product Evolution

What systems constitute an e-commerce shopping website? This is an issue that everyone engaged in the IT industry is attempting to understand.

In this chapter, various systems of the entire JD core business chain will be uncovered: Open Seller Platform, storage, logistics, after-sales service, finance, interior office, and more. This is the first time to disclose two issues that everyone wants to know about, namely how JD.COM developed and evolved, and how JD.com, Yixun.com, and paipai.com were integrated.

- Developmental history of the shopping website
- Integration with Tencent ECC
- POP legend
- Supply chain with sovereign experience
- After-sale system
- Evolution history of financial system
- The course of internal informatization

CHAPTER 5

The Great Era: Development History of the Website

Bronze Age

In 2003 when SARS wreaked havoc across Beijing, there were a few visitors to physical stores in Zhongguancun and it was the same case for JD. At that time, for the sake of employees' safety, Lao Liu decided to close all stores to fight against SARS. However, after the stores were closed, the available funds were expected to support JD's operation for half a year at most. How to keep running the company became a big problem. By a chance, Lao Liu found that the merchandise could be directly sold to customers through online forums and this approach could avoid physical contact with the customers, thus preventing SARS infection. Later, JD kicked off its journey of online sales.

And so, after a period, the online sales volume kept climbing. Online sales broke new ground for the company. Through careful consideration,

Lao Liu decided to close offline stores and turn to online sales. However, online sales could not solely depend on public forums, and so JD had to build its own online sales platform, which would be the leading channel for JD's business in the future. It was praised as the lifeline of JD.

There was a legendary story about the development of the first version of the website. In 2003, Lao Liu began his attempt to sell products through online forums. His marketing methods were quite distinctive. The customers were allowed to try the product first before buying it and didn't need to pay in case the product turned out to be unqualified during trial use. At an offline trial meeting, here came the key figure of this story, Cao Peng. He was then working as a programmer in a foreign-funded enterprise, which had a great demand in optical disks. He attended this trial meeting for the purpose of checking the quality of JD's merchandise. After trial use, he admitted that JD provided high-quality and licensed goods at competitive prices. Then Cao Peng formed ties with JD and became well acquainted with Lao Liu.

In 2003 when Lao Liu intended to build a website, he thought of Cao Peng. Another programmer was also invited along with Cao Peng. Cao Peng recalled that, at that time, there were only two of them developing this website with ASP technology.

At the beginning of 2004, the website was formally launched, bearing the name Jingdong Multimedia. This website displayed the commodities in a relatively simple way and users could place orders smoothly. After an order was placed, a primitive operation procedure was applied, where someone would print out the list and then pick up the goods in the warehouse. After all, it was the first online sales platform independently developed by JD as well as an important milestone for JD's e-commerce undertaking. This platform allowed users to experience online buying and shortened the distance between JD and its users. After the website was released, the sales volumes surged at a surprising speed.

From 2004 to 2006, a staff of less than five took charge of website development and management. All work relating to the system was undertaken by them jointly. Lao Liu paid special attention to customer feedback from the forum to the self-developed website and fell into the habit of maintaining close communications with customers and replying to their comments. He attached great importance to the website development. As some senior employees recalled, he held two posts in the company, one of which was in the R&D Department. He also provided instructions for website design, copy writing, and more.

In the first half of 2005, Lao Liu, who prevailed over all dissenting views by deciding to shut down 12 offline stores and focus on online sales. The online sales volume increased by over 200% annually. By June 2007, the number of daily orders had exceeded 3000.

In August 2007, JD obtained the first venture investment, putting the company on the fast track. Increases of order quantities also posed a great challenge to the systems. JD was badly in need of an excellent technical talent who could lead the team and lay a solid foundation for the business expansion.

In May, 2008, Donny joined JD and held the post of Head of the R&D Department. After careful research on the existing systems, Donny found that these systems would be unable to accommodate JD's future business growth, and the system architecture upgrading was imperative, with .Net replacing ASP. Meanwhile, we took this opportunity to revise the front-end pages in attempt to improve the customer experience.

Silver Age

On August 20, 2008, a minivan stopped in front of a three-story villa of an upscale neighborhood located in the Tongzhou District of Beijing. Out jumped 3 young men, looking around curiously. Several people immediately came out of the villa. They greeted the newcomers and moved several computers, displays, routers, and patch panels out of the minivan, and entered the villa talking and laughing. JD's future website architecture was born in this three-story villa.

Frank, who just joined JD 3 days ago, was among these 3 young men. He left Sohu and chose JD, expecting to bring his talent into play in the grand tide of e-commerce. Unexpectedly, the first task for him was an enclosed development program lasting nearly 3 months.

Head of R&D Department Donny acted as General Director of the enclosed development program and was called Lao Li in the company. Lao Li joined JD in June 2008, being the second vice president of JD. He was a typical southerner, not tall but shrewd, and always talked slowly but with cadence. All of us felt that his speech was as appealing as Ma Yun's. Lao Li offered a proposal for JD's website reconstruction based on the target of reaching the sales volume of RMB ten billion. After the 618 Mall Celebration Campaign, he led a small group leaving for Tongzhou to carry out the enclosed development program.

This enclosed development program involved around 14 participants at the earlier stage, and some other colleagues would join in to give support after entering the critical stage. In the initial phase, the group comprised 1 product manager, 2 front-end developers, 2 designers, 1 testing personnel, and around 8 developers. Conditions for the enclosed development were arduous. Although the program was in the villa, in it there were only had two sofas and one bed put at the third floor. Lao Li was senior, so we left the bed for him and other young men made a bed on the floor. It was tolerable in August, but it was getting cold in October, with an unbroken spell of wet weather. The villa was not furnished with heating installation, so they fetched thicker quilts. The daily schedule began at 10 a.m. and ended at around 1–2 a.m. Fortunately, most of the group members were young and they could handle it well. But there was one unhappy thing, a colleague snored loudly. If he fell asleep earlier, the rest would have to be awake, so others urged him to work later for the sake of others sleep quality and vigor for the work assigned for the next day. Meals were good. A middle-aged woman was hired to make three meals a day for us. Her food was tasty and we had good meals every day. The most restful thing we did was to take a walk in this deluxe villa area after lunch and dinner.

We won't go into the process of the enclosed development here. We tackled difficulties, had emotional discussions, and restarted painfully, as well as experiencing pleasure and joy in this process. At the later stage of the project, there was not much time left for development. Various problems would emerge in the process of joint debugging and testing for brand new bottom systems. With the time passing by, everyone made desperate efforts to work against the clock. In this phase, Lao Liu paid a visit and invited us to dine together in a restaurant nearby to cheer us up. The food's taste had been forgotten, and everyone suffered mental stress.

Three months later, with everyone's effort, the enclosed development program wound up successfully. The new version of JD.COM was launched in early November2008. Despite some bugs and performance-related problems were found during interaction with the customers, the overall customers' satisfaction and conversion ratio were greatly improved after repairs. In this revision, there were 4 significant changes made for the website page. First, not all commodity categories were listed any longer and a mode of secondary pop up layer for the categories was employed; second, a commodity ranking list was added; third, highlight on the login part was removed and the space was saved to display more products; and fourth, the shopping cart was shown on the home page for convenience of customers' checkout at any time.

The new website laid a solid foundation for JD's rapid growth from 2008 to 2010 and increased the daily number of orders from several thousand to hundreds of thousands. At the same time, after three months a new R&D team was born. Members of this team also grew into the backbone of JD's technical systems.

Golden Age

Focusing on the user experience has always been the tradition observed by JD. From Lao Liu to workers at the production line, everyone in JD puts customers first and attaches the most importance to customers' interests.

After revisions in 2008, the performance of JD's website was greatly improved, but various user experiences need to be continuously refined. In 2009, Lao Liu proposed to open a new function named CEO Online on which Lao Liu and other senior executives regularly answered questions raised by net citizens and helped them solve problems effectively.

CEO Online triggered active reactions among netizens. Lao Liu and other senior executives were really on line to offer help. Later, along with perfection of the website's functions and continuous promotion of services, JD had fostered a professional customer service team capable of solving various questions for customers, so the CEO Online was retired successfully.

At the primary stage of development, questions about logistics were among the most asked. However, with improvement of logistic service quality, these questions declined gradually. In this process, the Order Tracking system played a vital role.

Where is My Package?
JD's logistics system also underwent swift development in 2008. Barriers for competition were set up and JD gained a good reputation thanks to its fast delivery in the first-tier cities. Apart from fast delivery, Lao Liu also wanted the commodity's logistics information to be clearly displayed for customers to put an end to their misgivings and make them rest easy when buying and awaiting the products.

In 2010, Lao Liu suggested product managers in charge of order display to get down to designing the Order Tracking function. It was a simple function which was designed for recording and displaying key nodes of the whole service link, beginning after the order was placed, and enabled customers to check where the things they bought were, what the status was, which courier was delivering their products, and contact number of the courier, all whenever they opened the web page.

Viewing from the page content, it was a very simple information display process, but the realization mechanism behind it was not that simple, as JD's information system should record all circulation information from the moment the customers placed orders. Besides, this required a connection and interaction of all related systems, such as the order system, warehousing system, dispatch system, distribution system, site administration system, and delivery information system so that every message could be completely and accurately displayed in front of customers.

JD made it. When the order tracking system was released, it was well accepted by customers and led to a sharp decline of customer service hotline calls and rise of customer satisfaction rates. The feeling of "everything is under control" fully satisfied customers. In this age when e-commerce required acceptance and trust from more people, this kind of service really hit the nail on the head and was imitated by other e-commerce service providers. Although Order Tracking is a standard configuration of e-commerce now, JD was the pioneer of this function. Such focus on the user experience and innovative spirit propelled JD to advance quickly.

In 2012, with reinforcement of the warehousing and distribution system, perfection of process system and accumulation of big data, JD launched an Order Timeliness Promise system, which could forecast when the order would be received and allow customers to be informed earlier when they could receive products by considering inventory status, location of warehouse, place of receipt, order time, and distribution capacity. For example, if a customer in Beijing placed an order before 11 a.m. on Friday, he/she would be informed that "the package is estimated to be delivered before

6 pm. Therefore, the customers could take delivery of the goods at his working unit without being concerned about the place of receipt (home or workplace). From the service perspective of Order Promise, it was a shopping promise made by JD. Certain compensation would be made to the customers in case of delay in delivery. Meanwhile, the big data team would repeatedly calculate the data to find out problems and how to predict more accurately. JD was strict with itself to unremittingly improve the user experience. "JD's Fast Delivery" was recognized and publicly praised among customers.

JD took advantage of analysis methods of big data not only in the domain of logistics service, but also for analysis of the customers' browsing habits for the guidance of the website design. Then how to collect truthful data about users' browsing habit?

Establishing User Experience Room

In the end of 2006, a book named *Don't make me think* became popular in Internet circles, particularly in the product design circles. Hereafter, greater importance and attention were attached to the user experience. Every internet company was thinking about what good user experience is and how to provide a better user experience, and JD was no exception.

To provide a good user experience requires frequent interaction with users. Lao Liu set a good example for JD's product managers. He was present at the netizen meetings, answered customer service phones, and participated in the online exchange personally. To keep in touch with the users, the first step that should be taken was to find users quickly. One place immediately occurred to JD's product mangers: the JD self-pickup center. At the initial development stage, customers still entertained the idea of shopping at JD. The habit of payment on delivery led a lot of customers to select the shopping mode of picking up goods after payment at JD's self-pickup centers, which served new and old customers of different genders and ages. The centers' location had a great visitor flow volume, so in earlier days, the self-pickup centers became the optimal place for product managers to do user research and interviews.

In 2009 and 2010, JD's office was located near Suzhou Street in the Haidian District of Beijing, near where the largest pickup center was set up. The pickup centers were equipped with two computers used for order inquiry or goods selecting. When users were using the computers, product managers would stand behind them, watching how they used JD's website, where they stopped, and what operation mistakes were made, and observing their reaction and follow-ups. Such behind-the-back observations would obtain accurate, natural results. User research at these pickup centers provided product managers with the first-hand data for the optimization of website experience.

In the beginning of 2011, product managers and designers felt restricted just doing observations behind users. We called for better environment and needed to make an in-depth exchange or tests with users, so with strong support from the company, JD's R&D Department planned to establish user experience rooms. The user experience room was comprised of 3 rooms: the interview room, the test room, and the observation room. The interview room had a rectangular table for focus group interviews with users. The 6-8 users sat around the table and had discussions with a leader. The test room was relatively relaxing, being equipped with bookcases, a sofa, and green plants as well as m two computers and one expensive eye tracker used for recording the users' mouse action and eye movement data. The observation room was interesting as it was covered by a one-way mirror. Viewed from the outside, it was an ordinary mirror, but people behind the mirror could see the scene outside, therefore product managers could sit in the observation room to watch the users' operations. What they said and operation interfaces could be transmitted to the observation room via microphone and display screen, so it was very suitable for real-time observation.

The eye tracker, called X120, was produced by the Sweden company TOBII. Through the corneal reflex mode, information was collected by an imaging sensor, and the eye tracker could calculate the location and gaze orientation of the user's eyeballs and construct a planar reference diagram, overspread with points of regard using sophisticated and complicated image processing techniques and algorithms. With this device, we could figure out where and how long the users watched, where they clicked, and draw very accurate and quantitative conclusions through data analysis, thus assisting the product managers to optimize design schemes.

The establishment of user experience rooms laid a foundation for the redesign by JD in 2012. In the latter half of 2012, JD initiated redesign of the front-end web page. The core aim of this redesign was to show JD's image as a comprehensive shopping mall, make the website more pleasing to the eye, and attract more attention from female users.

After the newly designed website was launched, it was found through data comparison that the homepage conversion rate rose by 4.74% and the user experience was further improved.

A Company Not Avoiding Negative Comments

After the redesign in 2012, the brand awareness of JD was greatly improved and more and more people began to pay close attention to JD. Minor flaws in the website would compromise the shopping experience of many customers. The product managers also treated every improvement more cautiously. Taking the evaluation system as the example, it had a long historical standing and was subject to ongoing reforms.

JD is the earliest and best e-commerce company in commodity evaluation, without exaggeration. The reasons why JD focused on the feedback of consumers should begin with Lao Liu, who was in favor of interactions with customers. To this day, he still sticks to delivering an order in person once every year in an attempt to be closer to customers. In the eyes of Lao Liu and other colleagues, trusting, respecting, and allowing customers to help each other are the most effective way to narrow the distance to our consumers. The following factors contributed to the success of JD's product comment function.

First, JD first carried out communication and sales in a BBS, and thus fostered a rich community ambiance. Those loyal customers formed in the BSS and fanciers of hardware had a strong awareness of sharing and this batch of users was highly qualified and their feedback was of great value. Like snowballs, high-quality comments would attract more customers, who in turn give the commenter more incentives and a stronger sense of honor. Then JD was more like a grand community for hardware enthusiasts than a platform.

Secondly, a rule was set for the comments, which only allows customers who have bought the product to write comments. This rule may prevent many customers who intend to say something but have not bought yet from making comments, but it is reasonable to set such a rule because those who have used the product are best qualified to comment and can provide the most reliable and valuable feedback, which is also helpful for other customers in making purchasing decisions. Bad money drives out good — the customers who are helped will be happier to help others to purchase and transfer the help they have received.

Moreover, JD also provides bonus points for thoughtful guidance. For example, the number of bonus points varies with comments on the products in different categories; the first five comments are rewarded with multiplied bonus points; the higher the membership grade is, the more bonus points given; and high-quality comments are accompanied by additional bonus points, and so forth. These incentives lead customers to be willing to write high-quality comments to gain awards.

JD's product comments soon become its valuable feature. Baidu collected a great number of JD's comments and brought with them vast quantities of customers. Many customers will repeatedly review comments before purchasing, and these comments represented the product's degree of popularity, and were regarded as the basis for purchasing decisions.

Furthermore, JD's comments function falls into 3 Tab pages including "good," "medium," and "bad," which can be used by customers to review all the negative comments on certain products. Will these negative comments make customers give up a purchase? Initially, product managers had the same concern, but at Lao Liu's insistence, it was finally adopted. Data observations showed that the total order quantity was not reduced. Knowing the product's disadvantages, customers can carry out comparisons on an integrated basis and thus finally determine an optimal purchase plan, and we surprisingly found that the sales returns and complaints declined. Meanwhile, we have specially-assigned persons in charge of overseeing those products with too many negative comments, negotiating with or even punishing suppliers of such products. This is the best case for the rule of survival of the fittest by market-based means and best reflects that JD is dexterous in the basics of internet commerce.

Later, we also conducted an interesting experiment in which different comments and rankings were considered for Tests A and B to find out the content portfolio as the basis for optimization. Three teams attended this interesting and valuable competition with different algorithms and all teams could improve the algorithms. This competition lasted for over 3 months, and the team from the Chengdu Research Institute won the competition. The new screening and sorting algorithm raised the conversion rate by more than 20% and showed us the technology's value and the working spirit pursuing perfection.

Today, JD is still optimizing its product comment function, and tag, sharing, and Q&A are added to create a fair and transparent transaction environment to provide our customers with the most value-added services.

In the future, JD will continue to focus on the user experience and what we pursue is to provide the best user experience. We should endeavor to make everything simple and joyful, from every shopping process from the customer's single click through such experience optimization. This is the mission of everyone working at JD.

JD never stops moving forward and JD.COM is also being improved and optimized. There were only 42 BBS users at the very beginning, but as of the second quarter of 2014, the active users have reached 38.1 million, witnessing the course of JD's rapid development in the past ten years. Behind this lay the unremitting efforts made by many product managers, engineers, and project managers, and it is their youth and hard work that has accompanied JD's advances.

Author: Wang Yu

CHAPTER 6

Brotherhood: Integration with Tencent ECC

Before Integration

On the morning of March 10, 2014, JD Group and Tencent Holdings Limited announced the establishment of a strategic partnership. JD acquired 100% of equity, logistics employees, and assets of BUY.QQ.COM and PAIPAI.COM, which were respectively a B2C platform and the C2C platform of Tencent, and minority stakes of YIXUN.COM, and purchased the remaining stock rights of YIXUN.COM; Tencent purchased more than 350 million common shares of JD at about US$ 215 million, accounting for 15% of JD's circulating common shares. At the same time, Tencent offered the primary entry to Wechat and Mobile QQ Client as well as supports of other platforms to boost JD's development in the physical e-commerce domain. Both parties would also cooperate in online payment services to improve customers' online shopping experience.

Group Photo of OFC Development Team and Testing Team

This strategic cooperation was internally defined as integration. ECC business is handed over to JD and the latter will make plans and accomplish a seamless joint venture from employees, businesses, and systems. As the strategic project management team of the R&D system, we will undertake the work for system integration.

For this strategic cooperation, both parties set up the following cooperation frameworks:

1   Both parties will develop strategic cooperation in the e-commerce domain;

2   Tencent provides JD with cooperative support regarding mobile platform applications;

3   Both parties will cooperate in mobile payment;

4   JD will be Tencent's priority partner in several cooperative fields;

5   Tencent will no longer engage in the businesses that have a competitive relationship with JD.

To be specific, at the business level, all e-commerce businesses in the possession of Tencent such as buy.qq.com and paipai.com (including logistics) will be integrated into JD, and yixun.com will continue to operate as a separate brand. JD will subscribe a minority of stock rights and enjoy the right to buy the remaining ones. Meanwhile, Tencent will provide JD with primary entries to its strategic-level mobile products such as Mobile QQ and Wechat as well as support regarding other key platforms, thus helping JD develop a mobile e-commerce business.

When speaking of this cooperation, Haoyu pointed out that its impact on JD was obvious. First, the B2C business which relied chiefly on self-operation would give place to a complete an e-commerce ecosystem comprising of a self-operated B2C + Platform-based B2C + C2C. Secondly, the traffic from mobile terminals and Tencent Wechat as well as coverage of third-tier and forth-tier customer groups would complement JD's advantages.

The Road of Integration really began at this moment and there will be another challenging and exciting journey ahead. Afterward, JD's e-commerce business will step onto a wider platform.

Integration with ECC: yixun.com

JD Shop at yixun.com

The way to merge the businesses of JD and yixun.com was to set up a JD Shop in which customers can select products supplied by JD. Then JD undertook order fulfillment in a bid to enrich products at yixun.com and maintain its existing traffic and fixed resources.

In April 2014, both parties formally kicked off cooperation in logistics. After placing orders through yixun.com, customers could find out that the delivery method had changed to "Yixun JD Express Delivery" or "Third-Party Delivery by JD." On May 9 of the same year, JD set up a "JD Shop" at yixun.com to further enrich the product categories at yixun. com. Customers could select major household appliances from JD Shop at yixun.com and JD's operation center for major home appliances will fulfill the orders. Subsequently, articles of daily use and 3C products were also gradually pushed into JD Shop at yixun.com.

The R&D Department was responsible for the technical docking with yixun.com mainly for merchandise, orders, and inventory. To put it simply, JD's merchandise inventory was shared with yixun.com and orders placed at yixun.com were taken over by JD to dock with all links including order placing, distribution, warehousing, and after-sale service. With the team's efforts, the system docking was launched on May 9, 2014 and the whole program was nearly completed. The next step was to push products into JD Shop at yixun.com as planned by the personnel in charge of purchases and sales based on the business needs.

It was not an easy task. The system integration was much more complicated than expected. Both parties were large in volume. Yixun had more than a dozen mainstream systems, and JD also had dozens of mainstream systems. After being acquired by Tencent, yixun.com made several adjustments to its systems, and you can imagine how complex they were. The technical integration was a major subject beset with difficulties for the R&D teams of both sides. How to solve the problems and launch merchandise as soon as possible were great tests for both parties.

Rapid Communication and Accelerated Integration

When recalling this process, the product manager, Baohuan, told that they entered a commodity into the systems of yixun.com and planned two-for-one offers. All data was error-free and nothing could theoretically go wrong after the data entry. But during the actual execution, only a discount on a single item was available, so they had to re-modify. "Originally, we took it for granted, but the thing was always not that simple. Every system has its own merits and demerits in design and there are always minor differences," said Baohuan. The solution to these detail-related problems was communication.

R&D systems of both sides were enormous and over a hundred people were involved in the system docking. How to find the person in charge during communication and how to accurately transfer the information were problems that troubled everyone at the beginning. Communications by phone were not clear sometimes, so we would take business trips for face-to-face communication. Many people working in Shenzhen, Shanghai, and Beijing became frequent flyers between these three locations.

Henry from the ECC Team is Delivering a Team Introduction

Colleagues from Shenzhen, Shanghai, and Beijing in discussions in Beijing

Intermediate Conversion Interface Matching Data

What impressed He Fang was that when he went to Shenzhen to confirm some details with several R&D colleagues and back again, JD, Tencent, and yixun.com made joint efforts to put forward three or four proposals. It was a process beset with hardships. When the final decision was made, to fight against the time and raise efficiency, they directly discussed and communicated in meetings one by one instead of following established procedures to ask for instructions, thus determining the plans efficiently and submitting to the leaders. "We were a little silly and fearless then, and independently made a lot of decisions by ourselves. At that time, there must be someone undertaking due obligations," said He Fang.

Prior to start of integration, we specially assigned the big data department to extract the orders in the last year from the systems from both sides to conduct comparison and analysis. After obtaining the data and then communicating with leaders responsible for R&D and business (multiple sets of supporting data were supplemented), the team found that preferences of customer groups of both websites really differed significantly, with little overlap, thus raising stricter requirements for the integration. Customers and traffic were the most important assets for the e-commerce platform. Our product docking and system design should take the user experience as the priority and the user experience could not be changed in any case. Otherwise, customer loss and traffic reduction may be the result. However, the systems of both sides had been independently operated for many years and greatly differed both in user experience and business scenarios. For instance, at the distribution link, yixun.com delivered three times a day and JD delivered at fixed time. For the warehousing production link, one adopted a third-level address and the other adopted a fourth-level address, and so on. These could not be united in a simple fashion, but should be compatible and the user experience must be continuously enhanced. There were dozens of such similar differences and the final solution was to provide a middle conversion interface for analysis and matching of data docking on both sides and auto-match was realized through historical memory.

In-

Announcement for Formal Launch of JD Shop at yixun.com

depth Cooperation with yixun.com: Reinforcement of the B2C Field

Yixun.com continued to operate as an independent brand and would integrate with JD's pioneering advantages to explore operating models. Besides, both parties would set improvement of customer experience as the common goal, incorporate mutual advantages, and develop cooperation in platform construction, product marketing, and expansion of customers and regions.

Integration with ECC: buy.qq.com

Initial cooperation

In the first week after JD and Tencent signed the strategic agreement on March 10, 2014, Manager Ma of the Marketing and R&D Department led

a group to Shenzhen and conducted the first round of technical proposal discussions and docking on how to sell JD's self-operated and POP merchandise via Wechat and Mobile QQ in the future. This trip gave birth to a great decision which determined that the commodities supplied by JD would be sold in Wechat shops and Mobile QQ through the ECC system. General guidelines should be put into practice as soon as possible after they were set and the personnel in charge of products and technicians based in Beijing and Shenzhen instantly kicked off discussions and docking for specific implementation plans. The curtain of the integration was drawn apart.

Start of the Integration

In late March, 2014, the integration strategy set by ECC and JD began, and the integration of JD with buy.qq.com was quickly put into operation. After several rounds of discussions in Beijing and Shenzhen, the goals of integration were quickly set: first, by April 30, 2014, JD's POP merchandises must

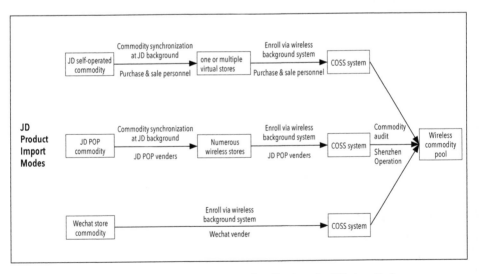

The Process of Importing JD's Merchandise into the Wireless End

be synchronized to the Wechat end and the background systems relating to all transactions should be made through JD's existing systems, and the original COSS system should materialize publish and display of the merchandise at the front end of Wechat. Within one month or so, systems associated with merchandise display, transaction process, promotion logic, and after-sale service had to be connected with and be aligned with the original systems employed by buy.qq.com to complete a one-stop and closed-loop shopping experience in the scenario of Wechat. On this basis, functions such as releasing self-operated merchandise to Wechat Shop and align with the host station.

Without hesitation, a special project team was set up in Beijing and they used an exclusive conference room as the command post for emergency use since JD suffered from crowded conference rooms. Principal members of this project team immediately picked up their packages and settled in, marking the launch of the integration project for Wechat Shop, Mobile QQ and Wechat.

When the initial demands were assigned to them, there was not much

The Command Post for Emergency Use

time, so the leaders reduced the description their task to one sentence: "JD's merchandise needs to be sold via Wechat." This was seemingly simple, but in fact, the integration required countless communications, modifications, and careful thought made by several teams in charge of business, products, and R&D based in Beijing and Shenzhen. According to the initial scheme, Wechat provided to entries for JD: the secondary entry was "My Bank Card" → "Featured Products" and the primary entry was "New Findings" → "Shopping." After entering the home page of JD Mall, 3 items were set, respectively "New Findings," "Brands," and "Special Offers." "New Findings" was for those first launched, pre-sold, and fashion merchandise, "Brands" for preferential branded merchandise, and "Special Offers" for general products at a special price, such as group buying.

JD had never undergone such integration before. Integration of different

Recommended reasons: single item + theme, group buying, gathering limitless traffic	Recommended reasons: brand + time-limited sale, including international brands and domestic famous brands	Recommended reasons: new products + fashions, fostering the most popular series by themed activities and fashion circle
Special offers: single-item latitude Attract price-sensitive naive users and it is similar to JD Group Buying. Without brand restriction, special offers with themes are held for high-quality and low-price commodities from seasonable and popular categories	**Brands: brand latitude** Attract brand-oriented intermediate users and it is similar to JD Flash Shopping. High-quality brands (including luxuries) are selected and great discount is provided.	**New findings: single-item latitude** Attract the senior users pursuing high-quality commodities, including firstly released, exclusive, new and special products, product cooperating with celebrities etc. It is like JD Funny Shopping, JD+ and Leading Edge.

Special Offers, Brands and New Findings

cultures, different territories, and stand-alone systems was confronted with a variety of differences in technology, commerce, manner of working, and other issues. The project team was overwhelmed by various problems from all directions every day. New problems or risks may emerge at all links such as the seller, merchandise, order, payment, or after-sale service at any time. Issues concerning needs and technology or problems to be confirmed arising from the balance of interests of all stakeholders came one after another, like meteoric showers over the command post. Fortunately, all members developed tacit cooperation. Biao and Caibao were assigned to deal with requirements raised by Shenzhen's team in the whole, Biao oversaw problems relating to interface and network interconnection, and Fei was responsible for following up POP sellers and product development. In the face of intense, arduous, and highly concurrent work assigned every day, having a reasonable work division was particularly significant. However, in early April 2014, after demands in setting up Wechat shops were raised by POP sellers and when the members were still excited about the integration, the team from Shenzhen (colleagues working for buy.qq.com) dispatched a highly capable delegation to Beijing and the second round of large-scale exchange subsequently started.

The Shenzhen Team

During this trip, the Shenzhen Team proposed new targets again. JD Search must be subsequently introduced while enabling POP sellers to set up shops via Wechat, and release of JD's self-operated merchandise must be materialized at Wechat. Most importantly, JD held an anniversary celebration campaign on June 8 every year and all of June was JD's celebration month. The promotional campaigns kicked off on June 1, 2014, and all relevant needs must be comprehensively met by the end of May 2015, to open the primary entry, thus catching up with the grand promotional campaign in June 2014. If this chance was blundered away, we would have had to wait until November 11. The primary entry was set under the item of "Game Center," and small red dots must be taken into consideration for the 618 Campaign. It was really a period with one problem after another. Time was wasting, and the only thing we could do was to get to work! At the meeting on April 16, 2014, the launch date of this version was specified to be May 25, 2015.

Wechat Shop for JD's Self-Operated Merchandises

The Project in Progress

At 10:10 a.m. every morning, the phone of the Amsterdam conference room started ringing. Colleagues of the Shenzhen Team called us as scheduled. It was time for the mandatory morning conference held by the Beijing Team and the Shenzhen Team for the integration project of buy.qq.com. Both sides must exchange ideas on existing problems and all principal persons concerned were required to be present. At that stage, the Amsterdam Conference Room was always packed with people. After the morning conference ended, if you thought you could take a breath and take a relaxed look at the Bird's Nest, the famous 2008 Olympic venue not far away, you were wrong, because there was no time to chill out. After the morning conference call, phones of many colleagues rang to talk about requirements to be confirmed, problems to be solved, or various sudden events. Such status lasted from early April to May and till the 618 Campaign. The requirements descended on us like an avalanche, discussion meetings came one after another, and countless problems emerged just as one problem was addressed. You had to learn how to cope with multiple urgent and important problems simultaneously. For instance, you should answer the phone about one problem, and at the same time solve another problem via e-mails. In those days when I was working overtime, I often doubted if the colleagues in charge of R&D were strong enough to persist working overtime, particularly those of the transaction team, who often worked till until the wee hours for a single launch. But Heaven rewards the persistent, and all our hard work was finally repaid. We stuck it out until the first functional POP seller system was successfully released in mid-April 2014. What came next was to launch other systems in succession. In the meantime, new requirements were constantly raised and every week saw release of new iterations. The colleagues responsible for the user experience told me with excitement that they saw another new function! Well, when we were happy with every phased achievement, the agenda seemed to be tighter and tighter with time.

Busy days fly very fast. In a twinkling, April 30 of 2014 witnessed the first important milestone of the project for integration of Wechat Shop, Mobile QQ, and Wechat — launch of the first stage! Thanks to unremitting efforts made by everyone, the whole process was solemn and tense at this critical joint. Within a day, colleagues from Beijing, Shenzhen, and Suqian developed positive teamwork and orderly coordination and various validation procedures were successfully fulfilled. We had gotten ready for sitting up all night, but at 11:00 pm., Zhang Q, who was responsible for the test interface in Beijing suddenly showed up in the conference room, announcing with a big smile that all validation procedures had succeeded today. The happy news came so suddenly and all the anxiety and fatigue one of the last month were finally released at that moment. We could go home early and sleep well that night and then take a short vacation. On May 4, 2014, we ushered in the first order placed at the Wechat Shop! Then various functions, such as release of JD's self-operated merchandise to the Wechat Shop, paying on delivery, appointed delivery of large household appliances, and more, were all put into operation. By May 15, 2014, despite of various minor problems, all requirements for the pre-planned two major versions were all met.

On May 16, 2014 when Wechat entry was put into service, we felt that all our efforts had paid off!

April	• May 4	• May 26	• June 4	• June 18	• August 4
•Manual docking and stock-taking • Operation and vendor enrollment system	Release POP commodities to Wechat store • May 8 Release self-operated commodities to Wechat store	Release of Wechat entry gray level	Release of primary Wechat entry	Release of secondary entry for mobile QQ	Release of primary entry for mobile QQ

Timeline for Integration with buy.qq.com

At the End of the Project
We still remembered when the project had just kicked off, the leader of buy.

qq.com, Fiona, once said, the launch of the access to Game under "Finding" of Wechat cost nine months, but it took only around two months for integration of JD and buy.qq.com until the launch of the primary entry of "Shopping." She believed most of us must be proud of it. An excellent team was indispensable to the project's success. In the whole process, although Beijing Team and Shenzhen Team were separated by thousands of miles, all of us developed tacit cooperation. Everyone sought common ground while resolving differences, respected each other, and struggled selflessly for the common mission and vision to successfully accomplish the project. We are particularly grateful to Allen, Double, Ray, and Xiaoyou from the Shenzhen Team.

This integration with Wechat Shop, Mobile QQ, and Wechat was just a start. There was a long journey for the real integration ahead, with a lot of tasks to be fulfilled as well as many variables in future. However, at this historic node, experiencing joys and sufferings from JD's reform constituted an integral part of everyone's growth.

Integration with ECC: paipai.com

Founder of paipai.com and Development

Dating back to the spring in 2003, traditional domestic industries were still tranquil and almost half of the retail industry was occupied by successors. People shopped at supermarkets and exclusive shops as usual. No one could imagine that the shuffle by fate came so suddenly. After the SARS epidemic hit China, the Internet-based e-commerce, with an acute business sense and convenient service sought its way into thousands of households. this new experience of online shopping was passed from mouth to mouth. Numerous e-commerce companies, including Taobao and JD, emerged at this moment and were well prepared to show their capabilities. Tencent, the overlord of instant messaging industry, was also developing rapidly.

On September 12, 2005, Tencent quietly launched "buy.qq.com," a C2C website, and joined this white war when the Internet industry had grabbed the limelight. From then on, the story of paipai.com began to spread: after operation for one day, its traffic climbed into top 500 in the "Global Website Traffic Ranking List" (data source: Alex), setting a record by entering the top 500 websites with the least time and first used the mode of "chatting while buying" and "sellers and buyers" credit separation system. After one year of operation, paipai.com had become one of three largest C2C platforms, together with eachnet.com and Taobao; in 2007, it leaped to the second place among Chinese C2C websites.

The Homepage of paipai.com in the Process of Reform

Reconstruction of paipai.com

With continual innovations, investments flooded into the e-commerce field. On March 10, 2014, the two giants, JD and Tencent, announced an alliance and planned to integrate the e-commerce and logistics sections of buy.qq.com and paipai.com into JD. On the base of the original B2C, JD set foot in the domain of C2C to enrich its e-commerce ecology and endeavored to comprehensively meet the consumer demands by introducing many small and medium-sized sellers and long-tail merchandise. During this time, the one who won the most users would conquer the industry. As an ordinary customer, I wanted to see if the reconstructed paipai.com was as convenient as JD on behalf of all customers.

Soon destiny unexpectedly tied us together with paipai.com. On May 5, 2014, leaders assigned me as the project manager to take charge of connecting JD.com and paipai.com. It was not difficult to understand that the login was the first step which supported all follow-up operation procedures, showing the importance of this project. What we undertook was to cooperate with the colleagues in charge of the ECC and introduce JD's account system into paipai.com so that the user registration and login system of paipai and JD could integrate.

New Homepage with a clear style of paipai.com

With great expectations, the project team had high morale and was exposed to various difficulties: team members were dispatched to Beijing and Shenzhen and as JD and paipai.com had completely different systems and design philosophies. There were system docking and personnel docking awaiting us, which imposed vitally important liabilities on our shoulders. As we knew, without account interworking and a seamless linking of systems as the foundation, having perfect functions and experiences would become empty talk. Considering the tight schedule and arduous tasks, colleagues in Shenzhen immediately departed and arrived at Beijing at the weekend without a stop. They ignored the fatigue of a tiring journey and threw themselves into discussions on the product and design schemes the next morning. The project team efficiently marched forward in a tense but orderly atmosphere. Through heated arguments, the final schemes were submitted to the supervisor and the latter would select the best one and a consensus was reached. Within one week, the project's product, research and development, testing, and overall plans were determined.

Scene Design of Logging at paipai.com with JD's Account

We grew very attached to this unforgettable process. Detailed designs, specific realization processes, technical proposals, and security policy were all carefully discussed by the project team with instant information sharing. All people concerned were united to care for this vitally important infant in its cradle. To achieve the common goal, we always fulfilled our duties and challenged our own mental limits, with countless proposals overridden, numerous ideas denied and numerous scenes filtered. The product staff conducted a real-time docking, developers worked overtime against the clock, the testing personnel gave up their weekends and the project team sent countless group discussion messages. Their efforts showed our resolution and executive ability. In the later stages, a little incident happened. JD had launched the systems, but by coincidence, the third-party payment platform, TenPay of paipai.com, planned to conduct a disaster recovery rehearsal. The project team was thus caught in a dilemma. If the reform of connected account system was directly launched without waiting till TenPay platform was upgraded, the project could be accomplished on schedule, but the original ports would fail to support customers who logged in paipai. com with JD's account to place orders and make payments; if we waited until the rehearsal was completed, the launch would be delayed. This was a strategic-level task and by rights no delay was allowed. The team was very anxious and hesitated for a while, and then decided to report to the leaders to follow their arrangements. As expected, the leaders finally instructed the project team not to sacrifice the user experience and to solve this problem by putting off the time of launch to be cautious and minimize the risk. When the system launch was completed in the wee hours, the project team felt a great weight taken off their minds. Online validation was successful and all participants in Beijing and Shenzhen held a long-distance party.

The Family: Group Photo of Beijing Paipai Integration Team + Shenzhen Paipai Integration Team for Celebration

When I sat in the bright and clean office again and input http://www.paipai.com/ while enjoying the sunshine, I saw the project that I had played a part in was smoothly operating online, my pride was beyond expression. Certainly, data and operation monitoring were particularly familiar to me. Whether logging in paipai.com with JD's account or registration of a JD's account at paipai.com was extremely smooth and so easy!

Login Page at Paipai.com

At this page with which I was very familiar, I typed in my JD account information and logged in → selected the merchandise I was interested in → added it to the shopping cart → filled in the delivery address → submitted the order. The whole process was smooth and fluent. It was just what our customers wanted, wasn't it?

Through the whole journey, the team members gained a lot of appreciation and gratitude. In the process of implementing the project, with the company and the department heads that supported us all the time and colleagues in Beijing and Shenzhen who never left and fought side by side, we finally reached the Company's target by considering the formula of 1+1>2 and contributed our own value. Huang Xuan was responsible for background development of paipai and through communications with him, we may catch a glimpse of the real epitome of paipai.com:

"I had worked at Tencent for 5 years. I started with a post in charge of

QQ Membership and then was transferred to shop.qq.com, buy.qq.com, and yixun.com, and then assigned to paipai to oversee the background development. The Internet is an industry which combines the cutting-edge technology with traditional services and enables us to try many new things, so I stayed in this industry. I have undertaken a number of businesses, each of which required me to get familiar with the content and structure in a short time and then pitched into the work. Now I can handle these with ease.

"The most unforgettable experience for everyone engaging in e-commerce must be the big promotional campaigns, especially seeing the smooth operation of systems optimized with much effort. Yixun's website system had general anti-pressure ability at the beginning and probably could not be opened when the traffic reached a certain high level. We spent three or four months improving its website and the feedback from all parties showed that the website operated more steadily than the previous year during the year-end promotional campaign this year. This gave us great pride.

"JD's advantage lies in its commercial ideology. In the past, the e-commerce companies such as Tencent might engage in the e-commerce with their attitude toward and experience in the Internet products, so the products they developed did not relate to traditional commerce. JD's thorough commercial understanding plus Tencent's technical assistance made it possible to generate new effects. Take paipai.com for example: the strategies adopted after it was taken over by JD enabled me to see different thinking patterns. We expected to exploit this old brand's potential and bring it to a higher stage."

Dream of paipai.com

The newly constructed paipai.com reignited hope. In Mid-May of 2014, JD's merchandise could be imported to paipai in batches. Next, the second-hand commodity auction service at paipai.com docked with JD's spare parts store to enrich and supplement the second-hand channel at the newly constructed paipai.com. Apart from changes in rules and experience, the newly constructed paipai.com will adopt an innovative business model and prioritize the second-hand auction market, 3C, maternal and baby products, automobile, garments, overseas shopping, and agricultural products. In future, paipai.com will grow into a fair, faithful and reliable e-commerce platform. It will put effort into the mobile end and reconstruct the principle of traffic distribution depending on new technology and the support from JD and Tencent to drive the development of the mobile e-commerce industry and create new values for the sellers and the whole ecological chain.

Currently, the e-commerce industry is facing a strong development momentum, but the road leading ahead will be complicated and confusing, with constantly changing conditions. Who will be the winner and who will be the loser are uncertain. As one of the colleagues who grow together with the e-commerce industry, I would like to wish that paipai.com could set sail with the company from a new start to realize the company's value and social value and the value of JD!

After Integration: J+T= Today

Through the integration, JD took a progressive step toward construction of a complete e-commerce ecosphere. Tencent has completed a real large life circle closed loop: the construction of a new mobile e-commerce ecosphere. Both parties have joined hands to provide better e-commerce services for Internet-based users and mobile Internet-based users in China.

Behind the blueprint for both parties' strategic cooperation, there are thousands of people working for ECC, who have to make choices and cherish the efforts made in the past. They have formed a vision for the future and are expecting new platforms on which they can fulfill larger dreams, and joining JD marks a brand-new start.

We loudly shouted: "Hello, we are a part of JD and we come from Tencent."

Authors: Zhang Aiwen, Bao Dan, Wang Xiaoqiong, Li Ang

CHAPTER 7

Rise of the Planet of the Apes: The Legend of POP

A Brief Introduction to the Plan of Open Platform (POP)

Throughout the development of various Internet applications, the ultimate fight in essence should be the competition of the open platform. Based on the sufficient traffic resources and powerful infrastructure, leaders of different industries support the growth of the disadvantaged small and medium-sized enterprises (SMEs). With time passing by, these leaders become industry incubators and set various universal industrial standards. POP (Plan of Open Platform) is an open platform of JD and the foundation stone to realize JD's Mega-platform Strategy.

No one knows what kind of the open platform is before JD decided to build one, but JD was clearly aware of the fact that a platform should not only highlight the quantity, more importantly, qualifications of vendors and quality of products must be guaranteed as it is the foundation of the open platform. In the face of a new business, the staff of JD positioned themselves as an entrepreneurial team with the attitude and resolution held when they started the business. POP is another start-up business and may be the largest entrepreneurial program to date as well!

In March, 2010, JD formally initiated the POP project and entered a tense stage of product planning. As time was limited, we specially reserved Conference Room 202 located on the second floor of the Yinfeng Tower, Suzhou Street, Beijing for semi-closed development. The team worked from dawn to dusk and brainstormed on critical nodes and key issues. Manager Ma worked together with us every day and arranged his office desk in a corner of the Conference Room.

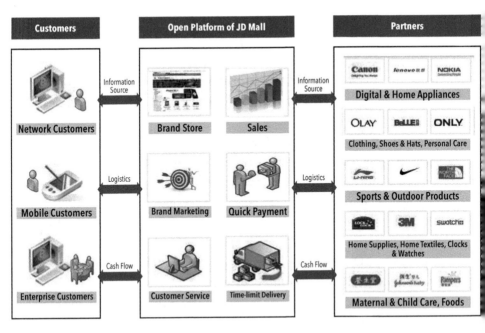

Business Mode

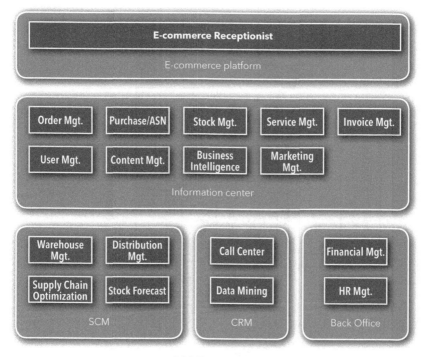

POP Framework

According to the domestic status quo, significant adjustments and improvements were made to the model and a variety of modes for cooperation with vendors were devised to give full access to JD's advantages in warehousing and logistics, and allow qualified vendors with relevant resources to access JD's open platform and remove their potential anxiety.

1. FBP (Fulfillment By POP) Mode: the vendors adopt services ①②③④⑤⑥, store their products in JD's warehouses, use JD logistics, support self-pickup and payment on delivery, and issue invoices for JD;

2. LBP (Logistics By POP) Mode: the vendors adopt services

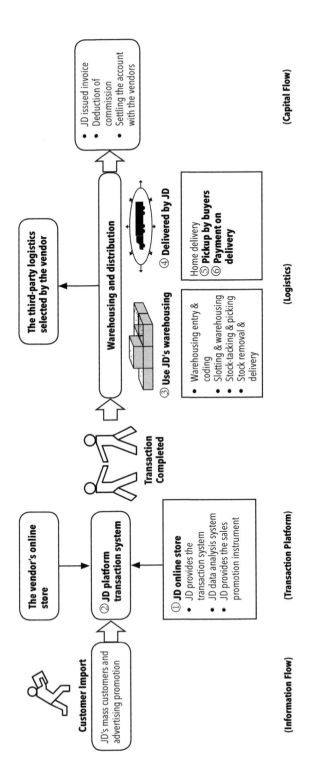

POP Transaction Process

①②④⑤⑥, excluding the warehousing service, send the orders to JD's distribution center, support self-pickup and payment on delivery, and issue invoices for JD;

3. SOPL (Sale On POP Logistics) Mode: the vendors adopt services ①②④⑤⑥ without using the warehousing service, send orders to JD's distribution center and support self-pickup and payment on delivery; and invoices shall be issued by vendors;

4. SOP (Sale On POP) Mode: the vendors adopt services ①② and use the third-party logistics; and the invoices shall be issued by vendors;

5. LBV (Logistics By Vendor) Mode: the vendors adopt services ①② and use the third-party logistics; invoices shall be issued by JD.

Invention of POP cooperation modes earned Ma's team the nickname of "the inventors." To link up all modes, members in charge of R&D penetrated into suburban warehouses, sorting centers, and distribution front lines, discussing and communicating with other departments to make these modes realizable and operable at the business level without affecting JD's self-operated businesses.

As an entrepreneurial team, the POP team had always been stable and united with tremendous vigor. The members were often locked into a bitter dispute on one problem, thus obtaining a great number of good ideas. The product manager would take the prototype he designed and seek for advice from other members, and then make modifications every evening. With a team effort, the system's functional framework was basically set up.

After the business modes and overall framework were determined, major function modules including the POP Channel, Vendor Management, Shop Management, Merchandise Management, Order Management, Warehouse Management, Logistics Management, Customer Service / After-sale Management, Marketing Management, and the Report Form Statistics were also confirmed. The modular planning and process setting was to be performed by product managers.

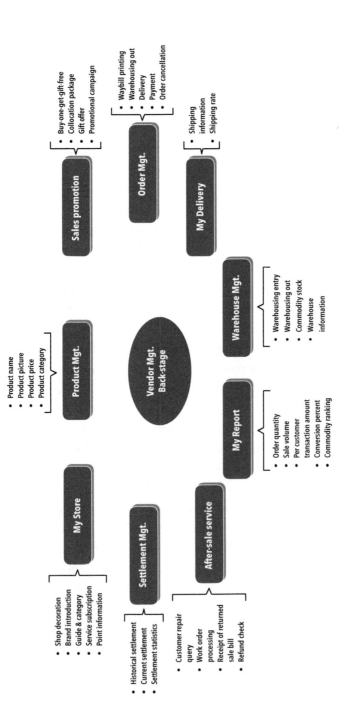

POP System's Functional Framework

Through internal labor division, product managers performed their own duties. They should communicate with the Financial Department or the Legal Department and repeatedly amend the processes, rules, and contracts for vendor entering; conduct commodity management over optimization and search of categories, commodity attribute, sales attribute, commodity codes, pictures, SEO; penetrate into the warehouse and logistics department to know more about the WMS system and the logistics distribution system in a bid to ensure the platform could access the current ERP system smoothly; exchange ideas with the after-sale and customer service staff and transform the platform's reverse process; and build a brand-new POP settlement system with joint efforts made by the financial staff of the ERP system and colleagues in charge of the information system.

Product managers should attend meetings, show up on the site, get familiar with the business and understand the detail logic in the daytime and sort out the information collected in the daytime and the business logic on the basis of the flow chart (UML), then they translate the information into technical languages, thus converting function modules to system prototypes operable for business segments using Axure. These prototypes were subject to the internal initial assessment, and then repeated modifications in case of any problem, followed by the Business Department's review and a comprehensive correction based on comments and requirements raised by the Business Department.

After getting off work, product managers would submit their assignments to Manager Ma, who would review prototypes and point out problems to help product managers make continuous progress.

Upon repeated reviews and modifications, sub-module prototypes were finally built and the next step was to integrate these sub-modules, including connections and correlative dependence management in respect of functions and logic. Product managers needed to clearly describe these prototypes, logic, business scenes, and field information by using PRD following the first draft for the overall vendor management background and operation management background.

Group Photo of the POP Product Planning Team

In May 2010, POP platform prototypes and PRD were successfully delivered to R&D, marking that the project had entered a tense state of development. In the whole course of R&D, the developers kept communicating with other departments with respect to the business and logical problems.

Building of the POP Platform

Building of the R&D team and product planning were carried out at the same time. Back then, JD's technical architecture was built on the base of .Net which would be transferred to Java in the future as expected by Lao Li, the head of the R&D Department. Therefore, the Java-based architecture was used for the POP project. However, all developers at that time were specialized in .Net and there was an urgent need in experts specialized in the Java technology. Siyong showed up at this point and became the pioneer of Java technology in JD. Although there were two regular Java developers (Lao Yang and Yang Kai), the R&D team of POP still decided to start to prepare for building the platform in March 2009. When Lao Ma and Lao Yang were worried about the slow progress in recruitment, a Java R&D team joined JD at exactly the right time.

Accession of the Team of Qianxun.com

Through a rapid growth in 2009, JD was aware of the need for extension of categories. The fashion e-commerce represented by clothing among the non-standard items was the most popular then, but how to step into this field? Qianxun.com, which was a subsidiary to SK Group then, came into Lao Liu's view. It stood out in the fashion e-commerce field and possessed talents and experience in the purchase and sale of fashion categories as well as an excellent technical team headed by Wang Biao.

By the end of March 2010, Wang Biao joined JD, together with his team's core members including Li Wenli, Gao Fei, Sun Bingwei, Zhang Feng, and Han Shichao, and set up a core member team for the POP project at the business startup phase. Wang Biao remembered that two employees of JD came to him when he just joined JD and said that they heard of Qianxun's technical team before and intended to learn something about Java from his team. Xue Tao was one of them; he was one of members of the initial R&D team for the POP project and then made distinguished contributions after being assigned to other product lines such as the POP platform, group buying, virtual products, and more.

In early April 2010, discussions on technical proposals kicked off. Qianxun.com adopted a platform mode in which all product information was translated, edited, and launched after they were synchronized from the ports by vendors in Korea. Orders were also transmitted to Korean vendors and then returned the information via these ports. This was quite similar to modes of the POP platform, hence the data sheet design and process management for the POP platform were relatively smooth.

R&D Story Excerpt: The First POP Item

Requirements were first determined by vendors and commodities, so the corresponding work was set out earlier. Design of the list structure was started in April 2010 and the development began in early May 2010. The initial design draft regarded the POP commodity as the master data, but too many modifications were required on the system for synchronization of self-operated merchandise. The major force was put into preparations for the anniversary celebration campaign on June 18, so there was hardly any manpower left for such modifications and we had to change the plan by deciding to synchronize POP merchandise to the self-operation system. It is well known that the most complicated part of commodity data is the category attribute, of which mapping and synchronization are the hardest links to realize. Moreover, the commodity data structure was so complicated that it involved over a dozen data sheets and required mapping of every field. Zhang Feng was transferred to undertake this arduous task. With 3 months of effort, the first POP item was finally launched.

The First POP Item

Comments of Netizens

Gao Fei, one of the developers, recalled:

"Back then, I was a 23-year-old newcomer of the e-commerce industry and followed with enthusiasm my head leader Wang Biao to join JD for Internet technology in March, 2010. JD arranged its office area in Yinfeng Tower on Suzhou Street where I soon met a group of outstanding and experienced R&D personnel, and we all came here from other Internet-based companies to realize our dreams."

"The POP Open Platform project was initiated in early 2010. The commodity was the origin of all businesses and this justified the commodity's role as the most important and urgent technical barrier: from standard to non-standard categories, fixed to flexible items, and the existing commodity system to POP-supported commodities. The most complicated part of commodity system was the classification and attributes of commodities. However, the self-operated commodity system appeared to be incompatible with POP commodities. Yang discussed issues including commodity classification, attributes, release and foreground display, with Yang Kai and Zhang Feng to determine by means of brainstorming whether we should establish a set of brand-new commodity systems or reform the existing merchandise systems to make it compatible with self-operated and POP products. We finally resorted to Lao Li who chose the latter after considering the project's R&D cycle. This choice appeared to be quite correct now. All systems within the shopping system from foreground display of merchandise to warehouse & distribution were closely related to the merchandise design schemes and the state of pause and ponder would waste our heavy project schedule."

"After the direction was defined, we quickly laid down the plans: used JD's self-operated system for the classification attribute data, use POP system for the sale attribute data and POP merchandise data was synchronized to the self-operated merchandise database (SQL Server) via data synchronization, with the number field of SKU and War starting with 1 billion. This data middleware was developed by the most popular development language, .Net, in JD then. Through lots of overtime, those technical talents we looked up to before became our close friends. In July 2010, the gray testing was accomplished for the merchandise system R&D. Every operation starting from vendor establishment to the merchandise release managing page was testing our achievements. After repeated error reports and debugging, Yang Kai successfully displayed the first item on the POP foreground."

This SKU was the first POP SKU. Yang Kai just wanted to have a try and used the Nokia 2100 for the gray testing. He never expected the success of the release. This SKU showed up in the JD homepage for various reasons, attracting the attention of a great number of customers.

The Debut of the POP Platform
On September 15, 2010, after the product and R&D personnel spent over 4 months in semi-enclosed development and various business departments pulled together, the POP platform was formally put into trial operation, as announced by Manager Liu at the annual meeting of paidai.com the next day.

The POP team recruited vendors and operators during research and development of the platform. With a united effort, there were dozens of vendors joined in while the system was launched for trial operation.

In November, 2010, a special channel entitled "direct brand selling" for the POP platform went live.

Direct Brand Selling Channel Goes Live

The Evolution of the POP Platform

After it officially went live in September 2010, the POP open platform turned into a fast track of development, embracing a sharp rise of business by several hundred percent as well as geometric growth of the pressure and challenges to the system. When dealing with the business pressure, the technical architecture and business systems were dependent on the demand and subject to ongoing change and evolution. The staff undertaking the research and development of the POP also continuously grew under such challenges, suffering while enjoying.

Upgrade of the Order System

The transformation of the ordering organization (November, 2010): while the system was launched for just one month, a defect in the design of the ordering system was detected: the vendor ID on orders was the former order organization fields of JD; as JD's business models were established for different subsidiaries, the financial accounting and settlement must be conducted in every subsidiary, i.e. the organization; FBP and LBP orders adopted the commission pattern and required invoices issued by JD, so it should be implemented in a specific organization; in the case of SOP, the commission deduction points were incurred when the vendors issued the invoices, so an organization must be designated for the calculation and settlement. Thus, the organization could not be used to record the vendor ID, but the order list was too complicated then and could not be added with more fields, hence we added an order expansion table.

It was the first system upgradation after the launch of the POP platform. In this tense course, what impressed us most was that on the day of launch, the data transfer and cleaning continued until 3 o'clock a.m.

The offline production of orders (beginning in March 2011): The POP business grew sharply, bringing around 10,000 POP orders every day with three months' development. In the past, the vendors' viewing and order operations should call the order middleware in a real-time manner and the order bank relied on SQL Server for master-slave replication which suffered the delay resulted from overwhelmed database replica function. It often took two or three hours for demonstration in peak hours, so during 3-5 o'clock every afternoon, such peak hours when the vendors delivered the ordered commodities from storage, the vendors were unable to view new orders and the product personnel had no way out but to propose the vendors trying again after 8 p.m. Thinking back, we felt deeply ashamed. Database replication had become a hard problem to tackle. To tell the truth, JD had given the fullest play to the performance of Windows+SQL Server at that time and no more breakthroughs could be made in this direction, but it was of great urgency to solve the problem.

The only way out was to bypass the primary order banks and the order middleware and directly send a message to the POP system if new orders were placed. The system then analyzed the order information and saved in its own database upon receipt the message, thus data delay would be avoided. However, if we depended only on this solution, failure in expansion would turn up after a few years, as the POP orders kept climbing.

To totally separate the order production from order lists, the concept of offline products was put forward. All order production links targeted at the job orders which was just like a process on the assembly line, and the next job order was put into production after all processing links for the last job order were finished. The next step was timed filing upon the completion of the job order processing to minimize the data size in the task lists and optimize the performance. Meanwhile, the final order status was returned to the master database and order status synchronization also employed an asynchronous task model.

After the direction was defined, the order offline production project led by Li Wenli immediately kicked off. With over one month of effort, a new order production system finally went live. The launch of offline production function avoided the order delay and eliminated the awkwardness owing to the vendors' inability to operate during peak hours, thus getting ready for the subsequent continuous growth of orders.

A brief interlude: the most heated argument in the course of research and development of POP occurred when the solution to the order offline project was about to be finalized. Biao hoped to implement as soon as possible, but was unsatisfied with Li Wenli's solution and even struck the table. This argument ended up with using Li Wenli's design proposal. Such scene was very common in the process of POP entrepreneurship project. Although we were face flamed in the arguments for proposals, this project was unveiled at its best through these conflicts. When retracing these days several years later, we were full with emotions and admitted that it was the passion for startup.

System Splitting and Servitization

The upsurge of the number of vendors and quantity of orders led to an increasing order inquiry frequency among vendors and meanwhile, API's call volume also grew faster. The only way to address mass call was turning to caches rather than databases by using MemCached or Redis. However, the usage scenario for vendors' order inquiry was search inquiry under dynamic conditions and search engine was the best approach to replace the complicated query conditions in the database. Solr may be a good choice. At the same time, we decided to set up an order center for materialization of SOA, while selection of service calling framework became another challenge. Back then, JD adopted multifarious internal service frameworks such as the primitive Web Service or the lately appeared Ice. After overall considerations, the light-class Hession was finalized as the service calling framework and was in the charge of Li Yangfan who just joined JD in July 2011. The advanced research on the technology selection for building of the order center began.

Great modifications to the POP system. Vertical splitting of the system was imperative and only two systems were arranged at the very beginning in order to quickly set up the POP system: POP-vendor orienting POP's vendors and POP-Man orienting POP operators. POP-vendor was the Shop end where all vendor backgrounds were placed, including modules of the vendor admin, item management, promotion management, order, distribution, warehousing, after-sale service and BI report.

With participation of increasing developers, perfection of the system function and complication of the system, the quantity of code surged and it even took 30 minutes to compile in the contracting test environment every time.

In addition, an accident by the end of 2011 also accelerated exposure of this problem. Someday of a weekend, Manager Li called Wang Biao to inform him of the breakdown of vendor background and failure in warehousing-out and delivery for orders. Restart worked at the beginning, but before long the system broke down again. Although there were only two servers, the vendor background could not go so far as to break down. By fetching and analyzing Apache's access Log, we found that frequent URL accesses for commodity operation had blocked the access to other modules. In the same application, different modules may interplay and it would take very long time to find the root cause.

The best way to solve such plight was to split the system and break different modules into corresponding sub-systems. It was a big project which might take two or three months at least, and we could not bear such torture every day. He then immediately called several core technicians: Li Wenli, Yang Kai, Gao Fei and Guan Liangqi and assigned the following tasks:

Dear Mr. Li,

Yang Kai and Gao Fei handled it at about 12 o'clock in the company yesterday.

We will focus on the following tasks today so that all problems can be solved thoroughly.

1. Analyze the vendor's access logs and summarize pages with large page views but suffering long response time as the focus for performance improvement;

2. Shorten the timeout for calling of external interfaces to avoid blockage caused by slow external interfaces;

3. Separately deploy those important functional modules (commodity, order and promotion) to avoid interaction.

The code level would be skipped for the time being and was just separately deployed. The core functions were divided into ware.shop.360buy.com, order.shop.360buy.com, and fin.shop.360buy.com and we applied for six services for separate deployment of these three core modules.

The team kept working until 11:30 at night that day and accomplished the system splitting and deployment. As expected, both the order-related functions and speed got right.

But the system splitting had not been truly accomplished yet. The project team initiated the system splitting and materialization of SOA at once to separate the service center from applications and the system architecture shown on the next page was taken shape.

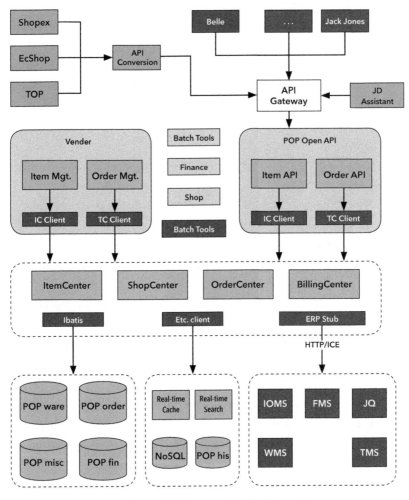

POP's System Architecture after the Upgrading

Building of the Online Vendor Recruitment Platform

In the first year following the launch of the POP platform, the vendor administration still stayed on the level of basic information management. The vendors' various information, operation qualification, contract and agreement must be administered in an offline manner, thus causing heavy workload on the business personnel, long interaction cycle, difficulty in the paper information management and retrieval, and low efficiency of the integrative vendor management. Besides, many vendors from other platforms of the same type entered JD, and through lateral comparison, they began to complain at the very beginning:

- A paper contract should be signed?
- The entering cycle will last more than a month?
- The brand qualification materials need to be mailed in an offline manner?
- The brand should be added by the operators manually?
- We are not provided with the secondary Domain Name Service!
- ...

There was a mountain of such complaints, which reminded us of the sheer volume of work to be done.

In that hot summer, the VP, directors, R&D head, managers, product managers, business personnel, legal personnel, financial personnel, and tax personnel of the business departments carried out multiple discussions to exploit the business features of JD vendor management. We redefined the vendor management and determined the following thoughts of development by analyzing competitive products of other platforms:

1 Systemize the business rules: truly integrate the platform's commercial rules into the IT system, reuse the relatively complete rules for physical commerce and incorporate the advantages of the IT system.

2 Improve the overall interaction and management efficiency through electronic processes: to informationize the business processes by separate steps and priorities to improve management efficiency.

3 Hierarchically manage vendors' data: to manage the core financial data, key business data, and non-key business data into separate authorities and roles to improve the management efficiency and lower business risk.

4 Enrich the vendor service functions: to provide vendors with more fundamental service functions.

5 Bring the integrated role superiority of vendor team into full play: to exploit the unique advantages of the vendor team to the full and integrate system resources to build a uniform operation and management platform for vendors.

The finalization of thoughts for development was determined and was followed by a business process analysis, product demand sorting, and development. Through continuous discussions with the business side, we finally determined the "Vendor Entering System" as the first sally port.

By the end of May 2012, the long-term goals of development for two cores and three main processes were determined considering the integrated system planning and the overall requirements for entering the system were finalized through discussions with business side. The VP of the POP platform and the director of the POP development team were respectively designated as the business principal and technical consultant for the follow-ups. It took less than 4 weeks to complete the development & testing and put it into trial operation after the product demands were determined. Within two weeks of trial operation, more than twenty function points were amended and perfected based on the business conditions and vendors' feedback, and the entry was opened in mid-July 2010 at the JD foreground.

After the vendor entering system ran online for one year, it attracted over 10,000 vendors, thus effectively supporting the business growth, but a knot remained, namely the online electronic contract, without which the entering efficiency could not be greatly improved. Through multiple communications with the business, legal, financial, and tax personnel, a full set of schemes for the electronic contract was worked out.

By the end of 2013, the phase-II development team for vendor recruitment was ready and waiting. Members migrated into the Moscow Conference Room for closed-door development to face the challenge of the stressful time and arduous tasks, but we finally removed the electronic contract from our mind and could not help shouting that we have realized the online electronic contract function and fulfilled the task for docking with the company's contract management system. This dream had lasted for one year, but we only spent one month making it come true. Within this month, we altered the working system from 5 × 8 hours to 6 × 9 hours, and 6 × 12 hours for the later stages and even stayed up all night for the joint debugging and testing in the last week. We were all workaholics. As you sow, so you shall reap. The systems went live as planned and all operating data suggested that we had taken one more step forward successfully:

1 The total number of vendors within 3 months exceeded the number at phase I;
2 Contract renewal and fee payment for tens of thousands of vendors were accomplished within 1 month;
3 The average time for single vendor recruitment was shortened from 15-20 days to two days;
4 Examination & validation, storage, inquiry, and retrieval of vendors' qualification data could be made electronically.

The business part of JD commented that materialization of electronic contracts could save several million yuan spent in mailing of paper contracts for vendors and the company annually. Perhaps this is the value of our team. The recruitment system needed to be improved and we kept improving it.

The member number increased from 6 to 14 at present (responsible for segments of products, R&D, and testing). We reviewed the thought for development we commonly set, and found there were lots of fulfillment waiting. The follow-up teams would focus on aspects of business rules, deep management of qualifications, quality control over the platform merchandise, integration of vendor information, optimization of the business process, and vendor ecology to keep pace with the growth of JD.

POP is Openness of Business as well as API

In 2010, when the development POP platform had just begun, we had considered that some major vendors may demand docking with the company's internal ERP system via the interface, then the API of POP was opened in such a way that Web Service was employed to call.

Web service

The Earliest Open Interface

The year of 2011 was crucial for JOS since users of JOS increased gradually. With more users and vendors without development ability, vendors' demands also increasingly expanded, therefore we began to productize our platform to introduce more ISVs to develop the software capable of satisfying the vendors' demands, set up a developer center enabling the developers to apply for APP and establish the concept of APP and developer. The former open platform lacked the concept of authorization and only provided the vendor ID as the sole identification. We imported OAUTH2.0 as the authorization standard to make the whole open platform safer.

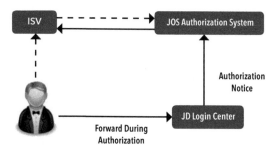

OAUTH 2.0 Authorization Process

Accordingly, we developed the Developer Center and Authorization Server, and transformed the gateways. Three programs were accomplished at one go and products on the open platform were launched to form an iron triangle for open products. As we recalled, the VP Li Daxue came up with its first name JDOS which was changed to JOS (Zeus) later because he thought that the former name was not impressive and could not be easily remembered.

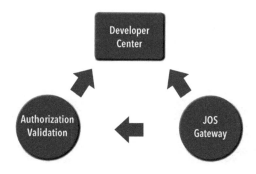

The Iron Triangle of JOS

In 2012, when it tended to be more open, developers held stricter attitudes towards API. We must add more APIs to the open platform. The former open mode was totally manual and our JOS developers had to open every API manually and write the documented SDKs.

Fellows in charge
of Opening   Jos

Manual Access Way for JOS

We had a lot more painful areas. For example, the parallel open API was restricted by JOS's personnel constraint or a team was incapable of understanding the businesses across the whole company. Accordingly, JOS platformization was put on the agenda. We set standards and drafted uniform interface description to standardize JOS-IDL which empowered us to convert and call any protocol.

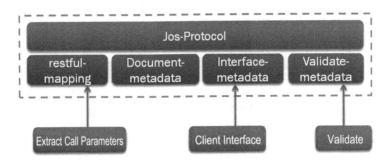

JOS Interface Description Specification

We also set up a service access platform, JHUB, to access services and automatically generate the document, testing tools, etc.

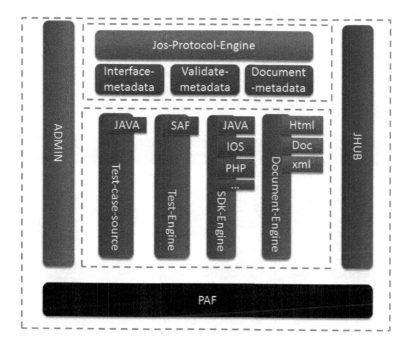

JHUB Architecture

Thus, the time of opening the API was greatly reduced and generation of API documents and test tools became automatic. API could be concurrently accessible, promoting the development of JOS. With increasing expansion of the data size, we also forged offline computing clusters and real-time computing clusters of our own to monitor the systems.

In 2013, the increase of API developers gave rise to problems in new product sales channels. At this point, we considered whether a service market could be established to satisfy the greater docking demands from developers and vendors. Then the service market was set up in JOS to further boom the ecology.

With the volume of calls increasing, we were aware of the importance of stable disaster recovery during calling, so we reconstructed the gateway and devised a structure applicable for API isolation. Asynchronization was the first step, which enabled us to take the control over disposal right of requests from the container and the channelization of internal calls to smoothly and dynamically degrade the processing businesses. After calling API, we improved the scheduling algorithm, replaced FIFO by weight and isolated the process of API calls.

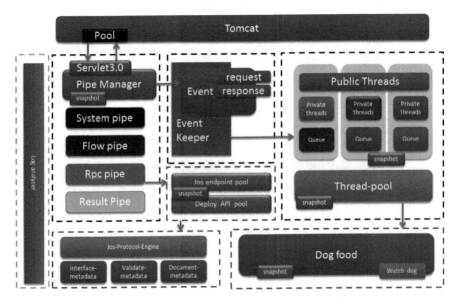

Processing Architecture of Request Asynchronization

The year of 2014 witnessed our rapid expansion. We kept obtaining the call status through real time monitoring as well as the performance information through real time analysis. The notification pushing system also went live and our documentation system was further upgraded to better serve users, continuously complete the data, and guide the system upgrades. JOS authorization buttons were also detailed and more open.

Task Drive Engine

The Oracle database used for the POP system broke down once early in 2012 as excessive Worker procedures kept scanning various task tables in the database. The indexes were available for the AQL filtration fields, thus leading SQL to basically execute full-table scanning. The department assigned Li Biao, who had just been hired, to develop an exclusive set of systems for task storage and management, and the task drive engine was born.

The task drive engine is a task storage and management system based on Redis and MongoDB to provide high-performance and stable task storage and management services. From the perspective of users, the task drive engine is endowed with four main functions: task storage (Push), task consumption (POP), task submission after consumption (Commit), and task rollback in case of consumption failure (Rollback).

The task drive engine receives and processes the above-mentioned four requests from the Client as shown in the following figure. After the task drive engine is applied, the task is stored in the queue to be executed by Redis. After consumption, the task is transferred to the queue which is being executed; when the task is submitted after consumption, it will be transferred to the completed task table of the MongoDB; in case the task fails and rolls back, it will be sent to the queue to be executed by Redis or the failed task table of the MongoDB.

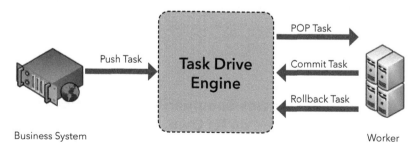

Sketch Map of Interaction between the Task Drive Engine and the Business System

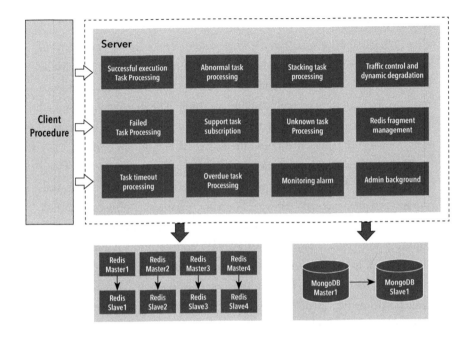

Function Structure Diagram of Task Drive Engine

Since March 2012, when the task drive engine was put into service, it has made great contributions to the stability of the POP systems. All POP systems introduced the task drive engine, which could process nearly 100 million tasks each day and provide high-performance and stable task storage and management services for all POP systems.

New POP Businesses Shouldering Responsibilities on Its Own

Due to the natural genetics of openness, the POP platform could better embrace new business and provide fast and convenient support, so many new business models in the company were expanded based on the POP platform. Moreover, manager Ma, the leader of POP business then, was established as a "new business inventor," with business innovations like a roaring and endless river. A variety of new businesses such as group buying and virtual products were implemented under his instructions. POP business has thrived since then.

The War of Group Buying

In 2010, the group buying industry was on a roll, suffering the "Hundred Regiments Offensive" in the first half and "Thousand Regiments Tangled Warfare" in the second half. As the leader of the self-operated B2C industry, JD naturally could not sit idly by. We received an urgent task from the company to formally launch the group buying website before Christmas, headquartered in a small corner of the R&D Center located at Suzhou Street in November 2011. We had only 20 days to do it.

When being informed of the company's plan to quickly set up a group buying platform, members of POP R&D Department immediately came up with a feasible solution. With little time left to do this arduous task, and with no one having experience in the research and development group buying business systems, how could we work this out and put it into operation before Christmas, as required by the company? Upon lengthy reflection, there was only one seemingly workable way: apply open source software to generate a system which could integrate into JD's information systems. We finally picked up open source software for group buying after a strict selection, quickly executed the purchasing process, and obtained the most primitive copy of the codes. The following problem was that the procedure was written in PHP, but most developers of JD were specialized in .Net and Java, so we were left scratching our heads again. And Xue Tao and Han Xiaoyue, two amateurs with PHP, decided to bone up and try to see if they could work out this system. After the personnel and time limits were determined, Yang Kai led them to start the development and improvement of the group buying system. Hard work paid off. They spent less than 20 days and nights linking up JD's user system, order system, payment system, merchandise system, and settlement system, and then integrating this purchased procedure perfectly into JD's information system. The first group buying program went live on December 14, 2010, when the first order was successfully paid and the discount coupon was granted, the three persons who had been busy as a beaver finally could stop for a breather and have a good rest.

Game Cards

With the POP businesses on track, fast expansion of the business volume, diversification of the merchandise types, to meet the Mall's developmental demands, provide better a one-stop service experience for users, and create higher turnover, expansion of new merchandise types was not needed, and we should introduce virtual products. The virtual business was free of storage and the delivery link from placing orders to successful purchases, and involved a rapid and simple process. Even if an order could only gain ½ RMB, a profit was made at least.

The following memories were recalled by Yang Kai, the head of the game card program.

"Game Card Passport/Direct Recharge" was the first virtual business of POP. I feel honored to have had a chance to lead the research and development of "Game Card Passport/Direct Recharge" program to support the Company's first virtual business.

At that time, I was baffled by three difficulties in the process of system design. Choices I made for them seem to be right from the perspective today, so I would like to share the difficulties with you.

1. The virtual products could not be put in JD's commodity library.

Before February, 2011, every product in JD came from its commodity library. However, the virtual products are greatly different from those physical ones. They are not provided with the necessary data like JD's other types of commodity and have flexible and diverse contents. JD's commodity library may be unable to satisfy them, so it needed to be improved. The data size of virtual products cannot be assessed through the experience in the real SKU, so in case that virtual products are put in JD's commodity library, and may cause some hidden system troubles. On this occasion, we decided to build a virtual commodity library and create the detail pages and list pages by ourselves. From the long view, we could connect the virtual products from various virtual service providers and design the website experience for current business at will, to freely take the plunge.

2. Make the virtual Business order system and the JD ERP order system operate concurrently.

The financial settlement directly depended on the JD ERP order system in which the order statuses were insufficient for the virtual business. For instance, the status of "during recharging, recharge succeeded, recharge failed" existed in the game card passport recharging business. It was also extremely difficult to incorporate other virtual businesses such as lottery and air ticket with various order status into JD's order system. Through analysis, every type of virtual business was found to have unique order statuses, so I decided to build an exclusive order system for virtual businesses to meet their individual needs. JD's order system was still in service and mainly used for account checking after online payment was made. Meanwhile, POP vendor settlement system was utilized to settle accounts for virtual service providers so that the demands from customers and vendors were satisfied at the same time and no transformation was required for the order, financial and settlement systems. This scheme then relieved the whole project team.

3. Set up a gateway system to provide the payment and financial services for all virtual businesses in the future.

Without distribution, a majority of virtual businesses had the online payment dependent on JD's online payment system and after-sale service via the after-sale refund system. There was a scene called "reverse instant notification" in these businesses. For example, the game recharging system must be

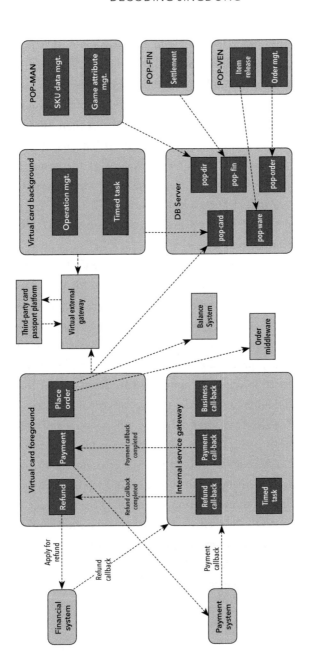

Architecture Design of Game Card System

informed after a successful online payment or financial audit for refund. Virtual businesses, including lottery, air ticket, and cellular phone recharging had such a business scenario and we could not require the financial system and after-sale system to coordinate with our transformations, so we set up a reverse notification gateway to receive all reverse instant notifications from the virtual businesses and determine the specific virtual business system to be notified, so that the variables were under our control, thus truly meeting the design requirements of high cohesion and low coupling.

Today, the size of virtual game recharging business is a lot larger than before, but the design experience accumulated in the R&D process for the first virtual business system has been serving all the subsequent virtual product lines and this is probably the value created by technology.

Cellular Phone Recharging

In March 2011, the POP R&D Department was assigned to undertake the research and development of the cellular phone recharging system. However, the POP R&D Department suffered from a significant shortage of resources, and since the POP platform had just been launched, with both business development and demands breaking out, it occupied most of the resources for development. After overall consideration, Biao sent Ding Qiong to be in charge of the research and development of cellular phone recharging system, Chen Bao'an, who was just transferred to the physical team to link up the vendor recharging interface, Zhang Tan of the game card team to develop the foreground functions for recharging, and Tu Hao from Chengdu Research Institute and came to Beijing for training to develop the background functions for recharging. These four quickly constituted a development team and coordinated with product managers to comb through the business process and complete the system prototype design. The final version of PRD was determined in late April 2011. Upon completion of the requirement review, the team instantly started the system design, with design review completed in mid-May 2011, development of the whole system completed in early June, and system testing completed by the end of June 2011. The online application and database environment were set up and the pre-lease environment testing was finished on June 23, 2011. Through a week of internal trial operations, the whole recharging process was connected and a new recharging system was formally opened on July 1, 2011. JD experienced a sharp rise in the speed and stability of recharging after this new system went live. The effect sketch of the new system's order center is shown as follows:

Cellular Phone Recharging Order Center

JD Lottery

The recharging project was followed by the need of a lottery, which was proposed in May 2011. Biao transferred Guan Liangqi, then in charge of the POP billing system, to help the research and development of the lottery system. Through two months of hard work, the lottery system was successfully launched in July 2011 and a new chapter for the JD Lottery was opened.

Page for Lottery Channel

In early 2012, to expand the customer base, we decided to employ a playing method named "quick drawing," with one drawing every 10 minutes and 84 drawings in one day, thus attracting a number of "short-attention" customers. After one month and a half of a required survey, development, and testing, "Xinshishi Lottery" went live in March 2012. However, it did not come up to expectations and suffered from low sales. However, the good news was that the sales of "Number Lottery" grew steadily. This reflected that, although new lottery types failed to drive up the order quantity, new customers were attracted and we became more mature.

Interface of Shishicai Lottery

The 2014 World Cup came much more strongly than we expected and could be seen as a nation-wide carnival. Nearly everyone around us was talking about teams, players, and coaches, as well as the "lottery" tied to the World Cup. Because of substantial growth of the sales of "Football Racing Lottery," enormous pressure was put on the system, especially the hour prior to the beginning of matches, when customers flooded into the website to place orders, thus creating unprecedented challenges against the system's capacity. Fortunately, the lottery system had been functioning well in this period and this was a cause for celebration.

The World Cup drove the sales of JD Lottery up to a historic high and led us to find out what our values were, but it was not the finish line. JD Lottery is just getting started and there was a lot of work to be accomplished. We will continue to escort the development of JD Lottery.

JD's Road of Special Selling

With increasing expansion of the POP open platform, new business formations were required to realize the surplus traffic and improve sales volume, so since 2012, the businesses such as overseas shopping, vehicle and house selling, auction, and others were carried out on the POP platform. The company achieved a very satisfactory sales performance and attracted much attention within the industry. The growth of these new businesses was supported by our technical team. When it came to the support for new POP businesses, Shanshan must be mentioned, who was always there in the technological realization process for every new business. She is a typical forthright girl from Shandong, and had a catch phrase for projects: "Anyone who has too many lice feels no itch and who gets in too much debt does not need to worry."

Previous and Present Life of Flash Group Buying and Flash Shopping

By the end of 2012, the group buying segment was separated from the POP platform to set up a tier-one division. A greater strategy had to be implemented to adjust constituents of the group buying business. The management layer held a series of discussions and in early 2013, the "Flash Group Buying" was born, which was designed to provide quality goods, special discounts, and flash sales. A warehouse for this business was also specially established in Chengdu.

In the initial stage, it took a long while to define the project scope. Commodities of FBP, SOP, LBP, and SOPL as well as JD's self-operated commodities had demands in warehousing for the flash group buying, but the concept of "open platform warehouse" was not invented. Only the FBP and self-operated commodities could be put in the warehouse, so vendors adopting other cooperation models needed to open an FBP store. But the self-operated merchandise was different from the POP's structure, hence was not taken as the priority for the first phase. Efforts were concentrated on working out the FBP's warehousing mode.

The FBP's warehouse attribute puzzled us. In the past, vendors stocked up in 6 places where the warehouses possessed variable coverage. While the flash group buying, business required stocking up at Chengdu only to support delivery of goods throughout the country. The parallel stock just began, without a matured model for warehouse-out priority. An SKU would not be put in the ordinary warehouse if it was listed in the flash group buying warehouse, otherwise a delivery disorder might be caused. We eliminated the possibility of being put into two warehouse types at the same time from the source and only allowed the commodities which participated in the flash group buying campaign to be put in the flash group buying warehouse. The stores must release new SKUs for the flash group buying and then label these commodities to distinguish them. Commodities with such labels would be directly bound with the attribute of the flash group buying warehouse and warehouse entries would not be issued by the ordinary warehouses in other six places.

There were other difficulties baffling us, such as order cancellation in 30 minutes, reverse processing, and other problem areas. Due to a lack of conference rooms, a vacant VP office at the second floor was temporarily used as the "flash group buying workshop," where the project managers and product managers discussed the operation plans and all processing charts for the flash group buying program was born. In the course of the program, we kept discussing, communicating, analyzing, re-discussing, re-communicating, and re-analyzing.

The processing chart on the next page was obtained through collating and modifying nearly 20 systems. This scheme appears not to be a big deal now, but we really took many unnecessary long ways and discussed numerous details before finalizing it.

On May 22, 2013, the eve of the launch, principal members of the project team and several developers of WMS worked and solved the problems until 3 o'clock in the morning. The flash group buying system went live on schedule the next day and achieved a good sales performance. However, the flash group buying business was suspended in October 2013 after 4 months of operation due to strategic adjustments in the group buying department. What a pity.

But JD did not give up this business. Late in 2013, the POP Department proposed to restart it as the time was more appropriate for both preparation of the open platform warehouse (yes, the concept of open platform warehouse had taken shape, allowing the third-party vendors to store their commodities in JD's warehouses. The warehouses in Beijing, Shanghai, and Guangzhou served as the open platform warehouses) and selection of suppliers. Then the "flash group buying" project was restarted. To drive up the sales, which suffered a downturn around the Spring Festival, the business departments expected the flash group buying to go live in early January. With only one month left, we were pushed hard.

The first key issue for the system design was to determine whether FBP or SOP plus open platform warehouses was more feasible. FBP was a ready-made warehouse-in mode but lacked flexibility with low vendor independence while SOP plus open platform warehouses was a new mode which was estimated to have greater development capacity and unknown risks but was more flexible and was the direction of the future. Through discussions held by leaders of several departments and product managers, the mode of SOP plus open platform warehouse was adopted.

(FBP + Self-operation) Flash Group Buying Function Process Chart

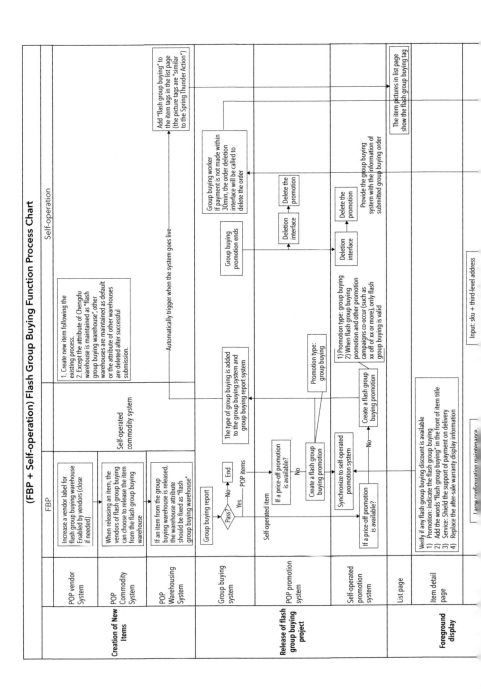

		FBP		Self-operation	
Creation of New Items	POP vendor System	Increase a vendor label for flash group buying warehouse Enabled by vendors (close if needed)			
	POP Commodity System	When releasing an item, the vendors of flash group buying can choose to release the item from the flash group buying warehouse	Self-operated commodity system	1. Create new item following the existing process. 2. Except the attribute of Chengdu warehouse is maintained as "flash group buying warehouse", other warehouses are maintained as default or the attribute of other warehouses are deleted after successful submission.	Add "flash group buying" to the item tags in the list page (the picture tags are "similar to the Spring Thunder Action")
	POP Warehousing System	If an item from the group buying warehouse is released, the warehouse attribute should be fixed as "flash group buying warehouse"			
	Group buying system	Group buying report → Pass? —No→ End; Yes→ POP items. The type of group buying is added to the group buying system and group buying report system		Automatically trigger when the system goes live	
Release of flash group buying project	POP promotion system	Self-operated item; If a price-off promotion is available? No → Create a flash group buying promotion	Promotion type: group buying	Group buying worker; If payment is not made within 30min, the order deletion interface will be called to delete the order	
	Self-operated promotion system	If a price-off promotion is available? No → Synchronize to self-operated promotion system → Create a flash group buying promotion	1) Promotion type: group buying 2) When flash group buying promotion and other promotion campaigns co-occur (such as xx off of xx or more), only flash group buying is valid	Group buying promotion ends → Deletion interface → Delete the promotion; Deletion interface → Delete the promotion; Provide the group buying system with the information of submitted group buying order	
Foreground display	List page				The item pictures in list page show the flash group buying tag
	Item detail page	Verify if any flash group buying discount is available 1) Promotion: indicate the flash group buying 2) Add the words "flash group buying in the front of item title 3) Service: Shield the support of payment on delivery 4) Replace the after-sale warranty display information			
		Large configuration maintenance	Input: sku + third-level address		

System Process of Flash Group Buying

Customer shopping

- settlement page
- ...from flash group buying warehouse
- ...based on the ordering address
- unit=consignee, the delivery mode is determined according to the existing process, but if not, delivery by express will be shown.

Order system — Submit an order
1. If an item participates in the flash group buying promotion, the discount for this item should be shown as the flash group buying promotion in the discount details.
2. If an item is marked for the flash group buying promotion or the warehouse attribute is Chengdu Warehouse 151, the mark of "flash group buying" should be printed in sendpay;
3. The settlement page and order center pass the parameters on to the payment page to provide a 30-min payment remind.

Payment page — Pay
Remind the customer at the order submission page that if payment is not made within 30min, the order will be canceled.

Flash group buying discount
The warehouse that the order belongs to → Order status

Order production

Order middleware — Transfer to the flash group buying warehouse in Chengdu
Configuration file modification

OFC

Warehousing — Produce in Chengdu flash group buying warehouse

Distribution — Pre-sorting: JD distribution or third-party distribution
If the sendpay is for a flash group buying order, then:
1. Consignee=consignor, judge by the existing logic;
2. Consignee≠consignor, express distribution is adopted

→ Sorting center

After-sale service
1. If the order warehouse of sku is Chengdu flash group buying warehouse or the order has the flash group buying label, then only sale return and maintenance are available.
2. In case of Chengdu flash group buying warehouse (with special warehouse number), the label of "unit +warehouse number +flash" should be added during unpacking

---

Reverse process

Spare part warehouse
1. If the customer rejects to return the package, thus causing logistics loss: deliver to the 3C spare parts store at the customer's location according to the reverse logistics type, and the spare parts system obtain and record the flash group buying label via the call interface and return to the spare parts store of flash group buying warehouse providing the rejected items according to the information flow, and the spare parts store will return them to the supplier.
2. In case the customer applies for sale return: the returned items are delivered to the 3C spare parts store at the customer's location according to the after-sale type, and the after-sale system must provide "unit" + "flash group buying warehouse" information to the spare parts system which will record the label, and then return to the spare parts store of flash group buying warehouse providing the rejected items according to the information flow, and the spare parts store will return them to the supplier.

The overall scheme was finalized, and then the project immediately kicked off. This project fell into three major parts. The first part was front-end pages, including the channel pages, campaign pages, and detail pages, etc.; the second part was transformation of the background system process and various links; and the third part was linking up the open platform warehousing services. Every part was assigned with product managers to follow up.

With experience in system foundations for the former "flash group buying" project, Shanshan felt it was labor-saving this time. The set pattern was similar, but the design of background system process required more effort. The flash group buying business used JD's warehousing and distribution systems, then two schemes were proposed. First, vendors participating in the flash group buying would be marked by a label to identify the subsequent order and after-sale process; second, the flash group buying, JD's warehousing system, and JD's distribution system were marked by three different labels to identify the subsequent processes separately. As the flash group buying business was based on SOP and the model services of SOP + service in the future must be decoupled, it was more feasible to mark respectively by three labels. To facilitate the operation, the systems were linked to automatically activate JD's warehousing and distribution services when the flash group buying business was operating. Such linkage would be removed when the flash group buying was independent from JD's warehousing and distribution services (in fact, this requirement was raised shortly thereafter).

The highlight of this project was linking with the warehouse. The warehouse-in and stock canceling were relatively easy with FBP as the reference. Linkage of the stock with orders caused us a lot of troubles and required participation of the architects. As the time pressed, many schemes were finalized during development. We had no time for careful sorting of the reverse process, particularly refunding to locked orders. SOP's process required that, the locked order could not leave the warehouse, but we were unable to stop it after review during the actual warehousing operation, so even though the systems had rejected to store-out requests after review, the package could not be gotten back. It was a large loophole in the process. However, to maintain the project progress, we had to put the review authority for manual offline communications before review. After several project risks were reported, the project finally went live.

Flash Group Buying Business "JD Red" Went Live

On January 8, 2014, the flash group buying business went live, with the nice name of "Red." But this did not relieve our product managers, because they had to address the problems existing in the reverse refund process. Then the project manager assembled around twenty people to thoroughly discuss the problems in a conference room and finally decided that the re-fund application will be pushed by the financial system to the warehousing open platform (JOSL) which asked WMS whether it could intercept or not, and if yes, the refund application would be automatically approved; if no, JOSL would ask the distribution system which decided whether it could intercept or not. After the systems concerned were developed and went live based on this scheme, everyone was finally relieved.

The flash group buying lived up to our expectations and was on the up-and-up. In July 2014, the flash group buying had become an independent tier-one division and the eighth sales and purchasing segment of JD. Its teams kept expanding and even a separate product team was set up. This business will be on a roll in the future.

New Period for Ecological Construction of the POP

In the second half of 2013, JD made great strides forwards in the e-commerce area and pushed its POP business into a new period. Many new models were introduced for the POP systems, including the reward-punishment system for vendors, a dynamic scoring system for the stores, flash group buying business, distribution business, LOC and Wechat shop — the first cooperative project after JD and Tencent established the partnership. These new models not only expanded the POP businesses, but also led POP's ecosystem to be more regulated and balanced.

Meanwhile, the entire POP R&D team was tired of business requirements in the earlier stage and the e-commerce business was featured by its logic, but inadequate emphasis was placed on the vendors' experience and we did not contact them frequently, leading to questions in the whole process. To better serve vendors and improve their experience in operating stores in JD, the POP R&D team was assigned with another duty since the second half of 2013: improving the vendors' experience.

Xu Jianwen recalled:

"I remembered that it was August 13, 2013 when I became a part of JD. After I went through various procedures for employment and received training in the daytime, and I thought that, anyhow, the first week must be relaxing."

"But on the first day, they gave me a surprise. At 7:00p.m., leaders asked me to attend a conference on something I didn't catch and I hurried from the second floor to the 16th floor. People one by one filed in the conference room and were reporting their work performance of that day and work plans for the following day. I learned later that this gory fight had an aggressive name, "Revenge Action," and we were assigned to the war zone of vendors."

"In the next one month or so, at 7:00 or 8:00 every evening, dozens of people gathered in the conference room to make a summary for the situation of that day. Outside the conference room, hundreds of colleagues were struggling in this fight. They were arranged in 16 product lines to find out product-related problems, make improvement plans, and notify vendors to make improvements by various means. Vendors could give recommendations for improvement after trial use and the corresponding product line would be subject to ongoing optimization."

"In the process of the revision, we interviewed 265 vendors, with 70% of major vendors. Small and medium-sized vendors accounted for 25% and new vendors took up 5%. 396 original requirements were collected, of which 304 were to be met."

Total number of requirements	396
Vendor group	49
Telephone interview	146
Operating personnel	40
Product manager	58
On-site interview	104

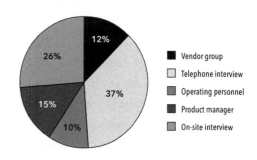

Statistics on Source of Demand

We put into 92 employees for the products, 276 for R&D, 42 for testing, three for design and one expert to perform work focusing on the following five core directions.

1. Availability: optimizing function points which had caused more complaints;
2. Efficiency: simplifying the operation process and optimizing the interactive interface;
3. Detailed operation: providing more function support;
4. Service: strengthening various types of assistance and initially systemizing vendors' ways of feedback;
5. Vendor ecosystem: perfecting the environment of competition for vendors and make it fairer.

By the fourth quarter in 2013, the vendors gave positive feedback and had full confidence in JD. This also set our mind at rest and proved that as you sow you shall mow.

Coexistence of Mission and Glory in the Future POP

More than 4 years passed since the POP platform commenced in March 2010 and ended in August 2014. This is an inspiring entrepreneurship march. Despite many twists and turns, the POP platform has obtained considerable development, provides diversified commodities, and become the greatest open exploration program for JD so far. JD's POP system has experienced several significant architectural upgrades and has successfully withstood the explosive growth year after year. The establishment of POP contributes to so many best practice cases and lessons learned for JD's IT undertaking and dispatches the R&D and product talents with rich e-commerce experience to all of JD's systems. We must extend our sincere gratitude to all participants in the POP platform project from the beginning and the success of POP was attributable to all of you, wherever you are working!

With JD's listing, the POP platform is bound to embrace a broader stage and encounter greater challenges. Every listed company will encounter the coexistence of opportunities and challenges. The cooperation with Tencent creates an opportunity to rewrite China's e-commerce history and the POP R&D Department will play a greater role and shoulder more responsibilities. We will adhere to the spirit of the entrepreneur team to improve the POP platform and add luster to the opening of JD!

Authors: Wang Biao, Ouyang Bo, and Tan Yuexian

CHAPTER 8

Fast and Furious: A Supply Chain with an Ultimate Experience

History of the Warehousing System

The First Exploration of Development of JD's WMS System: the Shanghai Old Warehousing System

JD adopted WMS1.0 for its warehousing system before, but it was a set of systems which had simple processes, lacked intelligent equipment, employed a centralized deployment mode, depended on the online production pattern, and provided a limited capacity for orders.

Since 2009, the company embarked upon research and development of the new generation of intelligent warehousing system. Back then, the Shanghai Old A Warehousing System, which could have been considered to be "new" at that time, was formally launched in November 2009 after four research personnel spent over half a year on concentrated research and development. Through a period of hardship, the research personnel finally worked out the first brand-new WMS system furnished with the intelligent equipment. JD first introduced the handheld terminals for order picking and the intelligent conveyor line for its system. The WMS1.0 system at that time not only was a high-end system, but also sharply improved the accuracy and production efficiency. Although the system can bear relatively few orders, with limited upgrading potential and is not favored by today's maintenance personnel, it played an important historical role in the development of JD's WMS.

Builder of Ecological Chain of JD's WMS: the WMS2.0 System

After the Shanghai Old A Warehousing System was developed and put into service, the company became aware of the benefits of the new system and was determined to invent a standardized general-purpose JD WMS system, which was officially named WMS2.0. Compared with WMS1.0, JD WMS2.0 made a qualitative leap in terms of business and technology. The system provided a great number of services which not only were complete, but also became business models for the subsequent WMS versions of JD's warehousing system.

JD's WMS2.0 system consists of warehousing entry, in-stock, inventory, warehouse-out, internal allocation, reverse logistics, and other modules, each of which was further divided, for example, the warehouse-out module had the sub-modules including positioning, task allocation, order picking, review, and packing. Functional nodes of these businesses enabled JD's special WMS business style to take shape. The business flow direction of following WMS systems developed by JD mainly referred to business nodes of WMS2.0 for the pre-design of a system framework or adjustment of functions. The business processes of JD WMS2.0 did not have complete designs at the beginning. Nearly all modules were subjected to re-development and many new business modules were added since 2010, when the system was launched. These results could not be achieved without validation and summary over many orders, feedback from the staff working in the warehouses and re-development after the collection of requirements. The invoice printing experienced the change from online printing to offline printing; express bills and collective bills were subject to centralized printing; multiple designs and re-developments were conducted for the internal order allocation module; warehousing transfer and replenishment evolved from artificial judgment to intelligent control; the task allocation and review modules were redesigned or re-developed; the order production data and status return were subject to several structural redesigns; line production was available for the warehousing entry module, and so forth. Improvement of WMS2.0 such as the re-planning and redesign of partial modules and repeated design and development of the production process made it possible for this system to provide valuable references for new generations of the WMS system. Furthermore, the WMS systems subsequently developed by JD for the large household appliances and synergistic warehousing were directly subject to secondary development of demand customization based on WMS2.0. WMS2.0 is not the best warehousing system, but supported the most orders for warehousing and production in China and has not yet encountered any production bottlenecks.

The Second Exploration of Development of JD's WMS System: the WMS3.0 System

In 2012, the company decided to use the new architecture design philosophy to research and develop the new generation of the warehousing system. Service-oriented design ideas of SOA were applied and a task engine was introduced to process the messages, enabling the data from various modules and sub-modules within the WMS system to interact by means of a service call. Such architecture design could address shortcomings such as high cost for single-warehouse deployment, decentralized data storage, and uneasy data extraction, etc. After module servitization in the WMS system, public modules and numerous warehouses receiving few orders could be deployed in a centralized manner and those warehouses for more orders were deployed separately. In addition, module servitization reduced the degree of dependence among different modules, facilitating the customization of modules.

However, for JD's warehousing team at that time, to do this thing was rather risky. The improvement of the original WMS2.0 system never ceased and the whole team could not be assigned to research and development of the new project. For the new generation of architecture design, fulfillment of many businesses became much more complicated, and it remained unknown that what kinds of problems we may encounter in the course of project research and development.

In this context, research and development for the new generation of warehousing system called WMS3.0 commenced.

As expected, this project encountered a lot of design-related problems and made countless modifications to the required design in respect to the business, products, and R&D. The whole R&D team for WMS3.0 system finally launched at No.98 test library in Beijing after the iterative development lasting more than half a year. Then the company decided to add open platform order business to this system and prove the feasibility of a multi-owner business model in which the third-party orders were made accessible via the open platform to JD's warehouses for separate production of the third-party orders.

WMS3.0 system was not popularized in a large scale since WMS2.0 was subject to ongoing business iteration and upgrading, which made the business functions of WMS3.0 system lag behind the WMS2.0 system. With launch of the Asia I system, the warehousing team encountered a situation where three warehousing systems, including WMS2.0, WMS3.0, and Asia I, were operating online simultaneously, thus WMS5.0 system was later developed to integrate these systems.

WMS3.0 system was not popularized and applied across the country, but it was still of great significance. The Asia I warehousing system could be quickly developed as its WMS improvements and requirement adjustments were conducted based on WMS3.0.

A New Leap of the JD WMS: the Asia I System

Kun had heard of JD's attempt to build its own warehouse capable of making highly automatic production — Asia I before he joined JD. The data about floor space, stock and so forth could be found on the Internet, so we needn't elaborate any more details.

This set of systems was comprised by WMS and WCS. JD had been versed in the field of WMS, but a WCS system was still a blank for JD.

Why was a WCS system applied? In addition to the conventional WMS management system, the automation equipment such as a hoister, stacker, and intelligent conveyor line were introduced in the Asia I warehouse of JD. Such equipment had built-in drivers, but how could we drive the intelligent equipment to work by orders of JD WMS through WMS's production message conversion? WCS was the solution and acted as the interpreter between JD's WMS system and the intelligent equipment's driven orders to translate numerous WMS business orders into actions done by a device or between devices. The processing mode for the equipment's abnormal executing actions and management mechanism to monitor the proper operation of equipment were also included.

Asia I system was more complicated than just adding the intelligent equipment to the conventional WMS system. As the WCS system was added, modules of WCS needed to have message-based communications with WCS and such communication mechanism was a type of extension of the existing WMS system. Moreover, WMS in the Asia I system was subject to a lot business changes to adapt to the automatic production. Compared with WMS2.0, the design of warehouse-out module, for instance, was significantly improved to support the production pattern of "one-for-one package."

After the Asia I system went live and was put into service successfully, JD's warehousing systems had climbed to new heights.

All-round opening of JD WMS: the WMS5.0 System

Three different warehousing systems including Asia I, WMS3.0 and WMS2.0 existed in JD's warehouses, which cast a heavy burden upon maintainers.

By a fortunate coincidence, the company planned to open JD's warehousing segment in an all-round fashion and integrate the systems to obtain a set of generally standardized WMS systems. The system development was based on the Asia I WMS system.

The R&D target of the system was to establish a system that possessed complete business functions and could replace all existing WMS systems in the future, and the most importantly, could help achieve the project's object — all-round opening of JD's warehousing segment.

The all-round opening was conducted based on the experimental opening of the WMS3.0 warehousing system and was expected to support inventories of JD's warehouses and generate a multi-owner management mode. This played a significant role in boosting reduction of operating costs and increasing profits for JD. Many witnessed the good development of JD's warehousing segment, so more third-party owners were drawn to experience and use JD's warehousing and production services, creating the opportunity for JD to enhance the impact and show the strength in warehousing. Additionally, opening of warehousing services could balance the production capacity among JD's warehouses and define another pathway to gain profits as the warehousing service was not provided for free after all.

Progress of the Logistics Distribution System

The value of e-commerce lies in cutting down intermediate links through operations featuring low costs and high efficiency to materially benefit the customers while realizing the enterprise value. The information flow, logistics, and capital flow have been elements which are commonly highlighted and researched. Despite of being only a constituent of commodity transaction, logistics can ultimately reflect the value of commodity and services. It stressed delivery of the commodity to the right place at the right time by a minimized cost by lowering the circulation cost and improving the supply-chain efficiency. The "customer-oriented" principle of logistics is reflected in the "the last mile" service quality and that's where JD's core competitiveness lies. Depending on the logistics distribution system set up in recent years, JD enables its customers to "enjoy the experience of shopping without going out."

JD's logistics network comprises core elements including warehousing, sorting centers, delivery terminals, and delivery personnel. Warehouses are responsible for arranging production for the customer orders including express bill printing, order picking, invoice printing and packing and production results are those order-based packages. Upon completion of production in the warehouses, packages are transferred to the sorting center which will conduct sorting, casing, sending out, and vehicle dispatching, and finally packages would be delivered to the distribution terminal as required.

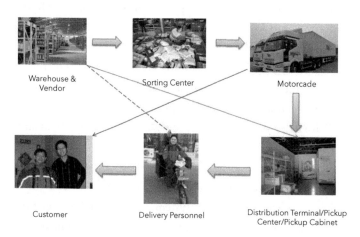

The Topological Graph for Main Processes of JD Logistics Distribution

The distribution terminal distributes packages to the delivery personnel after receipt and examination, and the delivery personnel is in charge of bring the packages to customers. Throughout the distribution network, fast circulation of the logistics, information flow, and capital flow ensures the timely delivery and recovery of payment and accurate information transfer.

Azure Dragon System 1.0

With expansion of the scope of business and growth of the business volume, JD's former logistics management system can no longer satisfy demands from the business expansion. To construct more reasonable business processes and a more efficient management information system is the fundamental way to address the bottleneck of JD's logistics and information flow.

With approval of JD's Technical Committee, the project was formally commenced on September 5, 2011. Its designation was Aladdin at the beginning and then was renamed as Azure Dragon proposed by our CEO, Liu. The name expressed the company's high expectations for this core system (The Blue Dragon is one of the Four Symbols in Chinese traditional culture and the chief of the Four Beasts. According to the Five Element Theory, it represents the east. "Dong (east)" in Jingdong is the leader of the eight directions and Azure Dragon is the chief of the Four Beasts, suggesting a close tie between Jingdong and Azure Dragon.)

The Distribution Project Planning Department, and the Product Department and the R&D Department of information segment cooperated perfectly from raising requirements, product design to system R&D and testing. With half a year, they finally completed the development and testing of the Azure Dragon System's infrastructure.

April 20, 2012

The Azure Dragon System under development went live for the first time, aiming at trial run of the system's basic functions, including the function test analysis, performance test analysis, system deployment scheme and other minor but important scheme tests.

Members of the project team promptly made a summary, put forward improvement suggestions and new requirements on the testing results so as to perfect system functions. In light of testing results in the first stage, developers dedicated themselves to the improvement work in the second stage. With continuous hard work for several days, the development of functions for Azure System Phase I was completed.

June 30, 2012

The first phase of functions had been ready for launch. Developers carefully examined the sub-systems, conducted gray level deployment and determined the online validation scheme. On July 9, 2012, all sub-systems were put into formal operation under the gray level environment. From July 7–July 9, 2012, a formal environment deployment plan was made. During July 11–July 12 of the same year, 5 terminals in Wuhan in central China were set as the experimental points. The team members gathered problems emerging in the experimental terminals and discussed the corresponding solutions.

July 24, 2012

It was destined to be a sleepless night for developers. The Azure Dragon System was applied to all sorting centers and distribution terminals in the Central China. It was also defined as a battle of life and death. The Azure Dragon System debuted and the achievement made by all participates through continuous hard works within numerous days and nights was subject to a strict inspection on this day. To assure stability and normal operation of the main process, the downtime exceeding 10 minutes was not allowed. Team members had made full preparations for the cutover, drafted a data migration scheme, and detailed the PDA installation scheme, log adjustment scheme, performance monitoring scheme, and the overall cutover plan.

To prevent the normal production from being affected, the cutover was conducted late at night. Developers who gave site instruction worked closely with those who were dispatched by the headquarters strictly followed the established schemes and then waited in worry. The wee hours finally arrived. The designated sorting centers and terminals began to use the brand-new Azure Dragon System. The outcome was inspiring. The cutover of Azure Dragon System was completed smoothly without significant problems that might impact the production. Some problems arose in the sorting centers and terminals, but they were tackled quickly by the developers. the low-profile and remarkable debut of the Azure Dragon System laid a solid foundation for the system cutover in all regions in China.

August 14, 2012

Cutover of Azure Dragon System succeeded in South China. Application of the Azure Dragon System in South China with greater order volume posed another severe test upon the performance of the Azure Dragon System. All developers were at work, with adequate preparation to guarantee a smooth and steady system cutover.

September 7, 2012

With experience from the previous two cutovers, the cutover of the Azure Dragon System was conducted smoothly in southwest China.

September 18, 2012

The Azure Dragon System was cutover in east China steadily and smoothly.

October 23, 2012

The cutover of the Azure Dragon System succeeded in northeast China.

November, 2012

The Azure Dragon System descended upon north China. By then, the system cutover had been accomplished across the country and the Azure Dragon 1.0 project was finished as scheduled, significantly upgrading JD's logistics distributions system and providing strong guarantee for the whole-process and detailed management of the distribution business.

The Azure Dragon System 1.0 was equipped with the whole-process management including pre-sorting, cargo handing over, sorting and handling, dispatching, examination, distribution by drivers, receipt and examination by terminals, and receipt and delivery by delivery personnel as well as the reverse logistics such as door-to-door replacement, collection, collection completed, order entry and packing of returned goods.

To satisfy demands from JD's high-speed development, functions of various sub-systems were fully addressed for the design of the application architecture of the Azure Dragon System, which clearly divided the roles of all sub-systems with due consideration to data sharing among different systems, providing support for the subsequent business expansion by design of the loose coupling structure.

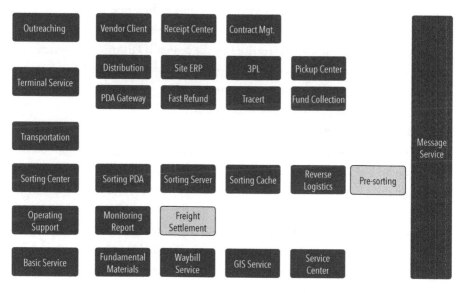

Core Sub-systems of Azure Dragon 1.0

Fundamental Materials

Reasonable setting of fundamental materials was of great importance to the systems. Setting of the Azure Dragon System was conducted for the basic objects such as sorting center, distribution terminal, delivery personnel, driver, vehicle, and third-party carrier as well as complicated documents such as vendor contracts and billing rules. Reasonable setting of the fundamental materials supported complicated business scenes.

The Sender Client and Consignment Receiving Center

The Azure Dragon System empowered JD's distribution to receive exterior orders and provide any vendors with the courier service if necessary.

The Sender Client enabled vendors to place orders offline and submit orders in batch. They could directly submit orders, track the distribution status and dealt with the subsequent payment collection and freight settlement via the client end.

The consignment receiving center served the vendors' exterior orders and delivery of the consignment to JD's distribution system was completed as soon as the consignment was received by the center. JD distribution system supported doorstep delivery by vendors and doorstep pickup by JD. The center was responsible for receiving management, express bill printing, consignment receipt, examination and return, etc.

Pre-sorting System

The pre-sorting system assigned the express bills to right distribution terminals based on the address of receipt in advance and delivered packages to the designated terminals according to the pre-sorting results. Therefore, accuracy of pre-sorting result was vital for the distribution system. The Azure Dragon distribution system adopted full-address matching, keyword matching, GIS geographic location information matching and other technologies to guarantee the accuracy and high efficiency of pre-sorting and highly efficient operation of subsequent links.

PDA System

PDA system was the core generation system of Azure Dragon System and the most powerful edged tool for site operation in the sorting centers and distribution terminals. The Azure Dragon PDA system was divided into the sorting system, distribution system, 3PL system and cooperative station system based on the application scenarios for all-round satisfaction of the demands from various business scenes in JD distribution segment.

The Azure Dragon System provided the delivery personnel with the POS-PDA AIO (all-in-one) system which realized the payment collection functions of PDA and POS and changed the previous working model (the delivery personnel must hold POS machine in one hand and PDA in the other). This sharply improved the delivery personnel's working efficiency, so this system was applauded by them.

Express bill System

The express bill system could record the basic information on the express bill such as the address of receipt and receive operating records from the consignment receiving system and the PDA system, providing full traceability of orders. Meanwhile, the express bill system allowed external systems such as settlement system to inquire status and mode of payment, etc.

Quality Control Platform

The quality control platform was designed to report and collect the abnormal information such as the logistics loss occurring in the process of business system operation, and the quality control personnel oversaw fixing responsibilities. The quality control system guaranteed prompt tracking of abnormal events during distribution and loss cut at the same time.

Monitoring and Report

The monitoring and reports provided the management and executive personnel with decision-making supports. The Azure Dragon System made the global monitoring possible by a centralized deployment plan. The Group could promptly monitor the operation of all areas and then made overall arrangements based on the varied smoothness of all links.

Financial Settlement

The Azure Dragon financial settlement system provided freight settlement service for third-party carriers, freight settlement. and payment collection service for outside vendors. JD would entrust nearly 100,000 orders to exterior carriers for distribution. The freight settlement in the past depended on manual calculation in Excel sheets with heavy workload and high error rate. The Azure Dragon financial system was designed for freight settlement and systematic management over the whole settlement process, thus the calculation accuracy and all-round monitoring.

GIS System

The Azure Dragon GIS system was established to explore applications at a deeper level based on the former order path tracking and site information presentation, including geographic information acquisition, distribution region division, GIS pre-sorting technology exploration, GIS statistical analysis of order volume and optimized division and setting of distribution regions, etc. Such exploration was expected to support the optimization of the distribution network by deeper application of GIS system.

The Azure Dragon System 1.0 was a large-scale SOA information system based on Java technology. In the process of R&D, the technical team tackled technical difficulties in the establishment of a large-scale asynchronous system, materializing gray level deployment, flexible control of service and unified monitoring and logs, etc.

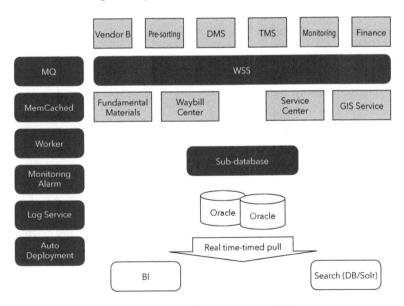

Technical Architecture of Azure Dragon 1.0 System

Improvement of Performance and Efficiency

The Azure Dragon System 1.0 addressed problems concerning imperfect information system and unreasonable system architecture, drafted more reasonable business process, at the same time built a more efficient information management system and realized the function of mass information processing which could fully meet the daily demands in mass data processing. The Azure Dragon platform reconstructed the former system to comprehensively improve the service ability of the sorting system and the distribution system. Simultaneously, the enhancement of system operating efficiency contributed to raising the working efficiency of delivery personnel, helped the continuous expansion of JD's sales, and created more convenient and faster shopping experience for customers.

Business Diversity

The Azure Dragon System 1.0 provided full support for JD's business diversity. It not only backed up the distribution business inside and outside terminals and pickup centers in the self-operation mode, but also was added with the supporting function for business types inside and outside the cooperative workstation in a non-self-operation mode. The Azure Dragon System was capable of supporting JD to establish self-operated terminals and cooperative workstations in the second-tier and third-tier cities so that more customers could access to the "211 Time-limited Delivery" service.

All-round and Detailed Information Management

The Azure Dragon logistics platform was endowed with comprehensive functions including forward operation functions such as cargo receipt and examination by terminals, receipt and distribution by delivery personnel as well as reverse functions such as door-to-door pickup and replacement, offering more convenient and faster delivery services for customers. In addition, monitoring and detailed management over the entire logistics link were available. The Azure Dragon System was comprised of four major parts: real time monitoring system, basic operation and sorting operation monitoring, distribution and delivery monitoring and cooperative operation monitoring, which respectively analyzed the distribution of order status at all major links and difference at all operation steps at the macro and micro level to provide reference for the company's decision making and operation and better satisfy business requirements from distribution quality control, sorting centers, self-operation, and third parties. Azure Dragon GIS positioning system could inform customers of the latest order status on a real-time basis.

Certainly, advantages of the Azure Dragon System were much more than these. It successfully applied the design principles of informatization, integration, and modularization. Firstly, the Azure Dragon System set up a complete and customer-oriented management application model to ensure all departments of JD could share and smoothly communicate the information with other enterprises. Secondly, it integrated correlative business parts and replaced the manual operation with automatic business processing mode.

Azure Dragon System 2.0

With the Azure Dragon System 1.0 going live and operating across the country, diversified demands which had been oppressed for nearly one year from the distribution business emerged, thus the Azure Dragon product and R&D team turned to the planning and implementation of version 2.0 by the end of 2012.

The Azure Dragon System 2.0 was mainly designed for quick and complete functions based on business demands. Hence, the items include vehicle management, dispatching center, reverse logistics, terminal-based cargo consolidation, order interception, appointed distribution, turnover box, internal quality management, return management, material management, business decision statement, statement pushing via e-mail, etc. With joint efforts made by the product and R&D team, plans were all successfully put into practice.

Compared with the 1.0 system, the Azure Dragon System 2.0 possessed more powerful functions.

Outreaching	Express Website	Vendor Client	Receipt Center	Contract Mgt.	Client Outreach
Terminal Service	Distribution PDA	Site ERP	3PL	Pickup Center	Self-Pickup Cabinet
	PDA Gateway	Fast Refund	Whole-process tracking	Stream Media	Fund Collection
Transportation Mgt.	Transportation PDA	Vehicle Mgt.	Vehicle Dispatching	Whole-network routing	Path Planning
Sorting Center	Sorting PDA	Sorting Service Station	Sorting Cache	Reverse Logistics	Pre-sorting
Operating Support	Material Mgt.	Quality Control & Mgt.	Knowledge Base	Aging Mgt.	
	Distribution Portal	Monitoring Report	Freight Settlement	Performance Mgt.	
Basic Service	Fundamental Materials	Express bill Service	GIS Service	Service Center	

Core Sub-systems of Azure Dragon 2.0

Vehicle Management and Dispatching

In the process of distribution, vehicles are the most important means of transport, so improvement of the working efficiency of vehicle management and implementation of standardized, scientific, and systematic management will directly raise the operating efficiency of the whole distribution network and cut the operating cost. The Azure Dragon System provides full-life-circle management for the vehicle's basic information, repair & maintenance, safety, annual inspection and insurance, as well as accessories.

This system improved the vehicle's operating efficiency, reduced the empty-loading ratio, increased the timeliness ratio of delivery, and raised the level of "211 Service" by means of the auxiliary dispatch. Meanwhile, standardization of vehicle operations was enhanced and monitoring data and performance assessment data were generated by a systematic operation management.

Self-Pickup Cabinet System

As a type of logistics distribution terminal, JD's Self-Pickup Cabinet could solve the difficulty of "The Last One Mile," improve the efficiency of distribution services and customer satisfaction, and collect the big data of logistics distribution.

JD's technology was also continually progressing while the Azure Dragon system underwent rapid development. The Azure Dragon team closely cooperated with the company's supporting technology team to conduct ongoing technical optimization of the System including SOA framework, distributed dispatching, Redis, MQ, distributed MySQL and so forth, which strongly a guaranteed stable operation of the system, improved the system efficiency, and made the supporting technology more mature.

Self-Pickup Cabinet Developed by JD Independently

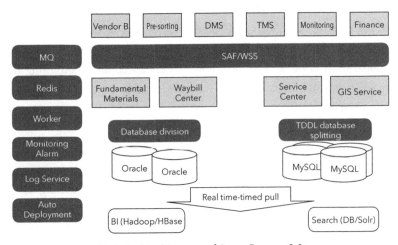

Technical Architecture of Azure Dragon 2.0

The success was in the details. Based on the specific situation of Azure Dragon System, the R&D team made various improvements to its technical architecture and achieved good effects. For example, Redis-based distributed dispatching was compatible with the existing database schemes and enabled smooth upgrading, avoidance of data loss after reboot, high concurrency, batch processing, avoidance of re-registration, and (auto and manual) switches in case of Redis failures.

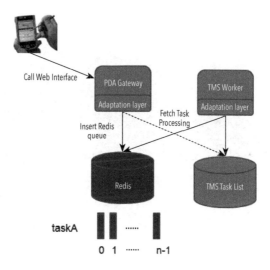

Architecture Chart for Distributed Dispatching of Azure Dragon System

After the 618 Campaign in 2013 when the Azure Dragon System 2.0 was under development, Liu led the senior executives to experience the distribution terminals and drew another main line of development for the Azure Dragon System — customer experience. Senior executives were discontent with the system's customer experience and put forward more than twenty recommendations for system optimization. Accordingly, we initiated a project with high priority for optimizing the senior executives' experience. The customer experience project was listed as a project subject to continuing improvements for which personnel in charge of project and R&D was regularly dispatched to receive training in the distribution terminals in a bid to constantly improve the customer experience. With a year's effort, during the 618 Anniversary Celebration Campaign in 2014, Liu spoke highly of the systems when he experienced a distribution terminal.

With the Azure Dragon R&D team's efforts for nearly one year, a far more elaborate logistics distribution system was established to meet demands of

Liu was Experiencing the Distribution Station during the 618 Campaign

Group Photo of Members of the Azure Dragon Team

our fast business expansion. Moreover, the team made great breakthroughs in numerous technologies, including the cache-based distributed dispatching and multi-level cache system and was granted with more than 40 technical patents as well as the company-level title of "excellent team" again.

Azure Dragon System 3.0

At the beginning of design, we had taken opening up into consideration and devised an open sub-system — Vendor System for the Azure Dragon System. However, both version 1.0 and 2.0 put emphasis on perfection and optimization of the system functions serving logistics distribution and did not give priority to development of the system opening.

The further expansion of business strongly demanded opening of the logistics distribution service. Foundation of Cainiao.com inspired managers of the distribution business to put the system opening in an overriding position, thus we also accelerated the speed and set out a journey for opening of the Azure Dragon System. Upon completion of some major projects such as SOP order docking and ISV linking, an outbound open platform began to come out.

In 2014, the Azure Dragon 3.0 took "opening up and establishing an ecosystem" as the most important strategy. Particularly with JD merging with the logistics segment of yixun.com and acquiring paipai.com, the entire system pattern underwent a significant change.

The Azure Dragon System's business mode was also transformed from JD's internal logistics system to a social one.

At the technology level, the R&D team also made breakthroughs in the system hierarchy and cross deployment since stricter requirements were raised for the stability, performance and customer experience.

With all-out struggles, the team achieved a great victory in opening the Azure Dragon System 3.0, set a new historical high of the external order volume and won full recognition by the company.

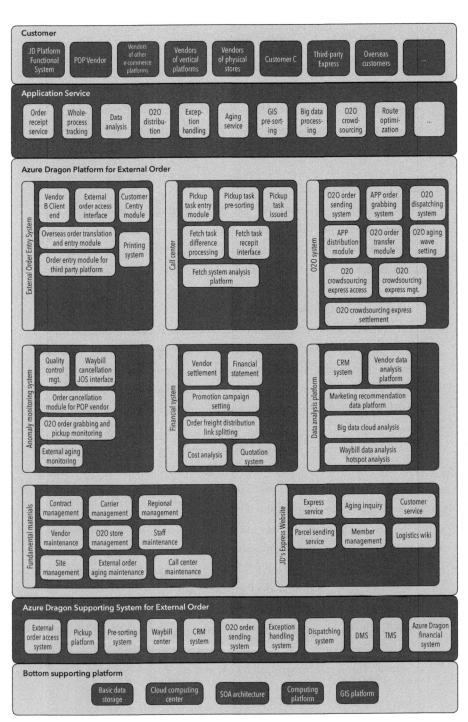

Module Diagram for External Orders of the Azure Dragon System

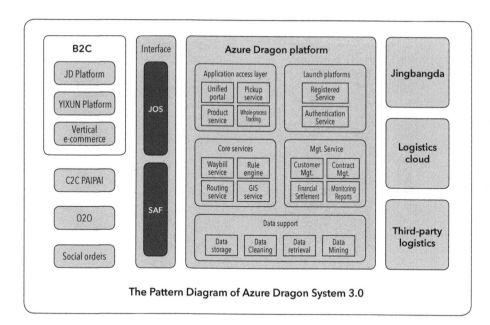

The Pattern Diagram of Azure Dragon System 3.0

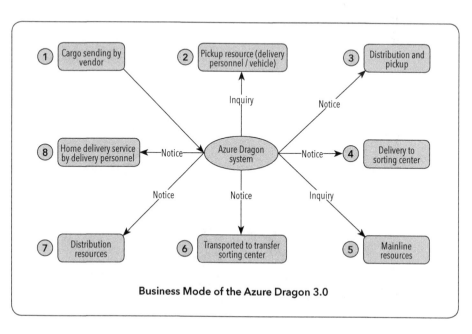

Business Mode of the Azure Dragon 3.0

Old Version

New Version

Example of POS AIO UED with Improved Interactive Experience for Delivery Personnel

Summary and Outlook of the Azure Dragon System

With the explosion of O2O, LBS, wearable devices, mobile phone App, automation equipment, air transportation and high-speed technical advance, stricter requirements were raised for the logistics distribution service.

Distribution Business and Technology Outlook

The Azure Dragon System started with version 1.0, which met the core functions and evolved into version 2.0 with basically perfect functions and the version 3.0 which has been an openly established ecology system. This system has taken giant steps toward the direction of open platform, become an integral part of socialized logistics and begin to set industry standards. A highly efficient, reliable, intelligent, and fascinating Azure Dragon System is coming towards us.

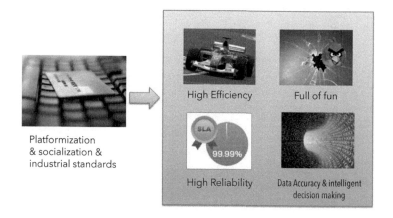

Prospective for Azure Dragon System

Authors: Chen Kun, Li Pengtao, Wu Xinhong, Wang Ru, and others

CHAPTER 9

Raiders of the Lost Ark: The After-sale System

Chasing After Business

In 2009 and 2010, e-commerce industry underwent the fastest development. JD was then called "Rough JD" due to its rapid development. When I joined the After-sale R&D team, the systems were, in a word, simple or even primitive, with many processes lacking system supports. Thousands of after-sale requests flooding in everyday were tackled by the customer service staff. I still remembered what I saw when I conducted survey in the spare parts storeroom for the first time. It was piled up with goods and there were not enough storage racks. Young colleagues were shuttling to and fro in this seedy room while many operators were still depending on Excel to record business documents. Apart from the colleagues who were working in the spare parts storeroom, after-sale service staff were also answering the phone while keeping records in an Excel sheet. Such "hand-to-hand tactics" might be workable for thousands of orders per day, but the order volume was undergoing a geometric growth, and so was the volume of phone calls and after-sale service requests. John resorted to our team and said that, "Get rid of Excel and establish informatized systems to keep pace with the businesses with 3 months".

Back then the After-sale R&D team comprised 4 members only, but two months after I joined, two of them quit to seek for occupational opportunities in other city because of the heavy pressure. John had to transfer several professionals specialized in WMS from other teams. JD's systems were established based on .Net platform and Lao Li had foreseen the need to transform to the open source platform. In such case, we were required to apply the Java platform to the CRM and production system for the spare parts storeroom.

We were facing a situation featured short-staff, complicated business, transformation of development language with short time limit for projects. At that window phase, we had no time to hesitate, and those young men in the R&D project teams did not flinch and were full of passion, just like the then JD.

CRM and production system for the spare parts storeroom commenced at the same time and were listed in top ten projects for the R&D Department that year. Lao Jia, with years of experience in WMS development, undertook the project of "production system for the spare parts storeroom" together with another 8 old hands including Liyao. Yang Shuai and I, both of whom were born after 1986, led a mixed brigade (consisting of fellows from other departments, newcomers, and personnel in charge of transforming .Net to Java) to be responsible for the CRM project. On hindsight, what we had at that time was the "fighting" spirit conveyed by Lao Liu to all people working in JD.

Despite of a variety of difficulties, we did not lower the standard for systems to be established. A target of building standardized processes to assist the business with detailed management was set at the very beginning. Despite a seemingly simple target, we got into trouble when project began.

The spare parts storeroom was a management warehouse for reverse recovery of commodities in JD's after-sale system as well as a department suffering the fastest oil spilling on "JD fast train." Due to the failed management of second-hand goods, the storeroom underwent severe loss, reaching around RMB 100 million annually. The business director of the spare parts storeroom personally participated in the project team to work with the R&D team for analysis of business requirements. We were surprised to find that the spare parts management system for self-operated commerce was so multifarious and disorderly and had numerous and detailed processes. Unlike the SUK management pattern for large warehouses, this system was designed to manage the returned goods on a one-order-for-one-commodity basis, particularly the RMA Manufacturer Repair mode in which goods were sent to the manufacturer for repair, but would be returned in varied forms, making it hard to accurately define the matching relations. Moreover, the inventory cycle time was long, with more than a dozen of stock in/out types. But how to import the existing data, how to cut over and go live, etc. baffled us most. We were facing great challenges for system modeling.

This was a real mess for a team lacking the experience in modeling of similar storeroom systems, and we even didn't know where to start. Liyao proposed to separate the primary and subsidiary businesses and make the production system independent of peripheral examination & approval and monitoring. With the B/S + C/S mode for its architecture, the core business logic was put on the Service End and developed by Java platform; the operating system inside the storeroom adopted C/S; Winform was generated using C# at the Client End and the B/S mode was used for monitoring, report and approval for convenience of the management layer. The production and operating system inside the storeroom were further divided into inventory, stock in/out, cargo space, packing for delivery, taking stock, RMA and other modules. There were several advantages by putting it this way. First, core business logic was encapsulated with enhanced re-usability for convenience of maintenance and upgrading; secondly, production and management were independent from each other, thus prioritizing the normal production; thirdly, linking with the peripheral system was subject to adaptive processing and replacement was made one by one to effectively control the scope of system transformation, facilitate linkage with existing legacy system. and data and guarantee smooth cutover and launch of systems; fourthly, the staff could make use of their advantages (.Net programmers were adept at development of the Client End, and those expert in WMS could well handle the storeroom management.

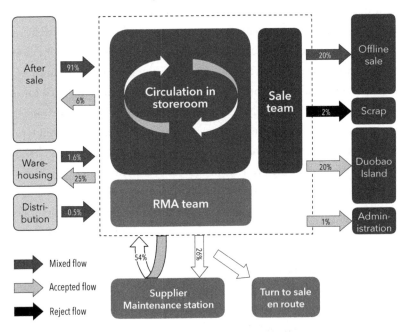

The Relationship Among Main Business Flows in the Spare Parts Storeroom Production System

A lot of puzzles were addressed by "brainstorming." In that suffering but pleasant stage, we encountered a variety of problems which challenged our team every day, but all of us derived a sense of achievement when we solved the difficulties properly. In the first half of 2010, the project went live and was released in advance, significantly raising the spare parts management level. We stopped year-on-year losses reaching over RMB 80 million for that current year. The business party also received acclaim that year and we reaped a brave and battle-wise R&D team for the After-sale Department.

Let's move back to the "CRM battlefield." Yang Shuai was in charge of product design and I was assigned for R&D. We lacked a good understanding of the call center system before and there were two problems in front of us: the first one was to integrate the phone system, prejudge and upgrade & transfer the incoming cases; the second one was to connect the sub-systems used by the customer service personnel in series and form a working platform for them with the events as a clue. Compared with the system of the spare parts storeroom, the processes contained in this version of CRM system were relatively simple, with a great many peripheral systems to be linked and integrated and requiring timely system response.

The architect Lidong and I led the team to finish system analysis and design. The Case was adopted as the core mode to converse various customer demands into cases, and then the customer service personnel tracked such cases which could be updated and transferred. The Case was also the clue for the connection of peripheral systems in series, with the systems including "after-sale service," "compensation," "reminder", "work order," "complaints," "warranty extensions," and "order management" as the Case's sub-tasks. Those peripheral systems interacted with CRM via message queue and dispatching task and such an architecture helped us achieve the goal of decoupling. There was a special context where the CRM system was deployed in the Call Center at Suqian, but other ERP systems were arranged in the machine room in Beijing, so a link connection was required. Lidong designed the system dependence relation and made it to be CRM's one-way dependence on other systems with assurance of a one-way proxy of the link.

A brief interlude took place. To integrate the phone system, we came to the phone system supplier's office together with our testers and developers. We still lingered around and wouldn't leave when employees of the supplier got off work. After several days with the supplier, the system joint debugging was finally succeeded. It was the first time that the peers witnessed the devotion to work of JD.

Yang Shuai took charge of arranging the principals of various systems to coordinate with the interface. There were more than a dozen systems with different sizes, so more interfaces were waiting and resources from several teams were needed for support. We thought that it might be risky, but it came as a surprise that other departments made positive responses and we should sincerely give them thumbs-up. The systems went live on schedule, but we suffered a setback the first day we went to Suqian for the on-site extension. The function of incoming screen popup took several seconds to activate. We were all in a sweat when we saw the customer service personnel talking with the customers by phone while waiting for white pages of the system. The database was heavily dependent on the remote procedure call. Our team members didn't sleep well that night and tried every method to find solutions. We performed various operations on the systems such as

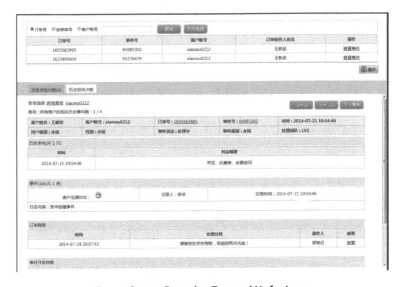

Popup Screen Page that Tortured Us for Long

splitting, cache, asynchronous message mechanism, SQL optimization, and so forth. Much valuable experience was accumulated in that period. The concurrent active users were around 1,000 and the number of primary cases per day exceeded 40,000. The number of cases on the 618 Campaign exceeded 80,000, so we successfully withstood the brunt of the first 618 Campaign. But now, the number of cases per day exceeds 160,000 and on June 18, this number climbed to 250,000. Others will exhale a sigh of relief at JD's fast growth, but only our team was clear about the bitterness and happiness on the journey.

In early 2012, the spare parts storeroom's systems and the CRM system had been completed, with a dozen of sub-systems and modules. Another core system — the after-sale system continued to be challenged by the business after constant revisions. Lao Xie, Director of our department, was keenly aware that, as the core business system of the after-sale customer service segment, the after-sale system was undergoing a dramatically growing trend and could be deemed as the main entrance to JD's reverse processes. The business expansion of marketing system would impact the after-sale system and its current architecture could hardly meet the development requirements of business in the future. Another hard fight kicked off. An R&D team consisting of 16 members spent two and a half months building a brand-new after-sale system which was officially renamed as "the after-sale service platform".

The current team lineup covering a half of "battle-tested" old hands was much stronger than the one two years ago, but there were many unprecedented challenges. As aforesaid, the after-sale system was the main entrance to JD's reverse processes and echoed the marketing transaction system. As the end of joint debugging for order production, it should positively interact with almost all core systems. Only one refund sub-system depended on over sixty external services. On the one hand, it was resulted from the small team pattern bearing data-island style in JD; on the other, it also reflected that various systems were growing dramatically and employed SOA-based service interaction. Our after-sale service platform set a record, being one of the systems having the most interactive interfaces with external systems.

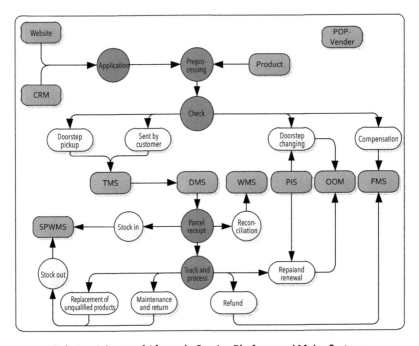

Relation Schema of After-sale Service Platform and Major Systems

As to the business, the process complexity was not inferior to that of any other systems. We substantially divided the systems into two parts: self-operated after-sale system and autonomous after-sale system. The self-operation after-sale system accounted for 60% of the total business volume, which involved "changing or refunding," "maintenance service," "large appliance installation and maintenance service," "virtual products after-sale," and more. The autonomous after-sale system enabled vendors and manufacturers to directly serve customers by accessing to the system, which included "vendor (seller) autonomous after-sale system," "manufacturer (direct selling) autonomous after-sale system", "O2O after-sale," and Others.

By the end of 2012, the troika for JD's after-sale customer service system, i.e. CRM, after-sale service platform, and spare parts storeroom management system had been completed. The After-sale Customer Service R&D Department also grew from a four-member group to an R&D team comprising 40 members.

Customer Experience First

As said by Lao Li, R&D covered three steps: "supporting the business," "driving the business," and "leading the business." We spent more than two years pursuing businesses, at a full trot and without idleness, as we never forgot our highest mission, to drive and lead the business. By the end of 2012, after-sale customer service systems were required to be "simple, professional and fast", aiming at great improvement of the customer satisfaction, which coincided with the development planning for our systems. To be simple, profession and fast must, we should rely on the systems.

For the After-sale Customer Service R&D Department, our service objects included internal customers, terminal customers (JD's members), vendors & manufacturers and brother departments. By the end of 2012, we had made significant automatic upgrading for system products in order to accelerate businesses and enabled our service objects to waste less time on waiting.

Regarding terminal customers, i.e. JD's members, we focused on customer demands and figured out that there were several key factors causing their dissatisfaction:

1. To make customers be informed of the response speed and handling progress, and achieve service process;
2. To provide broad, convenient and prompt channels for communication and feedback;

3. To grant more autonomous rights and provide human-based services.

Keeping an eye on the above-mentioned factors, we succeeded in doing a lot of work using some targeted technological means. The most typical example was that we opened a service entry to the mobile end and enabled online IM. A minor detail adjustment became the most typical case. I am not sure whether or not you have noticed that there is an item called "progress bar" in the channel, "My JD → Repair/Changing or Refunding", for JD's PC end while enjoying JD's after-sale services. This progress bar could be, so to speak, the most complicated and changeable progress presentation tools in JD or even in the whole e-commerce industry. A small progress bar can form nearly 20 events such as what the current status of your application form for after-sale service is or when the next response will be made, etc. so that our customers can be informed of the handling progress of their service requests at a glance. Don't underestimate this function, it is the result of painstaking efforts of our R&D personnel who should active branches of dozens of processes in a configuration form, and this is also an innovation.

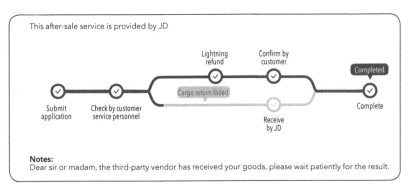

Changeable Progress Bar

To grant greater autonomous rights to the customers and enable them to enjoy human-based services, we gradually improved the system functions. For example, you had submitted a service application request for replacement, but would be on a business trip this week and only had time to get the parcel next week. In this case, the former solution was asking the customer to submit application form next week, but quality guarantee period would be exceeded by doing so, then we added a function of "making appointment for pickup," which readily solved such problems and greatly raised the pickup success ratio. There was other similar system improvement. For instance, customers could make an appointment for the customer service personnel to call back, without being anxious about failure of getting through to the customer service. This seemingly small step was significant in the enhancement of customer experience.

For the internal service objects, i.e. after-sale and customer service personnel, Yang Shuai took great pains, together with other product managers. They conducted surveys on every operation step of systems and worked out a great number of proposals for operation simplification and process optimization. The spare parts storeroom was equipped with pre-processing modules for purchase and sale to accelerate the circulation inside; the sub-system work order in CRM removed communication barriers between business departments, making the trans-department collaborative services be responded to promptly; the after-sale service platform was added with "auto check on change for new and refund", "lightning refund," "pickup preposition," and so forth, on the basis of previous feature service "doorstep changing for new." We provided a service with a cool name in an attempt to enable our customers to get back the payment quickly in case of sale return, but through which link can we shorten the waiting time? A variety of automated treatments had compressed the time for order check to a minute level. We finally targeted at the step of pickup of returned goods. Could we change the conventional thinking and refund the customer before taking the returned goods back? This practice seemed to touch on madness and be out of all reason in the traditional industry, but we made it!

Then, how could we control the risk? We should be particularly grateful to fellows in charge of the big data R&D. In an age of big data, we were provided with all data about customer behavior in JD and then built their credit model by extraction and mining of such data. With this model, our systems could intelligently recognize those customers with high credibility and we would offer them the preference of refunding before taking the returned goods back.

Yes, we unveiled an intelligent era for the after-sale customer service system depending on the big data for the first time.

Promoting the Business

Data not only laid the foundation for the development of system intelligence, but also provided the basis for operation monitoring, continuous optimization, and decision-making support. The year 2013 saw the build of a "whole-node monitoring" platform for the after-sale system which displayed various operation steps on the leaders' work bench and large screen board for the front-line workplace. Problems arising in any step or service form were clear at a glance, thus effectively reducing customer complaints.

In 2014, whole-process monitoring system for the spare parts storeroom went live and those in charge of R&D introduced visual effects to make reports vivid. The business personnel could customize and drag to generate reports. The timely database project of BI team was also a milestone for system intelligence as indexes such as anticipation of the stock loss rate and repair rate could be predicted in an intelligent way.

Speaking of the data power, there was a typical scenario, which may arouse echoes in those members who called for customer service before. JD's master station was provided with a function named member portrait description and a similar one was also set for the CRM system. When getting a phone call, our customer service personnel could call your name immediately, asked if you had any problem about certain commodity and knew your credits or preferences. Sometimes you might even feel that the customer service personnel were as cordial as your neighborhood. This also depended on the big data mining by which the customer service personnel could make prejudgment against your problems based on the description information in CRM, thus improving the efficiency of communications with our customers, bringing us closer and improving customer satisfaction.

Three major systems for the after-sale customer service had trodden a path from automation to intelligence. More and more developer components and frameworks avoided a duplication of efforts taken in R&D and the automated testing platform AMP solved the difficulty in regression testing of complicated processes. These automated tools were strong guarantee for avoidance of failures or major bugs in our systems over the years.

Integration and Opening up

The year 2014 was extraordinary for the after-sale customer service systems as it witnessed JD's integration with yixun.com and paipai.com. It took less than two months on system connection and launch after the integration program was announced. The integration posed challenges brought by connections and completely new business models. The after-sale systems and CRM system had to be opened to yixun.com and paipai.com and support service requests from different marketing platforms.

Before that, we were also exploring various open models for after-sale customer service systems. For example, the spare parts storeroom system related to the supplier's VC platform since 2012 to completely informatize RMA processes; the forwarding system was opened for convenience of connecting with carriers; a competitive sale platform went live, enabling the competitive sellers to sell the spare parts on a competitive basis; the after-sale system was connected to JOS and opened API so that vendors could integrate JD's after-sale system into their own ERP systems. Generally speaking, two open models were adopted in this phase: the first one was to establish systems through the public network accessible to external customers, and the second was to open AIP so that ISV could help service integration.

Oh, there was one more thing. We had an internal sale platform that was opened to our internal staff. After this system went live, it was said that no one would leave to go to the bathroom at 10:30 a.m. so as not to miss goods at 50% off. This preference was specially conferred on our staff to buy commodities in the spare parts storeroom at 50% off, with certain limited times. This system, equal to an internal second-kill system, caused a company-wide sensation. Everyone tried to make friends with fellows in charge of this internal sale system and wondered if there was a "back door." Certainly, it was a joke, but influence of our team was expanded then.

Models of yixun.com and paipai.com gave us the opportunity to see more clearly about the advent of an era for comprehensively open systems. Technically, core API must be peeled off for linking up external and internal systems and platforms or building systems into reusable and marketable products; from the perspective of product and business planning, what we tried to open was JD's service capability, which included computing resource as well as all customer service and after-sale service system resources.

CRM2.0

In fact, our systems had started on the road to open transformation. In 2014, Chen Wenfeng headed the CRM R&D team to develop CRM2.0 accessible to multiple business units. Informally, apart from JD's businesses, other vendors, manufacturers, and e-commerce platforms could link to our systems by a simple customized configuration. Currently, CRM2.0 was launched after half a year of R&D.

New Mode

If we said that CRM2.0 was a new model practice for open systems, then the maintenance center system was an exploration for the opening of professional proficiency.

On March 15, 2014, "doorstep after-sale service" debuted at JD's press conference. One month before this conference, engineers of our team kept preparing for this service all through the night.

Upon receipt of your phone call or online application, JD's maintenance engineers would come to your house and services are accessible even if you are staying at home. There were very many home-stayers who became target customers of this service. In a short while, JD's members no longer had to rush here and there for any problems arising in the goods they bought (whether such goods were bought through JD or other platforms) and be wary of bad maintenance service providers who charged exorbitant prices. They could purchase maintenance services online via our systems that made open and transparent offers in the whole process.

It is an attempt as well as progress. JD's brand image has gained public praise among our customers, and few e-commerce companies stepped into the maintenance service zone. Our maintenance center system currently supports maintenance service within the warranty period and authorized maintenance service. New models will be launched soon. Then, services will be a type of products. JD's members may enjoy more convenient and transparent maintenance services via our system. This is also an important transition from cost center to profit center, and we named this system "Spread the Wings."

Since 2009, after-sale customer service systems have kept writing remarkable chapters. Now a new chapter is opening, like a butterfly that is fluttering and is going to soar high. We believe greater values will be added to the industry.

Author: Zhang Hua

CHAPTER 10

Wall Street: The Evolution of the Financial System

The Secret of JD's Fund

JD's financial system included three modules including settlements, invoices, and funds, each of which is equipped with different functions. For example, the module of funds involves forward and reverse payment, refund process, and so forth. We will show you the little-known financial system of JD below.

The evolution of the fund system fell into three stages as follows:

First Stage: Single Means of Payment, Fund Decentralization, and Manual Reconciliation of Orders

This stage saw the outset of e-commerce community in which a single means of payment was employed, online payment had to rely on e-banks and only cash against delivery was available. Customers were clear about these deficiencies. However, what they did not know was that JD still conducted manual reconciliation for orders, and in case the payment made by customers was transferred to a recipient account in consistent with the order unit, the cashiers of recipient company and the company to which the order belonged had to communicate and carry out fund allocation.

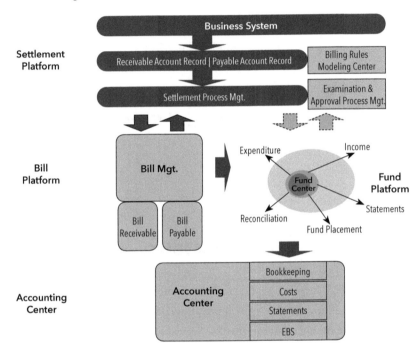

JD's Financial System

Second Stage: Increase of Means of Payment, Fund Centralization, and System-based Reconciliation

At the beginning of business, methods of collection and reconciliation could meet business demands of various branches. However, with expansion of JD's market share, the volume of orders surged. Order operation costs and communication costs for trans-department orders and receipt or allocation of follow-up fund orders were subject to ongoing increases. Therefore, the

Financial Department and Function R&D Department made up their mind to utterly change this situation, where everyone acted independently.

In the conference room, De Ge, the product manager and Lao Chen, Lao Niu, and Lao Xie, engineers on the business side were silent all the while. In fact, they knew the cause of current problems and had upgraded the systems for many times, but failed to really solve the problems.

The business party, Juan, did not want to announce that this conference ended up with the decision to upgrade systems, then she threw out a heavy bomb the Financial Department was ready to consolidate the order payment collection and transform collection by branches to collection and reconciliation by the Group, so that the funds could receive unified management. The product manager and several R&D developers were suddenly enlightened. If the Group carried out unified management of the funds, then the design system could be re-designed. Apart from satisfaction of business demands, understanding of JD's businesses and future expectations could be combined to design and plan a more efficient and perfect system. They joined JD for the purpose of planning a blueprint. With the promise made by the business party, all participants of the conference vied with each other airing their stands on system planning, business improvement, etc., with great confidence.

However, the reality was that the Financial Department had set up the Suqian Order Center for unified management of orders by the Group, but where was the system? We couldn't let the fellows in Suqian process orders manually and spent two years in research and development. Everyone had to compromise in the face of reality. In 2010, the first phase of the project for unified settlement was set up in this context. The idea of making a perfect plan was relinquished. Based on the current situation, we should confirm core and emergency functions and several fellows enabled the most basic functions in the shortest period of time so that the Suqian Order Center could operate normally.

To satisfy the business party's requirements, the second and third phases for unified settlement kicked off. Upon completion of three phases, the systems could basically meet business requirements, guarantee order flows and financial settlements so as to plan and set up core systems for finance. After repeated adjustments and alterations or even re-designs of the scheme, the systems finally went live and were well received by the business party.

Third Phase: Diversification of Means of Payment and Unified Management of Funds

In 2012, the sheer volume of business posed new challenges against the unified settlement system at that time. The functions of payment collection and reconciliation could neither meet the requirements for financial management and operation, nor support increasingly diversified payment demands from customers, such as consolidated payments, mixed payments and so forth. We were in urgent need of new reforms.

At this time, both the business party and the R&D Department dispatched their elites to work together on survey of the system status, problem analysis, and process combing. The problems were analyzed at the level of business and system. The R&D Department assigned 4 product managers, including De, Xie, Liu and Tan, and the business party's team was still led by Juan and added with Shang from Suqian Order Center and Shuang from the Fund Management Center. Three business personnel sorted problems and combed the business process according to the current situation. Four product managers conducted surveys based on the business types and analyzed every step from placement of orders to funds collection by division of work, with a survey scope involving more than thirty systems and forty business types. Four product managers conducted surveys during the day. They sorted the survey-related documents, exchanged experience, analyzed problems and discussed solutions into the night. They spent two months finishing surveys on the current situation of systems. Through careful product surveys, the Function R&D Department provided detailed and perfect product design based on existing problems and future planning.

After the scheme was made, the business party and personnel in charge of products and R&D conducted a comprehensive review. Juan, Shang, and Shuang proposed a lot of special business types and business that is probably usable in the future. Four product managers of the R&D Department were responsible for system establishment by designing and simulating various system flow situations. With various business scenarios normally operating in the simulated scenes, gradually they started to be at ease. Under the product design philosophy of making perfection more perfect, the fourth phase of unified settlement not only met the customers' payment demands, but also helped build a financial system to lay a solid data foundation for subsequent fund management and monitoring.

Completion of the product design only signified the first step for system implementation, and the follow-up R&D and system cutover was the main priority. As a variety of systems were involved and the scope was wide, it took half a year for the system coordination and cutover. Within this period, existing problems in the systems were detected and solved in a bid to guarantee stable running and high compatibility of systems in the later phase.

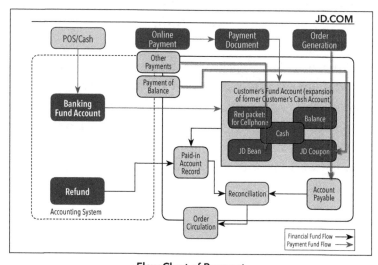

Flow Chart of Payment

The fourth phase of the unified settlement could rapidly support various payment demands of customers and realize decoupling of payment means and order reconciliation. After re-planning of the fund flow, customers knew better about usage of funds in JD, thus strengthening their sense of belonging. Establishment of banking fund accounts wound up the situation of decentralized funding as long as eight years in JD, changed the way of fund statistics by documents, and really enabled monitoring all fund flows by one account book in the JD Group. Based on banking fund accounts, JD Group realized funds allocation and transfer for payment against orders. Supported by direct connection of banks and enterprises, JD Group could automatically generate a Bank Balance Reconciliation Statement by the banking fund account to intensify control and management over the funds. The banking fund account was also taken as the most important and accurate account book.

Settlement – A Story We Must Tell about JD and Suppliers

JD settled accounts for its suppliers in a semi-automatic way prior to January 2011. When the purchasing staff needed to settle accounts for vendors, the Settlement Center would submit a paper form to be completed by hand to the financial staff and then the Cashier would click the system to settle according to the Warehouse Entry number on the paper document. In the Settlement Center, one settlement clerk was responsible for several or many suppliers and would be tired out if he managed the settlement history by paper documents.

At the 2011 Annual Meeting, the Financial Department required that online settlements must be enabled. The system for online settlement had been developed in mid-2009, but it did not go live and was still in the testing stage due to lack of understanding and ineffective communication. On January 10, 2011, this system which had been under development for one year and a half was finally launched. But it was soon taken offline because of too many problems. The supplier settlement system was back online on January 20, 2011 after various functions were sorted out and all account records with unclear functional orientation were removed. Although there were still some problems, the system's basic functions were OK. We kept collecting and analyzing the problems during operation of the system and redesigned processes and worked out an updated version, which repaired various bugs in October 2011.

The supplier settlement system was the first system furnished with online management of outbound settlement in the Financial Department. Then the systems such as e-book settlements, warranty extension settlements, and POP settlement sprang up like bamboo shoots after a spring rain. However, these systems became the prelude to new problems. Too many settlement systems greatly drove the maintenance cost up. on the one hand, a supplier might have to do with several settlement systems, thus vendors may think that JD's internal management systems were in disorder. On the other hand, if a vendor defaulted in one settlement business, other systems would remain unknown and the Financial Staff was unable to see complete data about JD's payables. Thus, the R&D Department planned to set up a settlement platform in 2013 to solve these problems.

But the most critical issue in front of the financial R&D team when devising a scheme was how to make such a settlement platform. The project team analyzed the merits and demerits of existing systems and exploited rip experience from the packed systems. The journey of scheme determination was full of hardships. When one idea was put forward, refutation appeared immediately. We had to address so many problems, such as whether billing functions should be wiped out, how to keep account records, what page style we should adopt, how to optimize the business process, and so forth. Meanwhile, a lot of factors needed to be balanced. The ideal of all people was unified until those responsible for architecture design in the R&D Department finalized the business architecture and design architecture for the settlement platform. The project kicked off at the command from the leaders.

With this anchor, teams in charge products, R&D, and testing quickly finalized their project schemes. This step was stabilized and followed by a clearance journey lasting three months.

First Stage: Product

The product design was the start. Without premium product design for this "high-end, magnificent, and classy" system, we might be unable to set a good example for those in charge of R&D. However, as the project schedule was too limited and only two weeks left for product design, we had no time for elaboration. Seven product managers went all out to draw the prototype and conducted parallel work on different modules. Completion of the first version of prototype was followed by repeated discussions and amendments and prototype design was changed three times. Then we finalized the page, functions, and product description. After the R&D work started, product managers invited Fang, who was responsible for UED to re-design the prototype. After half a month, a product prototype of a fresh style was put in front of the product managers and they thought that this prototype was just what they wanted at the first glance. Please look at the following figure:

Second  **Stage:**

Product Prototype for Settlement Application

Product Prototype for Backlog

Development

Through unremitting efforts by the Product Department team, a system having powerful functions, clearly defined processes, and featured page style was made, but it was endowed with complicated businesses and multifarious functions. How could we swiftly understand the system's logical structure? How could we quickly complete the development files? And how could the project be accomplished within limited time and guarantee quality and quantity?

1. Understanding and getting familiar with the process and functions of the settlement platform with their time limited, architects could only complete basic development design documents, but developers were unable to quickly understand the system business and structure by referring to simple project documents and basic development documents, since a system design covered a sheer volume of business and complicated logic and functions. Hence, we familiarized developers with the systems by means of continuous explanation and detailing. After the developers had a rudimentary grasp of systems, the team held meetings frequently during which architects went over explanation and developers digested the knowledge and asked if they

did understand until the developers fully understood the whole system.

2. Allocation for project development

Due to the system's complexity, tight schedule, and shortage of development resources, the leaders instructed 99% of members in the settlement team to participate in this project. Some of them spent all their time on it and the remainder should spare efforts on routine requirements of the systems they were formerly in charge of. The whole development team was divided into three sub-teams according to the system modules. The first sub-team was responsible for system configuration, examination and approval process, interface, etc., the second one was in charge of settlement applications, and the third one took charge of the invoice module.

3. Development of the first phase of project and testing

Throughout the development process for operator settlement, we adopted a strategy pursuing all at once and the initiative, to wit, architects targeted at the current functions to ceaselessly detail the development documents; UED scripts were continuously detailed and completed; and developers tackled the identified function problems. Furthermore, the R&D team reported progress, summarized problems concerning development and set the development goal for the following day on a daily basis. The entire development process was highly efficient and orderly. With cooperative efforts by those in other departments, our developers completed function development, internal function testing, and inter-system joint bugging within the required time, and finally handed it over to testers for further testing.

4. Development of the second and third phases and outlook for later phases

Based on the results achieved in the first phase, we swiftly accessed POP T+1 settlement, campus cooperation station, and other systems at the second and third phases. In terms of development of settlement platforms at the later phase, we focused on detailing modules and producing the best settlement business with the minimum volume of development.

Third Stage: Testing

In the earlier stage of testing, in face of the unfamiliar new business, testers underwent a difficult period to understand it and the disconcerting logic disturbed their thoughts. Understanding of preliminary requirements took up a great proportion in the subsequent project testing process and led the trend of the whole testing process. Meanwhile, the success or failure of the project testing consisted of the completeness of design and use cases in the earlier stages. The testing team unremittingly discussed the design of use cases and convened use case review meetings to ensure that all possible business scenarios were covered and the use cases for testing were as complete as possible.

After countless requirement explanation meetings held by the architects for the R&D and testing teams, we gradually sorted out the business scenarios and had a deep grasp of the system design and module functions. Then compilation of the test plan and the first draft of use cases for testing were completed. Through joint reviews by the architects, the R&D team, and testing team, the use cases for testing subject to constant improvement and completion were finalized.

During testing, the Project Manager assisted us in communicating and coordinating with other departments to obtain testing resources and data, finding access through all the upstream links, and assure data guarantee for joint debugging and accurate provision of testing resources. With explicit divisions of labor, the testing squad strove to verify the system's logic and usability and continuously submit system bugs.

Following the first operator settlement business, other settlement businesses such as POP T+1 settlement business were introduced step by step and the project's setting up gradually became evident. The testing squad was familiar with the system's module design and dealt with the assignments with high proficiency. In the process of the ongoing iteration tests and verification, the project went from disorderly to orderly. Testers and developers kept discussing how to further improve the systems and made joint efforts in system optimization.

When the testing was near the end, all defects were corrected. The new settlement platform was finally finished and brought online under common expectations. The testing squad summarized several principles that must be followed during the test based on experiences in testing the supplier settlement system and problems arising in the settlement platform testing and insisted on these principles. The first principle was real time tracking of the daily removed and deferred defects. The second one was a periodic summary of testing data and results. And the third one was close communication with the Product Personnel in the early stages to ensure requirements were understood correctly.

After a trial period, we learned that if all members were of the same mind, their sharpness can cut through metal and the real meaning of software testing was to find errors rather than verify the software's correctness.

No matter how rigorous a test was, it would never discover all the software errors, but could detect most errors and at least ensure the software's usability. Therefore, in the process of follow-up usage, we needed to enhance the links requiring a quick response and combine the theories on software testing to identify errors and take the initiative to tackle them before the final Client End.

Launch of the Settlement Platform

In September, 2013, with struggle and cooperation of the financial R&D team, a completely new settlement system, the settlement platform was successfully in operation. Compared with former settlement systems, this new platform provided the entry to unified settlement, unified settlement processes, and a unified settlement account to lay a solid system foundation for integration of all settlement systems. This marked a critical milestone in the development history of JD's settlement systems.

Characteristics of the Architecture of the Settlement Platform:

1. A billing rule pool was built to provide foreground configuration and display function for billing rules to facilitate the financial staff to control risks of settlement billing;

2. Reconstruct account records for payables and receivables to decouple the business systems and clearly define the boundary for the functions of settlement systems;

3. Add the concept of settlement grouping and function of differentiating between settlement application forms and final statements to satisfy settlement demands from different purchase & sale businesses and improve the system's compatibility and extensibility;

4. Provide unified settlement framework and unified interfaces for settlement and invoice management system and paying/receiving management system to lower the risk arising from the system operation and maintenance and reduce the workload.

Course of Integration of the Settlement Platform
1. The Access completed
- Access of the operator settlement business in September, 2013
- Access of POP T+1 settlement business in October, 2013
- Access of the freight settlement business for the campus cooperation station and joint-operation points in April, 2014
- Access of the virtual operator settlement business in May, 2014

2. The Access to be completed later
- Access of the settlement business for the cloud platform service market in July, 2014
- Access of the settlement business for overseas purchasing and warehousing service in August, 2014
- Access of the freight settlement business for the Azure Dragon systems in October, 2014
- Access of the spare parts maintenance settlement business in

November, 2014
- ...

Future Planning of the Settlement Platform

1. Automatic settlement

In the process of accessing new businesses to the settlement platform, its functions would be gradually optimized, and we targeted the establishment of a more robust and flexible settlement system toward the automatic settlement.

- Individual settlement rule configuration — automatic submission for settlement
- Individual settlement examination and approval flow configuration — automatic settlement examination and approval
- Individual configuration for rules of invoice verification and reimbursement—automatic invoice verification and reimbursement

2. VC settlement

A supplier settlement platform would be set up based on the settlement platform to provide AIP interface for ISV to build an integrated supply-chain settlement ecosystem between JD and its suppliers.

The Invoice – the Past and Present Life of a Piece of Paper

In China, an invoice can be a receipt or payment voucher, warranty voucher, and tax certificate. Accordingly, JD issues invoices to every self-operated valuable item to make quality guarantee for self-operated commodities and commitment to customers. Therefore, the invoice system becomes one of those indispensable systems in JD.

Positioning of the Invoice System

The invoice system is a generative system and is placed at the lower end of the system chain. Up the chain stream, there are order systems, master data systems, and so forth. The invoice system is mainly designed to sort the data of upstream systems and issue final invoices to customers.

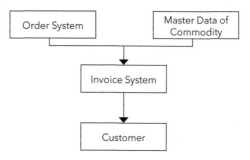

Positioning of the Invoice System

Structure of the Invoice System

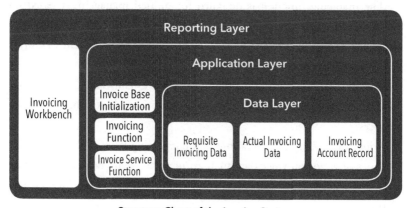

Structure Chart of the Invoice System

Through overall improvement of invoice system since 2013, JD has set up the basic data layer for the invoice system, including requisite invoicing data, actual invoicing data, and invoicing accounts.

1. Requisite Invoicing Data is the reference data for invoicing, with sources from the upstream systems, including the information about commodity name, unit price, quantity, discount, tax rate, invoice title, drawer, etc.;
2. Actual Invoicing Data is the information of issued invoices and is mainly used for recording the information on an invoice, such as invoice code, invoice number, invoice content, etc.;
3. Invoicing Accounts is mainly used to record invoicing actions and compare the requisite invoicing data with actual invoicing data to guarantee their consistency.

The application layer of invoice system is based on the basic data layer, consisting of three parts: invoice basis initialization, invoice drawing function, and invoice service function.

The invoice basis initialization is applied for configuration of invoice information, including invoice template configuration, invoiced content configuration, the drawer's information configuration, and so forth.

The invoicing function is designed for unified management based on various business demands, for example, "VAT Centralized Processing Platform" for VAT special invoices, "Application Form Management Platform" for issuing invoices to suppliers, etc.

Invoice service functions currently include "Qualification Verification" for VAT special invoices and "Invoice Mailing Admin" for the mailing of invoices.

Above these data and operations is the reporting layer of the invoice for statistics of various invoice data such as "unsettled daily requisite invoicing data," "invoiced daily data," "invoiced monthly data," and "discrepancy alarm".

"High-end, Magnificent and Classy" Electronic Invoice

We begin with the business of electronic invoices at the outset. The electronic invoice is essentially used to save the invoice's information in a form of data flow and enables the users to call the data through a PDF document or a QR code for reimbursement. The invoices are generated via data connection between systems and physical invoice buying, printing, and tax declarations are no longer needed. For JD, an e-commerce company requiring high working efficiency, electronic invoices can reduce manual intervention and sharply raise the production efficiency. You can read the following two questions if you have any doubt:

Question 1: It takes three minutes and one minute respectively for a warehouse staff to pack one commodity, and print one invoice and put it into the commodity's package. Completion of both tasks can represent completion of one order product. If this fellow keeps working for one hour, how many orders can be finished? If the paper invoice is taken place by the electronic invoice, without participation of warehouses, then how many orders can be finished in the same period?

Question 2: When financial staff are reviewing and verifying the refunds, the amount is undertaken by the system, and it takes one millisecond, but the invoice is dealt with manually and it takes three minutes to invalidate an invoice. In case of electronic invoices, without manual participation, how many refunds can be finished in a period of time needed for ten refunds in the past?

From the perspective of the e-commerce operation, this project saved substantial costs for JD. Suppose that the price for one paper invoice is RMB .3, then electronic invoices can save several million RMB per year. At the macroscopic level, electronic invoices can save vast resources for our society. We conducted data statistics before and found that, if we spread out all the paper invoices issued by JD within one year, the total area was equal to that of five times that of Beijing. If these invoices were put in Shanghai Asia I warehouse, they would occupy 3600 m² of that warehouse.

Authors: Liu Lei, Tan Nie, and Wang Chao

CHAPTER 11

Growing Pains: The Internal Informatization Process

JD's Featured New Employee Matching

The Function R&D Department subordinated to CTO Line R&D Department upholds a tradition that new employees must attend a training program named "Cao and JD in These Years" apart from the company-level values system training and the R&D Department-level vocational training.

This training program is a tea party attended by a young man who proclaimed himself "Lao Cao" and newcomers will listen to Lao Cao's easy and fluent talks about the JD development he experienced. This tea party is provided with neither dessert nor tea. I call it a tea party because its desserts were stories that happened when he sold optical discs and promoted sales with Lao Liu, such as the scene that they packed in the warehouse until 3:00 a.m. and were still present at the morning meeting at 8:30. This made me jealous when I heard that JD underwent rapid development at a rate of 200% every year and the individual wealth of these entrepreneurs also quickly increased. Lao Cao now holds the post of CTO at "Financial Group," a branch of JD Group.

When I attended this tea party, Lao Cao said, "JD is a trading company, not merely an internet-based company." It is well within my memory and I have gained deeper understanding of it because the informationization degree of the internal management business in the charge of HR and administrative departments under the tertiary sector "Comprehensive Function R&D Department" where I worked was far different from JD's title of "Internet-based Company."

For quite a long period, all information systems in JD were focused on e-commerce, so the informationization degree of commerce, customer service, warehousing, and distribution business was relatively high, but OA, process and HR management for internal management remained in an initial stage. Fortunately, through a period of centralized integrated planning and high-speed construction, the functional management information system had been dramatically improved. The products from two business lines of in-house portal and process platform were representative.

JD's In-house Portal System

I've worked in a software outsourcing company specialized in offering implementation services for heavyweight products such as ERP, SAP. and so forth to enterprise groups for several years before joining JD. I was deeply impressed that ERP is a big and all-embracing system designed for unified management of critical business such as production, manufacturing, financial affairs, sale, purchasing, processing, etc., in an enterprise.

Therefore, after I completed the entry formalities with the title of "Product Manager," when my immediate supervisor told me "Hong Tao, you are responsible for JD's ERP system," I felt weak in the knees. Sure enough, JD never doubts the person it hires and never hires a person it doubts, with reliance on a newcomer to take charge of such an important system. Later, I found I thought too much as ERP in JD referred to JD's in-house portal system.

JD's in-house portal system underwent three stages in chronological order, including old ERP stage, portal stage, and one-stop office platform stage.

Time-honored Old ERP

Interface of the Old ERP System

The above picture shows the system interface in front of me when I undertook the assignment for JD's ERP system development. Lao Liu smiled with fists clenched and appeared in my head with an image of a young entrepreneur with masculine and scholarly bearing.

This system was developed and launched in the spring of 2009 and kept operating until 2013. It can be called a time-honored system. From 2009 the present, the staff of JD increased from 2,000 to 60,000. Xiao, Chun, and others who were involved in development had become leaders of various R&D lines in JD. We interviewed some senior executives above the VP level about their requirements during development of "JD People @ Work" project (a project for upgrading of the Portal version of the ERP system), most of whom participated in R&D of this system before, including Lao Xu, a punster.

Lao Xu said, "This ERP system was developed by me together with my teammates, and why does it still serve as I have been gone for two years?" Lao Xu, the SVP of JD's Sales & Marketing Department, is a renowned punster in the internet-based e-commerce circle.

By the way, a fellow in my R&D team once told me that, when he was reconstructing a long string of old codes, he found a line of codes which may have been written by Lao Liu judging from the annotation, but he could not tell whether it is true or false. I asked him, "What do you think about the codes?" he answered, "I did not closely examine them. They were directly rewritten with an annotation."

It should be noted that this system now seems not to be cool and fashionable, but in terms of technical architecture, it possesses premium re-usability and expansibility.

For the system's permission control, Chun drew on RBAC permission model to independently developed a permission mechanism for the entire system, which laid a theoretical foundation for the UIM (Unified Identification Management) system. The UIM system is now overseeing more than 1,000 internal information systems and 3,000 resource points and controlling permissions of a staff of over 60,000.

Furthermore, after time this system won a lot of praise for its function design and usage experience, and many staff still felt reluctant to abandon the old ERP system after the new portal system had been launched for a long while.

"JD People @work"

December of 2013 could be a period of hardships and happiness for Lao Yang, the Manager of "Comprehensive Function R&D Department" in JD's CTO System since by the end of December, 2013, both the new portal system "JD People @work" and the process platform were brought online successfully at the same time.

Interface of the New ERP "JD People @work"

In July, 2013, the Company finally decided to replace the old ERP system which had been used by the staff for nearly five years with a new system. This heavy burden was placed on the shoulder of Lao Yang's team of the "Comprehensive Function R&D Department. "Since then, several brightly-lit windows appeared at the second floor, Block A, Beichen Century Tower beside Beijing National Convention Center.

New portal system was named "JD People @work" bearing a meaning of one-stop working platform for JD people. The following three objectives were prioritized for this project:

1. Coordination work platform: integrate all internal information systems and focus on building of two sections of "Group Portal" and "Work Center" to improve the coordination efficiency;
2. Transformation of technical architecture: change the databases from SQL Server to MySQL and the developer language from .Net to Java, and adopt Jetspeed Portal framework for the whole system;
3. Unified permission sorting: reclassify the existing over 3,000 resource points according to the business lines.

After setting the above objectives, Lao Yang personally acted as the product manager and led the team to start product planning day and night for four consecutive weeks. In late September 2013, the product's interactive prototype and PRD were finally completed.

Shenyang Research Institute subordinated to the Marketing R&D Department provided this project with orientation support back then. It was said that, one day in early October 2013, Lao Yang and his R&D team held a seminar lasting from 4 p.m. until 12 o'clock at night in a conference room located at the second floor of IT International Tower in the Angli Information Park, Yunnan New District, Shenyang. The focus of dispute was the project schedule. Lao Yang insisted on bringing the system online by the end of December, 2013, but the R&D team held that, there was no guarantee that the system could be launched on schedule according to the estimate on the basis of existing workloads. Then the theme of that meeting became a discussion on the time needed for every development task. Later, debates in the conference room turned to wine on the dining table, and those from Northeast China got Lao Yang drunk as expected. Fortunately, his drunkenness won him a new project schedule from the R&D team, specifying that the system could be brought online by the end of December 2013.

However, the period of difficulty awaiting the R&D team of Shenyang Research Institute had just began.

The first problem they encountered is the Jetspeed2 framework for the portal's foreground main architecture. Back then, JD and other large e-commerce companies in China lacked experience in building a large enterprise portal by Jetspeed2, so few technical documents in Chinese could be found on the Internet and many help documents could be downloaded only from Apache's official website. However, considering rich Portal techniques and flexible Portlet management mechanisms provided by Jetspeed2, the R&D team was determined to take up the challenge. The Shenyang Research Institute specially chose five experienced architects in Java and Portal's bottom structure to conduct deep research and recruited several postgraduates proficient in English for computer science to translate the technical documents.

Another problem that baffled project team was the migration of other systems integrated in the old ERP system. After completion of the foundation for the old ERP system, information systems for various business lines including operations, marketing, and so forth were continuously researched, developed, and integrated. According to a preliminary estimate, over 1,000 online systems had been integrated in the old ERP system when we undertook the assignment for version upgrading. The project team had to figure out how to smoothly migrate these systems into the new "JD People @ work" system. Through repeated discussions and trade-offs, the scheme finally adopted by the project team was "system single-point login, insertion of function interface, and centralized presentation of core functions". At the outset, the R&D team developed a unified single-point login mechanism for the ERP account and opened single-point verification API, requiring all online systems to access the single-point login mechanism. Meanwhile, we sorted and divided functions of various business systems so that function interfaces could be inserted into the ERP system and realize one-stop operation experience for the staff. Moreover, this scheme also allowed unified permission control over the function points via UIM. Centralized Portlet display areas were created by the portal framework of Jetspeed for core functions in different business systems.

The team members solved one problem after another through discussions and tests and gradually developed with effort many functions within three months. To ensure that the system could be brought online in late December 2013, all members volunteered to take one day off every week and even worked without intermission for three weeks in the later stage of the project. Despite of hardship in the process, such fast-paced project contributed to cultivation of an excellent project team. Up to now, those who participated in that project always say impressively, "We were quickly improved in those three months," when they are chatting and recalling scenes in the past.

The project was successfully brought online by the end of December, 2013. Favorable feedback was gained once the system was taken online thanks to our elaborate requirements and design stages as well as all-out efforts during development. Currently, this system is stably operating in JD's intranet and has become one of the systems which are most frequently used by JD's staff for the daily office work.

One-stop Coordinating Work Platform

Rollout of the "JD People @work" system was the inception for us to set up a one-stop coordinating work platform. From the day when system was brought online until today, we continue to supplement and perfect it. The visual schematic diagram of interface of "Online Admin Service Lobby" which was just brought online in the 2nd quarter of 2014 is provided below.

Visual Schematic Diagram of Interface of "Online Admin Service Lobby"

We plan to equip the initially formed "One-stop Coordinating Work Platform" with the following sub-systems":

1. Portal Center: a portal gathering the information about the group, branches, and different business lines;

2. Work Center: a one-stop window for routine staff work for collecting common functions in various business systems and displaying them by means of a portlet to meet customized priority requirements;

3. Task Center: a center geared to all staff and aiming at coordinating task assignment, tracking, and fulfillment;

4. Process Platform: centralized management of BPM;

5. Personal Space: staff personal space from anon-work perspective, thus establishing the enterprise SNS.

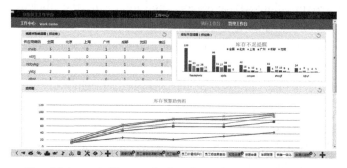

Visual Schematic Diagram for Interface of "Work Center" from Administrator's Perspective

---

JD's Business Process Platform

JD now has two process management platforms: the IT Service Platform and the Process Center. IT Service Platform is a process platform based on problems, events, and tracking management. The Process Center is placed in the OA Platform and used for examination and approval of routine information. I will introduce these two process management platforms respectively.

IT Service Platform (ITSM to ITSV)

The Company's growth speed requires business process management to be highly efficient and the best way for normal operation of various foreground businesses is to build efficient process management platforms. At this moment, a department head discovered ITSM product made by BMC Software, Inc., a leading company in the software industry, and introduced it into JD in early 2012 in a fast and efficient way. We cooperated with the IT operation team to set up a company-wide IT Service Platform, thus unifying IT fault/request processing entries, setting processing standards for IT system failure/service requests, and improving the efficiency of IT operation/maintenance to a certain extent.

However, this product was created outside China, so it included a variety of non-localized operation habits which caused some trouble in the process of usage. Therefore, our R&D professionals had a bright idea and found an efficient solution which enabled users to give feedback via e-mail and regard it as a problem report entry. The background support system would identify the problems and generate corresponding event list on the ITSM platform and then transfer it to the next operation step. These simple operating modes greatly improved the event processing efficiency, and thus efficiently raised satisfaction of all business departments in charge of customer service, sales & promotion, distribution, etc. with services provided by IT systems.

To better address the discomforts caused by the non-localized operational software, our R&D team was devoted to independent research and development of ITIL system (code: ITSV) based on the background of e-commerce industry since 2014.

The following two figures fully shows the values brought by the IT Service Platform:

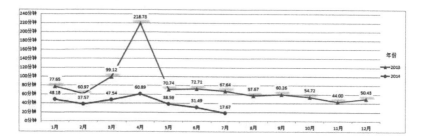

Tendency of Average Time Cost for IT Operation Work Orders in Recent Two Years

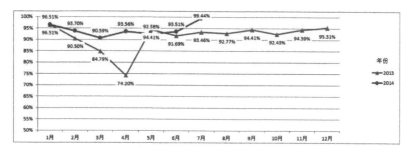

Tendency of Solution Rate of IT Operation Work Orders in Recent Two Years

Process Center

The Process Center was derived from a company meeting in late March, 2013. At the meeting, a senior leader pointed out that "Our daily routine process is still dependent on paper and it is a little bit outdated, so we must find corresponding IT solutions to abandon paper and step onto the path toward an electronic office."

After the meeting, our leaders led us to unceasingly find the information of enterprise OA platform in all large OA enterprises and deeply communicated and exchanged with several selected manufacturers in an attempt to pick up an OA platform suitable for JD. However, despite repeated communication with these manufacturers, we failed to find a satisfactory one. At this right time, Chairman Mao's words about "Ample food and clothing by working with our own hands" passed through our minds. Boss Li finally decided to create an OA platform of JD with our joint efforts.

After the target was set, Li appointed several product managers with rich experience to conduct comprehensive system planning for the OA platform. Since it covered a wide scope, the first step we had to take was to set up a process center so that electronic approval could be realized as soon as possible. The Process Center was finally positioned as a center with speed, flexibility, and convenience as core philosophies, which enabled functions including individual form configuration, process building, individual field definition for e-mail approval template, and more.

I remember that it was in September, 2013 when the development began. The R&D manager led a group of young staff into the Shanghai Conference Room at 6F. As this team was comprised by newcomers, they needed to learn more. At the beginning, the technical veterans discussed construction of technical architecture together and then everyone followed procedures to develop function modules. This process was filled with various difficulties attributable to arduous tasks, shortage of resources, time pressures, etc., but all members continued to struggle together and overcame difficulties one after another. The first version of Process Center finally came out.

In that difficult period, the leaders transferred us to the Guangzhou Conference Room, which was more bright and roomy, to provide better development environment for those in charge of R&D. Until now, the process team is still working there, but the conference room has been renamed "Washington" (it was said that a former conference room named "Washington" was exclusive for Lao Liu).

Although primary functions of the first version had been put into normal operation, there were still a lot of defects, such as nonsupport of the outbound interface service, not allowing individual process setup configuration for more businesses, cumbersome process setup work, etc. After a short time of function optimization and product upgrading, the Process Center platform independently developed by JD has now set up nearly 100 processes and successfully bears primary business processes in JD.

Looking back, during those years for development of this Process Center, the R&D team with less than 10 members started from scratch grew to support daily operation of almost 100 business processes and now can undertake unified backlogs and integrate approvals of other business systems into this platform. They improved our daily office working efficiency again and again. These figures and typical milestones have suggested that the Process Center is an indispensable platform for our daily office work.

Process Platform

My Backlog

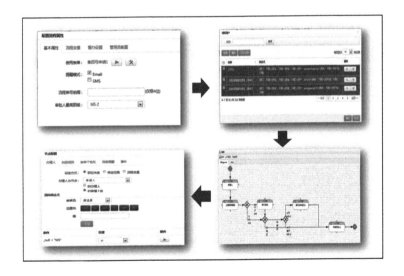

Implementation Plan

Authors: Yang Hongtao and Nan Jie

Technology Evolution

What technology architecture is used by JD'S R&D systems to support its mass businesses?

This chapter will show you the architecture of a mass processing system through several critical technology architectures including, SOA governance, middleware, and cloud platform, and for the first time unveils how JD switched step by step from .Net to Java.

- – From .Net to Java
- – Middleware
- – SOA Governance

CHAPTER 12

Life of Pi: From .Net to Java

Personal Website in the Era of ASP

I wonder if any of you still remember what JD's website looked like in its inception stage. Before I joined JD in 2005, I bought two barrels of Mitsubishi DVDs through JD's website, which was called Jingdong Multimedia then, and sold main products including CD burners and optical discs.

This version of the website was a set of ASP for online store software bought from the outside in 2003. The website now appears to be very simple and crude, but it was sufficient to support JD's business because of a small volume of business back then. There were only four or five members in the R&D Department, namely Lu, Jing, Mao, and Ping, who carried out maintenance and upgrading on the basis of this set of software and launched a variety of systems, including discount coupons, DIY Installer Master, Alliance, etc.

By 2008, the ASP website system which was purchased gradually revealed its restrictions. With increasing growth of visitors and order volume, the website sometimes was slow or had no response. At this moment, an important figure, Li, the first VP hired from outside, arrived.

Enclosed Development for the Upgrading .Net

The first thing Li did after he joined JD in 2008 was to enclose development for upgrading JD's system from primitive ASP to .Net-based architecture. On July 21, 2008, Li led six developers (Jun, Jin, Tao, Chun, Min ,and Tai, plus two testers Ning and Yong) and several others in charge of products and UED including Yu, Luo, Lei, and Rong, and entered a villa in the suburb of Tongzhou District, Beijing, throwing themselves into the enclosed development program burning with ambition. The above-mentioned predecessors are still working at JD and have taken important posts.

During the enclosed development, they started work at 8:00a.m., working until late at night. They kept writing code in front of computers except intervals of eating or going to the toilet all day long and sometimes worked until 2 or 3 a.m. or even the whole night. They stayed in this villa till Sunday, when everyone could go back home for a break.

In this team for the enclosed development, Li was the most passionate one. He personally participated in the architecture design and even wrote partial core codes. When others stopped working and went to sleep at 2 or 3 a.m., Li was still vigorously typing. When others got out of bed with eyes half closed the next morning, Li was still sitting in front of the computer! No one knew exactly whether he got up early or did not go to sleep. Later, his assistant Guang showed us a picture of President Wen receiving him when he was granted the title of "National Model Worker", and we understood everything — he proved himself to be a model worker.

In that period, Liu often visited us in the villa where we stayed for the enclosed development to inspect our achievements and provide us with better food by sometimes cooking in person. By September, 2008, the enclosed development program entered its final stage and Liu paid a visit to the villa almost every evening, checking the R&D results and putting forward some

Home Page of JD's Website in 2008

improvement suggestions based on which we would immediately make improvements. This satisfied Liu, who was fussy about user experience. Once Chun excitedly demonstrated a function he just finished, but by accident, he clicked an image of a sexy lady on the desktop. Liu tapped him on the shoulder of Chun, who felt very awkward, and Liu said, "Chun seems to be in the mood."

In October 2008, the .Net-based JD website was taken online. It was also the foundation system supporting the operation of JD Mall for three years. Although many technologies were obsolescent, it made a great improvement compared with the earliest version.

JD's website launched in 2008 after the enclosed development was the last version adopting the blue color and it was changed to a red color, expressing joy.

Upgrading the Architecture to Java and Servitization

In 2010, some systems adopted Java for development, but the core transaction part in the Mall was still using .Net-based system developed on the basis of the enclosed development program in 2008. After two years, the transaction system had become enormous, with numerous business branches. Its sub-systems even reached up to thirty, so it was difficult to upgrade the system. Helplessly, we had to continuously increase hardware. The more servers there were, the higher the maintenance cost was. Bringing the system online really baffled us. At that time, an auto-deployment system was not yet developed and those responsible for operation and maintenance had to deploy by hand, who eluded developers of the transaction system in the end. Moreover, an increase of hardware caused nonlinear performance improvement.

In 2011, once the Book Purchasing & Sales department held a 50%-off promotional campaign, which aroused the enthusiasm of customers. However, our servers could not sustain the pressure. Within the last half an hour of the campaign, pages of shopping cart and order settlement frequently suffered slow response or even could not be opened. Many customers failing to buy books they were interested in complained of feeling that they were cheated. Back then, Liu expressed his anger through Weibo and required to add three times more servers and hold one more promotional campaign the next day. He also posted a picture in which a knife was put on the table and he invited fellows in the R&D Department to "drink coffee." The knife in the picture was just a joke, but we were clear that this time addition of servers could not solve problems and the system's architecture must be upgraded. Architect Zhong, who joined JD in 2011, took on this heavy task.

Throughout the process of design of the Java-based architecture for the transaction system, leaders of sub-modules separately designed interfaces and physical business objects in the daytime and gathered in the conference room to conduct reviews in the evening. Sometimes such discussion was heated and they argued against the name of an attribute or parameters of an interface. In case of a deadlock, the Architect Zhong was responsible to make the final decision. Reviews often continued till 11 or 12 at night, and sometimes we ordered takeout as "flavoring agent." Discussions continued while eating. We are grateful to the delivery services of MacDonald, KFC, and Pizza Hut, regardless of bad weather, Thanks to them, we could accomplish projects in good spirits.

During the architecture upgrading, the first step was to change the development language from .Net to Java. We selected Java as the development language for two reasons. One, there were a great number of domestic and foreign websites applying Java technology, thus providing a lot experience as well as mature open-source frameworks to guide us. Two, .Net language was free of charge, but Windows operating system was not. Besides, the development tool Visual Studio was expensive. With the business expansion and increase of servers and developers, such optimization was necessary. Certainly, .Net technology had many advantages, such as ease for beginners, high development efficiency, and refined IDE. Moreover, Microsoft had recently also set up open source and cross platform for .Net and it was becoming more and more open. According to Paul Graham, the "Godfather of Silicon Valley start-ups" and author of *Hackers & Painters*, programming languages are half technology and half religion, and if you intend to compare different programming languages, you need to be ready for a religious war. Hence, you might have your own answers about which one was better, Java or .Net.

Considering the high-speed business expansion at JD, it was necessary to split the former centralized systems to simplify the system architecture and shunt the performance. The former centralized systems were separated by business types into User Center, Commodity Center, Price Promotion Center, and so forth. All systems were designed based on the SOA architecture to provide external services and direct trans-system reading was forbidden. We were grateful to those in the RPC Framework SAF team who provided us with such efficient and stable service frameworks. User Center, Commodity Center, and other services providing basic information constituted a basic service layer; above this layer, the Transaction Center, Inventory Center, and services with complicated business logic consisted of a business service layer; the top layer covered the shopping cart, order settlement page, marketplace, and other WEB systems. Through splitting, the system's architecture was basically changed to the following one.

Furthermore, the system storage was also upgraded and SQL Server applied for .Net was also replaced by MySQL. Systems with enormous data volume, such as orders, commodities, users, etc. must be subject to sub-library and sub-lists. Large fields were taken out of databases, such as order information snapshot and commodity's detailed information, and then put into JFS, a system independently developed by JD.

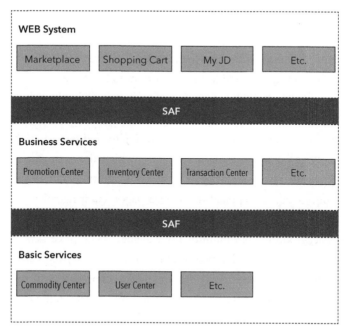

Sketch of Upgraded System Architecture in 2011

The last point was use of a large volume of caches. In the era of .Net, MemCached was widely applied in JD's systems by means of a hot data cache. For example, in case of the commodity information cache, to obtain a commodity's information, we must first check if there were any caches; if not, we read the commodity information in the databases and then put them into the caches. Within the period of validity of caches, if we needed to read information of the same commodity, such information could be obtained from the caches quickly. This method was valid in most cases, but in event that we needed to read information of some unpopular goods, the system would be very slow. Around 2011, Redis became popular and was widely applied by JD's systems. A lot of critical data about commodities, users, and prices was subject to full-volume caches. In this way, the service efficiency was greatly improved. For instance, one query took two or three milliseconds. The system memory was also low cost. With several servers with memory of 128 GB and cache data simplified and compressed, tens of thousands of commodities information and hundreds of millions of users information could be stored in the memory in full volume.

During this period, we made a cool improvement for the price system. The Architect Jianfeng developed a Nginx extension which enabled direct reading of price caches saved in Redis from Nginx and provision of HTTP services. We all knew the speed of Nginx, which drove up the speed of services provided by Tomacat by one order of magnitude. HTTP service by asynchronous call was applied to the web pages requiring price calls, thus not only realizing decoupling, but also improving the efficiency. A server placed background could monitor price changes. The price data in Redis caches would be upgraded background upon receipt of message about price adjustment for purchase and sale or start and end of promotional campaign.

Project implementation was, of course, never plain sailing. Given a shortage of time (we were always pushed for time during the project development), we were forced to bring a version with half Java and half .Net. The foreground WEB was based on Java, and partial background interfaces which we hardly had the time to upgrade, and some branch businesses still adopted the old systems based on .Net. The benefit was that we could provide achievements in a shorter period, but the down side was that we had to maintain Java-based and .Net-based systems at the same time. Furthermore, those old .Net interfaces always became bottlenecks. Then we spent half a year replacing .Net with Java for major businesses and another two years later, we replaced with Java for those branch businesses When the final .Net-based system was brought offline, those developers gathered and said in tears they would not allow the coexistence of two types of systems any more.

Cutover of new and old systems was also very shocking. Upgrading transaction systems for an e-commerce website which kept serving its customers 24/7 was no less than changing wheels for a high-speed rail moving at full speed or changing wings for a plane soaring in the skies. To complete cutover of the new and old systems, we wrote a complicated switch for the entry of adding commodities to shopping cart.

The first step was user cutover. Workmates deployed some internal user accounts for closed beta test. Next, they conducted cutover of business types. The part of online payment took the lead and was followed by payment on delivery and self-pickup; self-operated orders were cut over first and followed by orders of third-party vendors; orders without fictitious assets were cut over first and followed by those using discount coupon, gift card, balance, and credit points. Then cutover was carried out by regions and the traffic from three northeast provinces in China was first imported into new systems. The cutover by quantity was the next. We placed 100 orders using new systems and observed them for a period of time. Until these orders were passed downward to the warehouse and delivered to customers, and after we confirmed that there were no problems, we placed another 1000 orders under new system. The last step was cutover by percentage: 1% at the beginning and then 5%, 10% and so on until 100% of traffic was cut over. Unexpectedly, we spent more than one month on it.

After cutover of the entire system, Xiangzi, one of development leaders, was so boastful and said, "If nothing else, JD is the best in configuration switching systems. If anyone was unconvinced, challenge us."

During the cutover of new and old systems, to verify the correctness of new system's business logic, we also developed a comparison program to prove that orders under the new system were identical to those under the old system. The way we adopted to prove it was, after placing an order in new system, we immediately placed another order in old system using an asynchronous thread and the same information, and then compared the snapshot of order information generated by new and old systems; if such information was identical, the business logic of the new system could be proved to have no problems. The comparison way was direct as well. The objects of order information were serialized to XML and then were compared by using character strings. Staff in charge of writing the comparison program were beset by minor differences in format and sequence arising after serialization of .Net-based and Java-based XML, but such problems helped to create a great master in regular expression. Back then, we placed 100 orders in the new system and compared them one by one. In case of any discrepancy, the corresponding colleagues would find causes and correct bugs. After correction, we placed more orders to continue the comparison.

By May 2012, we finally brought the Java-based transaction system online. As June was around the corner, we had done more for the 618 Anniversary Celebration Day. The first one was to add a monitoring module on the system's response time. Monitoring was conducted over external services calling, external services providing, database reading, and other methods which were deemed important, and then we analyzed the causes of slow responses detected during monitoring and gradually optimized them. We would like to thank the team that developed the UMP system for all efforts they exerted. Secondly, online pressure tests were conducted. Before the system was taken online, pressure tests were conducted under the testing environment, but the effect was not favorable. The transaction system was particularly complicated and depended on a lot of services. It was difficult to establish the pressure testing environment for it, so we decided to carry out a pressure test in an online environment. Direct pressure tests on running applications, of course, was impracticable. We conducted pressure tests in hot standby machine room in an environment basically the same as the online environment, so the result of such test could reflect the facts. After getting the test results, we were fully confident in the system stability on the 618 Anniversary Celebration Day this year.

On the 618 Anniversary Celebration Day that year, systems underwent stable operations. We also nipped some minor accidents in the bud. By 10 p.m., when we were unoccupied and had nothing to do, we started to bet on the order volume that day. Since then, system breakdown resulting from large-scale promotion campaigns as mentioned above never happened again, and Liu never "drew his sword" any more.

Up to now, except for a few desktop programs, the basis of most systems of JD have been changed from .Net to Java. Occasionally you may see several pages with the extension of .Aspx, which are Java pages which had gone through URL rewriting.

Author: Wang Yuan

CHAPTER 13

Babel: Middleware

Service Framework SAF

A great number of middleware technologies are applied in JD's application systems. Critical components in SOA field include service framework SAF, workflow engine PAF, and message engine JMQ. First of all, we will introduce the service framework SAF.

With rapid expansion of JD's R&D system, RPC (Remote Procedure Call) among various sub-systems was increasing, but there was no unified solution inside the company. As a result, we applied a motley variety of technologies and developers for every system to find out how to realize clustering, load balance, failure-caused retry, etc. This greatly intensifies the intersystem complexity and raises developers' learning costs. Then there was SAF.

SAF is an important public basis component for system SOA (Service Oriented Architecture) applied across the company and the critical precondition for access to JD open platform (JOS) as well as the technical standard for system servitization and opening in JD.

Goals of SAF

1. The goal of SAF is to create an "ecosphere" with integrated SOA governance functions;
2. Collect service quality data by using RPC framework;
3. Set up a strong, simple and handy service management platform;
4. Find out system problems and figure out the optimal service instance combination through analysis of data which may affect the RPC framework;
5. Draw the outline of system dependence diagram and detect systematic coupling through analysis of calling relations;
6. Automatically change the size of service clusters through analysis of pressure data such as requests volume.

SAF 1.0

We drew on some existing practices in the industry and spent four months taking SAF1.x online, which provided highly efficient point-to point RPC calling function, service registration, and subscription function. Through months of optimization, SAF1.0.8, which could run more steadily was released. This version has experienced several big promotional campaigns and to date has remained stable.

Unified and Efficient RPC Framework

In the past, WebService, RMI, Hessian, REST, Thrift, etc. were used for intersystem calling, but now we apply SAF protocol (compatible with Dubbo protocol) for all systems. In this way, we could reduce the complexity of systems and communication and learning costs of developers, and improve the development efficiency.

RPC calling framework (SAF Client) has the following features:

1. Service calling is transparent without code invasion;
2. Developers could call remote services like calling local codes by simple

configuration and only need to focus on business code development without sparing efforts on the details of RPC (such as remote communication, load balance, transparency of call, synchronization/ asynchronization, failure retry, etc.);

3. Multi-protocol supporting;
4. Persistent-connection including SAF, Dubbo, Thrift and short-connection including WebService, REST, Hessian, etc.
5. Realize failover and support retry after failure;
6. In the event that any non-business fault occurs during service call, the system will automatically switch to Provider for retrial;
7. Multiple soft load balances;
8. Support multiple load balance algorithms such as random, polling, multicast, and so forth;

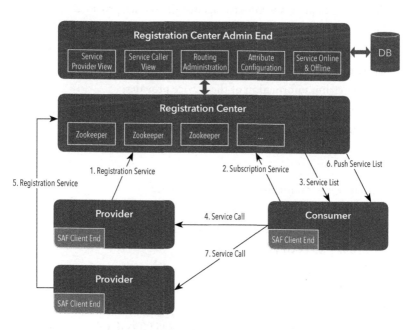

Schematic Diagram of SAF 1.x Architecture

9. Stable and efficient, with NIO and long connection-based SAF protocol as the default and TPS is 3–4 times greater than ordinary WebService.

Simple Service Governance Function

After the RPC call framework was unified, we used it to release services of SAF protocol, but how to dynamically find the problem of a service address after distributed deployment remained unknown? Obviously, RPC framework was not enough to completely solve the problem.

We introduced the concept of "Registration Center." The center saved the service provider list and configuration information. The service provider would register a service address and the service caller would subscribe to a service address at this Center to start up. After the service caller got the list, a RPC calling request was initiated against the service provider.

The Registration Center for the first generation of SAF was developed on the basis of Zookeeper. It combined a self-developed management platform to realize the following service governance functions:

1. Ownership information of the service provider;
2. Service registration and subscription, and changing dynamics pushing;
3. Service grouping and online & offline function; and
4. Simple function of service routing.

Currently, the online using scale is as follows:

1. Publishing 1620+ interfaces;
2. 2700+ access services (calculated by independent IP);
3. 21000+ accessed JVM instances;
4. 22000+ nodes provided by access services;
5. 63000+ nodes called by access services;
6. About 42% was taken up by the Marketing R&D Department; and
7. 500+ interfaces were connected with JOS (JD's development service).

SAF 1.x Management Interface

SAF 2.0

After another two years, the first generation of SAF was still running steadily, but with sharp rise in access volume and continuous evolution of JD's system SOA, we gradually detected some problems as follows:

1. The logic tasks of SAF Client were arduous and a lot of logic could be completed at the Registration Center to assure light weight on the Client End and optimize its performances.

2. The Registration Center based on Zookeeper was limited in various aspects, including failure in traversal retrieval of data from multiple dimensions and realization of business pre-processing caused by a dendritical structure, and failure in horizontal dynamic dilatation resulted from the Leader/Follower mode.

3. Lack of service quality management functions. We were unable to obtain statistical data on calling volume, concurrence, traffic, etc. and service quality (QoS) data including elapsed time, success ratio, and so forth.

4. Service governance function was relatively weak and shall become stronger. For example, attribution of call end, dynamic grouping, traffic limit, blacklist and whitelist, request priority, etc.

To solve these problems, a new generation of SAF was launched and various modules and components in SAF 2.x were independently developed to ensure flexibility, controllability, and high customization of codes.

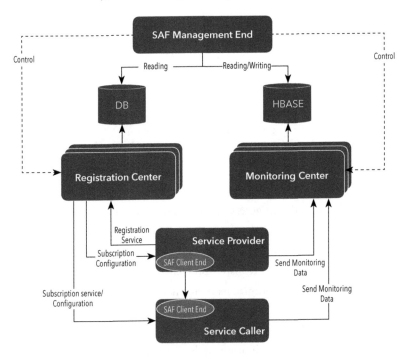

Schematic Diagram of SAF 2.x Architecture

The features of RPC module are as follows:
1. Light, stable, and efficient;
2. Calculation logic was put in the Registration Center and the Client End only focused on the results instead of the data operation;
3. High expandability;

4. Compatible with the intermodulation of new and old versions to provide rich access entry points for business expansion;
5. Real-time collection of the service quality data;
6. Send the statistical calling data by minute, instance, and methodology to the monitoring center according to the configuration rules.

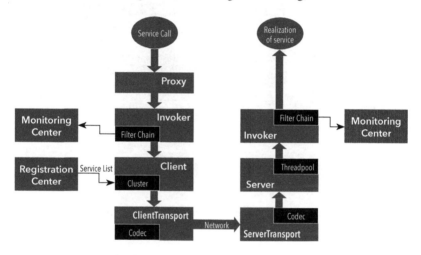

Schematic Diagram of SAF 2.x RPC Architecture

The features of Registration Center are as follows:
1. No Master, horizontal expansion, stability, and high efficiency;
2. Flexible calling methods and combination of data push and pull;
3. Business logic included and reducing the burden of Client End.

Features of service quality management are as follows:
1. Fine-grit data collection and compatibility with the data formats of new and old versions;
2. Flexible and automatic data collection and acquisition strategy;
3. Multi-dimensional data display and warning functions;
4. Calculation of service configuration through QoS and transmission to Client End.

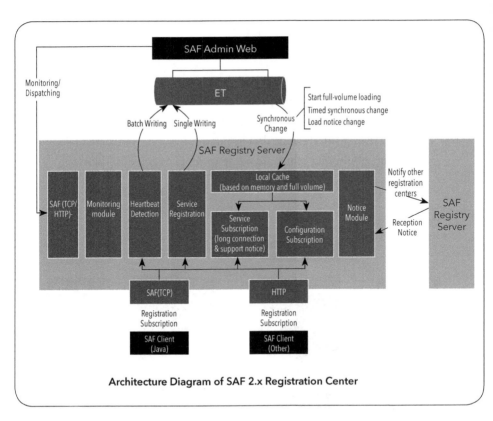

Architecture Diagram of SAF 2.x Registration Center

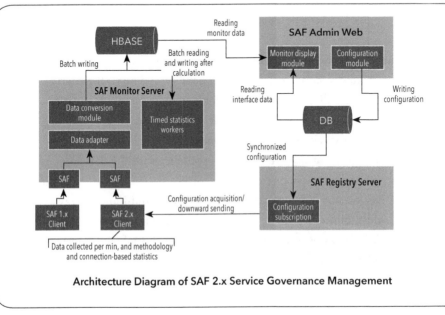

Architecture Diagram of SAF 2.x Service Governance Management

Workflow Engine PAF

Introduction to PAF

PAF (Process Architecture Foundation) is a workflow platform. Workflow is indispensable for large and medium-size companies. From the perspective of business, processes represent the automation and standardization; for developers of business systems, workflow can alleviate workload of process development, shorten the time for process change and maintenance, reduce usage rate of Worker of the system, and avoid judgment by business rules in the system.

Application Scenarios of PAF are as follows:

1. There are several or many manual approval processes, such as gift card/discount coupon approval, etc.
2. The project has frequently changed and complicated business logic and processes;
3. The project requires synchronous or asynchronous interactions with externally independent systems in sequence;
4. A number of complicated and changeable business verification rules in the project.

Advantages brought by PAF for the business system are listed as follows:

1. Alleviate workload of the process development;
2. Shorten the time for process change and maintenance;
3. Reduce the usage rate of workers of the system; and
4. Avoid judgment by frequent use of business rules in the system.

Creation of PAF

We followed "copinism" to create PAF and set up an internal workflow platform for JD on the basis of Activiti, an open source workflow system. The slogan "As Activiti is 'just a jar'" displayed on its official website was why we were attracted by this system. Activiti supported distributed deployment, but its core engines were only a jar and this greatly facilitated us to set up the platform. With simple design of architecture by the leader of the PAF team, horizontal expansion capability of Activiti was dramatically enhanced.

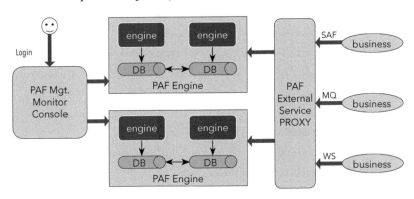

Deployment Architecture

The outermost layer was PROXY, which could receive various calling methods. Internal PROXY was set with routing rules used for allocating different business system calls to corresponding PAF engines. You may find functions of PAF engine are powerful and can be horizontally expanded without limitation. PAF engine generally corresponds to one business system, but if there are a few processes in one business system, multiple PAF engines can be allocated to this business.

Development of PAF

After PAF was brought online, purchase order approval and return business was first accessed. This was a fully automated process and required no manual intervention, so it only needed several interfaces of business system according to the rules. Hence, PROXY merely provided one interface and one method and users merely needed to start the process.

In the using process, the business would inquire current operating nodes and execution tracks of an instance from time to time. Then what was provided by Activiti was insufficient since it only displayed the current nodes. In such case, with design of Li, we can display the process as follows:

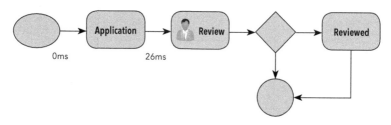

Schematic Diagram of Process Running

This diagram directly shows where the process is and which nodes it has passed.

The most direct application of the workflow system in the artificial field is the OA system. For access of ERP to PAF, numerous individual requirements were raised, such as IE version process definition designer, stimulation and calculation of next node, positive pullback, etc. Activiti lacked these features, so we had to develop it by ourselves. In fact, it is a drawback for introducing foreign workflow systems which could not support special requirements in China or accord with national situations, i.e. "environmental inadaptability."

Status Quo of PAF

After PAF was brought online, purchase order approval and return business, multiple financial processes, ERP system, and other processes were connected. Now there are nearly 179 process definitions in the online environment, 15 average process nodes and almost 100,000 process instances in a day.

Existing Problems of PAF and Continuous Improvement

Through performance tests of automatic processes, we also found some problems in Activiti. For example, during the testing, we arranged eight ServiceTask nodes to call external WebService services and set the response time of external services as 1s. Results of performance tests are listed as follows:

Total Requests	Number of Requests Failed	Request TPS	Average Response Time of Requests	Process TPS	Average time for process completion (millisecond)
141097	0	38.248	0.077	38.53	12559.96
157542	0	42.691	0.641	42.64	14582.48
175661	0	47.796	0.656	43.27	14599.648

Results of Performance Test

The test results showed that single DB could only support about 40 TPS at most and CPU and memory of various servers were idle. Only the linking number of DB server database reached the maximum. Through analysis, when Activiti was executing the nodes of ServiceTask, the time for calling external services would hold DB connection.

Both problems and causes were found and then everything was easy to handle. Whether we should continuously improve Activiti or independently develop a set of new workflow engines was the problem we had to consider and solve for the next version.

JD's Message Middleware JQ

Message middleware is an important middleware product in the course of information system SOA and it could be used for system decoupling, non-real-time system communication and asynchronous flow processing, etc. Message middleware mainly undergoes three stages.

Due to the narrow scope of application and small message volume at the beginning, JQ based on database storage was developed, but with expanded application of scope, JQ suffered increasingly prominent performance problems and database storage pressure.

To solve the problems of JQ, we needed to abandon database storage. To quickly bring it online and maintain the stability, the Company chose ActiveMQ, which was widely applied for customized development, and established a distributed Client End and a completely new management platform. Moreover, some functions of ActiveMQ were improved in the process of operation and maintenance.

The company saw a sharp rise in the business volume, with the daily number of messages exceeding one billion. The existing message platform AMQ failed to meet the needs resulting from business expansion. VirtualTopic could copy multiple messages according to the number of subscribers, leading to low sending performance; Slave did not support consumption, and when the Master in one group broke down while cutover conditions were not satisfied, the backlog messages could not be consumed in a timely fashion; consumption confirmed the need to delete indexes, leading consumption and production to compete for the same lock and affecting the sending performance; the large message backlog would seriously impact the sending performances; the processing capacity of AMQ failed to meet the demands of system with high throughput capacity. Therefore, we developed the new version of message platform — JMQ.

The technical details of various versions of message middleware will be illustrated below:

JQ Era

JQ was a message system on the basis of the database, with a Server End in charge of routing for message management and Client End responsible for loading messages from the database through timed polling. Consumed messages were deleted from the database regularly.

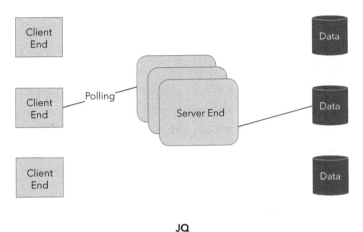

JQ

Disadvantages
1. The Client End adopted a way of polling to check whether there were new messages, thus affecting the timeliness for messages delivered to consumers, but frequent inquiry would impose great pressures on the database;
2. Message backlog would impose great demands on database storage and impact its inquiry performance;
3. Limited by the performance of the database, we were not satisfied with the distributed and large-scale message production and consumption.

AMQ Era

The secondary development was carried out based on ActiveMQ to greatly transform the Client End so that it could support distributed deployment and automatically perceive server cluster change. A management program with complete functions was developed to provide a function of consuming abnormal message and automatic retry, and functions including alarm, sending, and consumption audit log query were added.

Meanwhile, Broker of ActiveMQ also received great improvement, the copy protocol was rewritten, and the writing performance of VirtualTopic was optimized.

This product boasts the following features:

1. Technical Standards
- Follow JMS1.1 specifications;
- Use Zookeeper as a distributed coordinator.

2. High Usability
- Adopt Master/Slave mode for deployment to support failover;
- Employ synchronous sending and message persistence to avoid data loss;
- Distributed Java Client End supported loading balance and failover for multiple groups of MQ servers;
- Messages were filed with cloud storage asynchronously for the convenience of failure tracing;
- Unified abnormal message retry service enabled fault tolerance.

3. Expansibility
- Divide by type of messages vertically;
- Distributed Java Client End supported horizontal expansion, dynamic dilation, and load balancing.

4. Management Monitoring
- Cluster-based management control platform including management of message types, release and subscription, business system and servers, filing query, abnormal message management, operation and maintenance plan, and so forth;

- Support backlog alarm, survival alarm, memory occupation alarm, disk occupation alarm, connection breaking alarm, master/slave status alarm and alarm query;
- Mail reports for timed message statistics

5. Usability

- Integrate consumer abnormal message retry services and the business system mainly focuses on processing of business logic;
- Be compatible with the Client End interfaces of JQ.

The overall architecture is detailed as below:

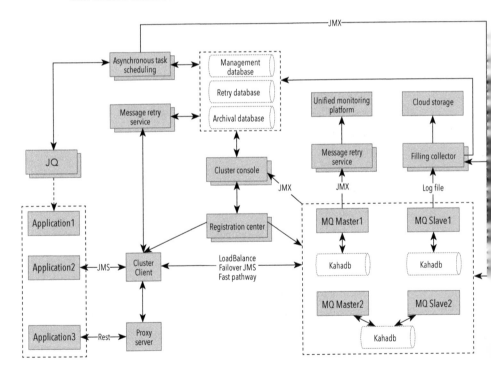

Overall Architecture Diagram

Duplication Optimization

We improved the message forwarding method based on ActiveMQ in the past by Master-Slave synchronous replication and changed it to duplication on the basis of message logs.

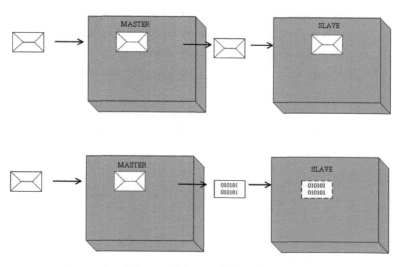

Comparison Diagram Before and After the Improvement

Optimization of VirtualTopic

After receiving messages, VirtualTopic internally forwarded them to the consumer queues. In case of several subscribers, single sending could lead to multiple writing and brushes, further achieve single sending and writing, and transmission for master-slave replication time by merging, thus improving the performance of sending.

Disadvantages

1. The storage engine Kahadb index uses the B-Tree structure, which requires modification to the index when sending messages and confirming consumption and leads sending and consumption to interplay;

2. Due to semantic restriction, the Topic has multiple subscribers. If the subscribers require internal support of multi-thread load balance and quick failover, VirtualTopic should be used. VirtualTopic creates an independent queue for every subscriber and replicated messages will be put in the corresponding queue. With an increase of subscribers, more and more copies should be replicated by the messages, thus seriously affecting the performance of sending;

3. Slave can only conduct data backup and has no consumption function;

4. The Client End has complicated logic and new functions generally touch upon upgrading of the Client End, which may discourage acceptance.

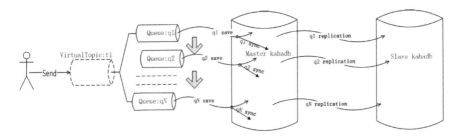

Sketch Diagram Before the Optimization

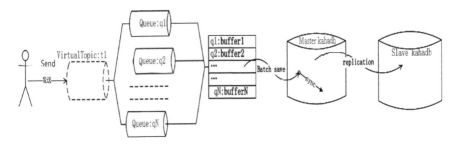

Sketch Diagram After the Optimization

JMQ Era

Learning from the experience and misfortune of AMQ, in the case of JMQ we redesigned the memory model and developed the entire application totally by ourselves. With the characteristics of the last generation of MQ retained, we provided some new characteristics and made it better than the last generation.

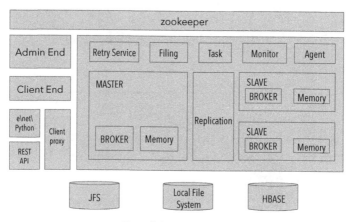

Overall Structure Diagram

Characteristics of the former memory were as follows:
1. Synchronously create index and B-tree structure;
2. The indexes share locks and queues share the index files.
3. The consumption affects production and consumption confirmation requires modification of index, deletion of consumed nodes, and occupation of the index file lock, thus impacting the performance of sending.

Characteristics of present memory are as follows:
1. Asynchronously create index and List structure, add in sequence and directly return after writing logs successfully in the stage of sending;

2. The consumption doesn't impact the production and consumption only amends the position of index cursor without modification to the original index structure or impact on the sending performance;

3. The consumption position can be reset, thus enabling playback.

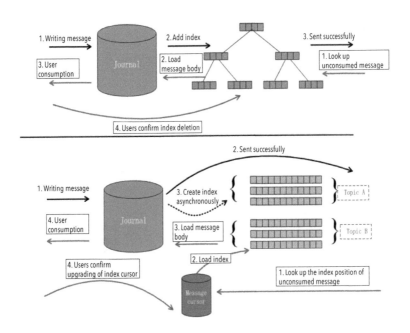

Memory Change Diagram

Topic Change

When a topic has several subscribers, such subscribers can share the same index and message body and multi-thread consumption is realized for single subscriber at the same time, through a separate record of every subscriber's consumption location.

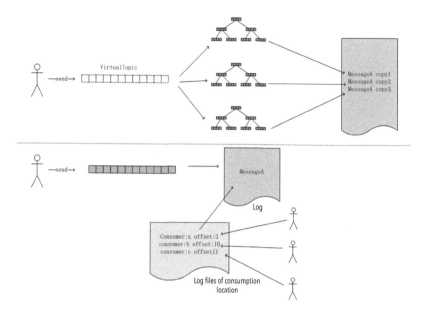

Comparison Diagram of Topic between AMQ and JMQ

Authors: Li Xin, Zhang Geng, Ding Jun, Gui Chuanghua, Wang Songlin and Liang Qiushi

CHAPTER 14

Transformers: Governance of SOA

The Start of Servitization

With the fast development of JD, the former technical architecture was not able to support the explosive growth of business. In this case, we stepped on a journey of discovery toward SOA. JD's practice in SOA is a process of continuously finding and solving problems as well as a course of interlaced separation and unification. Introduction of middleware and open source technology gives an enormous impetus to it.

In the early stages of JD's technological development, most business systems were directly connected with the database, thus bringing simplicity, reliability, and a high development efficiency. In 2009, with a vigorous growth of business, a great number of new systems sprang up. The impacts between systems, and between systems and databases became increasingly greater. Taking an order as an example, the mall's businesses were driven by orders, so every system should have logical codes for a single order. Once a system suffered any error in terms of the order logic, the order would take "strange" action. For example, when an order was canceled, but items on this order were still delivered to the customers. Furthermore, when new functions were brought online, the error ratio of systems continued to climb. We often encountered the dilemma where the transaction codes were amended, commodity codes became problematic, or commodity codes were amended, but problems arose during transaction. Back then, developers and DBA had to stay up all night to amend the transaction data, making them suffer a lot both physically and mentally.

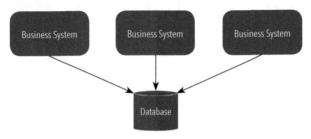

Schematic Diagram of Architecture Before the Transformation in 2009

To solve these problems, Donny put forward a concept of establishing five major business middlewares (differing from common middlewares such as message middleware) and led us to put this concept into practice. Business middleware abstracted and packed the public logic in business system and provided an external uniform interface to be called by the business system. For instance, the order middleware, which abstracted and packed the rules on changes of order status. The order status changed on a regular basis. Only when the former status was met can it enter the following status. For example, only normal orders could be transferred to the warehouses while canceled orders could not; JD set dozens of order statuses and particularly complicated rules. But the business system cannot and did not have to know these rules. All we need to do was to call the order middleware.

In this manner, several benefits could be achieved. First, reuse of modules. We could call the business middleware only in case general functions were needed, thus sharply decreasing the development difficulty; the second one was system decoupling. Changes in the general functions would never cause modification of the business system and conversely, change of the business was not the concern of the middleware, thus greatly improving the development efficiency; the last one was decoupling of application and memory. The business systems prohibited operating the data sheets from other systems and only permitted the business middleware to do so, thus fundamentally avoiding the "disordered skip" of the above-mentioned order status.

However, the aforesaid plan also led to new problems. Performance losses occurred due to remote calling. Moreover, breakdown of any middleware may give rise to a "butterfly effect" which could result in failure of other middleware. In the beginning, problems concerning network environment and improper resource management caused temporary unavailability of services and some adverse outcomes, which evoked the doubts of some staff on the servitization at that time and furthermore set back the progress of the servitization of JD.

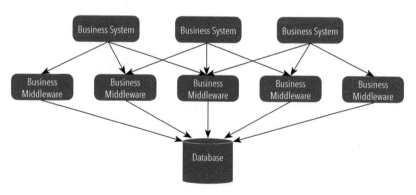

Schematic Diagram of Architecture After the Transformation in 2009

Service Splitting

In 2010, JD set foot in the book market, and held several exceptionally fantastic promotional campaigns of books. However, pressures on the systems had gradually exceeded the maximum capacity. To support the explosive growth of orders, upgrading of the architecture of the master transaction system was a task which could not be delayed. Then a gigantic and vigorous "reform movement" began.

The first step was to separate the master transaction system and the primary database. It was a long-running transaction and should take 200ms to save the orders placed by customers in the primary database. Furthermore, the primary database was for writing and could not be horizontally expanded, so I developed a service to receive orders. Just as its name implied, this service was responsible for receiving and saving orders in its order receipt library instead of the primary database. The order receipt library was equivalent and could be horizontally expanded, without theoretical capacity ceiling. However, there was another problem: the order number. The order number should be generated at the same time and could not be repeated (auto-incremental primary key in the primary order list was used in the past, but became unusable because of multiple order receipt libraries). Other systems were subject to interactions using order numbers and transaction systems. To this end, I developed another order number service, which utilized the equivalence relation of module congruence to prevent repetition of order numbers, enable a roughly monotone increase and sufficiently reliable of order numbers, and support horizontal expansion.

Payment system, promotion system, inventory system, commodity system, coupon and card system, user system, etc. were also separated from the master transaction system (five major middlewares only packed partial common logic, and the real business separation was carried out this time). Like the orders, these systems gradually migrated their memories from the primary database.

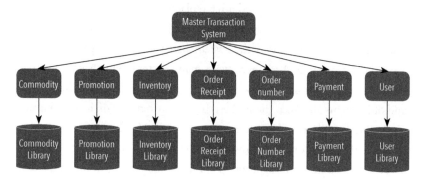

Schematic Diagram of the Architecture After the Service Splitting

After the transformation, the performance of systems was greatly improved. For example, the time taken for order storage dropped from 200 ms to 10 ms. More importantly, the system was endowed with the ability of horizontal expansion (addition of several machines could increase the system capacity by several times) and disaster recovery. Even if most services or databases crashed, the system could operate normally if one group was available (one application or one database). In fact, a group of machine could support all page views. To enable disaster recovery, four groups of machines were equipped). This disaster recovery service still supported cross-machine rooms. Even if the entire machine room broke down, the system could switch to another machine room so that the system could operate normally.

This architecture upgrading was re-birth of JD after the closed development in 2008 and as thrilling as "replacing tires for a racing car during traveling at a high speed." Hence, during the implementation, we had to carefully tackle every problem.

The first problem to tackle was how to migrate smoothly. As an internet-based company, JD gives the priority to user experience. Downtime should be prevented because of system upgrading, i.e. "the racing car could continue to travel at high speed after replacing the tires." However, it was easier said than done. The systems were subject to significant refactoring, but how could we maintain the system behaviors unchanged before and after the refactoring? And there were many systems which could not be brought online simultaneously, so how to guarantee compatibility of new and old systems and keep them operating concurrently remained unknown. Undoubtedly, this was a long-term process. Moreover, the data structure had changed after refactoring, so how could the new and the old data coexist?

To achieve a smooth migration of application layers, I put forward a two-phase scheme to cut the traffic. At the first phase, cut the traffic by users. We set a white list, which enabled those designated users to access to new systems and other users could only operate via old systems. At the second phase: cut the traffic by percentage (to assure the data consistency, schemes for different percentages were employed in different business scenarios, such as perform modulus on the order number or fetch hash values on user account before modulus). First, accesses to new systems were provided for 0.01% or less users and then observe whether there were any problems or not. In case of any problem, we should immediately switch to old systems until the problem was solved. If no problem was found, the limit on traffic could be gradually removed by 1/1000, 1/100, 1/10 or 1/2 until the systems were completely accessible. This was mainly applied for the public beta phase in the later stage after systems were taken online.

There were two more problems to be solved: how to quickly perceive and position in case of any problem and how to switch to the old systems swiftly. It's not easy to quickly position and switch in face of so many systems and hundreds of machines. Back then, JD lacked a mature monitoring system. We wrote a set of monitoring systems for rapid positioning and a set of configuration administration systems for a quick switch. The monitoring system was relatively simple and we added an Appender to Log4j to put the error logs and performance parameters into caches or MongoDB. On the admin interface, we could observe the status and abnormal information of systems on a real-time basis. The configuration administration system could open or close the access to new systems of hundreds of machines or adjust the size of traffic to new systems within 30 seconds like a water switch.

To solve the problem of the smooth migration of data layers, Andy proposed a four-phase cutover scheme. In the first phase, we wrote old databases synchronously and new databases asynchronously; in the second phase, new and old databases were written synchronously; in the third phase, we wrote old databases asynchronously and new databases synchronously; and in the fourth phase, we wrote new databases synchronously. In this process, we should also formulate a system rollback scheme based on the specific business scenario to ensure that the product environment would not be impacted because of system upgrading.

The migration process required verification on whether the logic and data were consistent in old and new systems for the application layer and data layer. Except for testing, data proofreading was necessary as well (processing results were reflected in the data). We conducted logic proofreading for the data of new and old systems. This process lasted very long and we allowed more traffic to the systems after proofreading millions of times.

Later, these experiences were absorbed by other teams and now have become the commonly used methods for system upgrading at JD. This is only two interludes in the process of architecture upgrading. We summed up a lot of empirical rules to ensure smooth upgrading of the systems in practice. (If there is a chance, we expect to summarize these empirical rules for you)

However, all these required exceptional vitality and willpower. Words can't describe the bitter hardships in this course. We remembered that during the closed development, Andy's daughter was born. He had to go to and from three places: the office, home and the hospital. Once he was so tired that he even felt asleep on the subway, but we never heard him complain. The office used for the closed development was not equipped with a heating system. It was during the severe winter, but our enthusiasm for work made the room fiery. However, one thing we expected to do then was to eat a baked fish in a small restaurant near the company. We often spent less than five minutes eating up the fish. The waitress was surprised at the beginning, but later became used to it.

For JD's information system, the architecture upgrading was an epochal change. Because of this, we could live through one 618 Anniversary Celebration and Double 11 Carnival after another and keep the systems safe and sound. JD has set sail on the road of SOA!

Service Governance

From 2011 to 2012, JD's old systems were continuously split up and new systems sprang up like bamboo shoots after a spring rain. System splitting brought many benefits. Every system and service could provide other systems with reusable modules for development of new businesses; the systems and services could be deployed independently and allow expansion at any time; the systems were loosely coupling and modification to one system would not affect the other; the development cycle was short and so forth. However, new problems arose. Interactions and dependence between systems were so complicated that no one could clearly understand them, and they were also changing every day. The system with higher dependence would need remote calls more frequently and higher network overhead, and suffer worse availability and performances. The "butterfly effect" of systems became more and more obvious, especially for the bottom services and systems. The upper systems would vibrate if the bottom systems shook. Breakdown of any one would cause failure of not a few systems and even the crash of the entire system. Management and monitoring of such a decentralized environment had become an impending task.

Later, Xiaozhong, a big fish from AliPay, joined us. He introduced a distributed service framework called Dubbo applied by AliPay (based on this framework, we developed JD's SAF framework). This framework solved the problem of service governance.

The service provider registers its service address at the registration center; service consumers could inquire the addresses of service providers he is interested in and send request to the service providers based on the address he obtains; both service providers and consumers must provide a monitoring system with their running conditions. None of these four roles were single points (service providers and consumers constitute a cluster) and any breakdown will not impact the whole system. Furthermore, the dependency relation among services is recorded by the registration center on a real-time basis and reflected in the admin system as it stands. The operation and maintenance personnel could monitor and manage it. For example, which systems will be impacted if a system is added with new functions? We can send emails or short texts to the principal of systems by depending on this service. The monitoring system can control and realize load balance for the system according to the running condition and dependency relation of service providers and consumers. If one cluster of service providers suffers prolonged response times, the monitoring system will automatically shunt more traffic to another cluster with a longer response time. When a new project is released, we can control certain clusters online and offline via the monitoring system, thus smoothly transferring the systems. In case a service provider has reached its system capacity ceiling, the monitoring system can conduct traffic-limiting protection to avoid breakdown.

At this point, JD's systems have separated after unification and unified after separation, and thus basically completed its progress of servitization. However, there were several more problems to tackle. The first one was the delay of data replication; the second one was the problem about how to loosely serve and effectively combine into business process to reuse it more efficiently; and the third one was how to solve the cascade reaction of services.

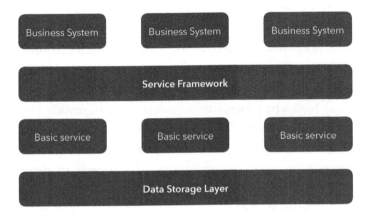

Schematic Sketch of Architecture After Introduction of the Service Framework

At this point, JD's systems have separated after unification and unified after separation, and thus basically completed its progress of servitization. However, there were several more problems to tackle. The first one was the delay of data replication; the second one was the problem about how to loosely serve and effectively combine into business process to reuse it more efficiently; and the third one was how to solve the cascade reaction of services.

Event-driven

The problem of data replication had long baffled JD. We may take two examples.

The price problem came first. JD often provided price-cutting promotions which attracted a great number of customers. Some of them added the commodities into shopping cart, but found the price has returned to the original one when submitting orders. The cache was to blame. The price service was exposed to billions of page views every day. To support such an enormous number of visitors, we set multilevel caches for systems, including page cache, CDN cache, service end cache, and so forth. The caches would expire, and short validity term would increase the system's pressure and longer one led to the above-mentioned consequence.

To improve the user experience, we decided to reduce the delay time by minutes to seconds, and the project of "real-time price" was launched. Through the event-driven mechanism, the data delay time was reduced. The schematic diagram of architecture before and after the transformation is shown as follows:

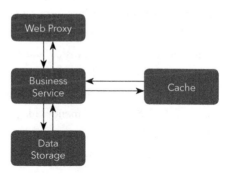

Schematic Diagram of Architecture for the Real-time Price Before the Transformation

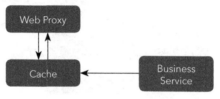

Schematic Diagram of Architecture for the Real-time Price After the Transformation

After the transformation, the Web Proxy layer could directly acquire data from the caches and its speed was faster than acquiring data from the business service layer by an order of magnitudes. The system's performance was improved greatly. The application system would update the data in caches if a business event was triggered, thus successfully shortening the delay time of replication to seconds. Later, the CND cache was removed. The price system was still firm as a rock and became veritable "real-time price."

Another problem was order production. When the customer placed an order, that order should enter a series of a generation process. Back then, it took 20 minutes from order placing to order being sent to the warehouse. Once the database replication was delayed, a backlog of orders would happen. To improve the warehousing efficiency and decrease the operating cost, the R&D Department launched another larger project named "211 Order Fulfillment Project," which completely transformed the primary process for order production and a business event would be triggered if the customers successfully placed an order. This event would push the order from links such as placing, splitting, transfer, and invoice to entering the warehouses. The time was shortened from 20 minutes in the past to about 10 seconds, thus greatly improving the order production efficiency and the technical status of the R&D Department. This project ranked the first among top ten projects in 2012 at JD because of its wide range, complicated transformation process, and great influence.

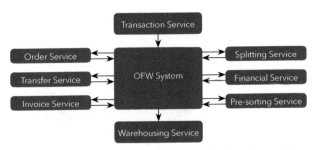

**Schematic Diagram of Architecture of Production System After
Introduction of the Event-driven Mechanism**

The event-driven mechanism confers the ability of quick response on systems. If SOA is compared to the extremities, then the event-driven mechanism could be assimilated to eyes and ears of a human being. When the eyes see a lion rushing to you, a message will be sent to the brain and then the brain gives an order to your extremities: run. Besides, the event-driven mechanism utilizes decoupling. During an interaction, it is not necessary to take all the services online. Temporary breakdown of a service will not impact normal operations of other systems. Taking the OFW system, for instance: it will store the data temporarily and then process until this service is available. Hence, it also plays a role in resisting the flood peak. In addition, the event-driven mechanism can enable process orchestration, which will be explained in the next section.

The message middleware MQ was introduced later and brought the event-driven mechanism to other systems in a simpler way. For example, in the financial reconciliation system, the reconciliation process would be triggered and the processing time was shortened from minutes to seconds if the change in receivables or proceeds occurred.

Process Orchestration

In early 2013, to improve the user experience, the company launched another project named "SOP Order Consolidation" with a far-reaching influence. The customers could place an order for the commodity operated by JD and sold by the third-party vendors. Meanwhile, the number of packages and distribution status of this order would be made clear. This involved almost all main systems such as the transaction system, financial system, splitting system, transfer system, etc. In the face of so many systems, we should also consider a cascade reaction of services. Downtime of a service would make the customers unable to view the order status.

Order Settlement Page

Submission of Orders

Stories in hide: coupon, card, balance, inventory system, Promise system, commodity system, promotion system…

Page of Successful Order

Successful Submission of Orders

Hidden stories: splitting system, order system, inventory system, OFW system, financial system…

Therefore, I introduced the event process engine to the transaction system and named it the "transaction engine." It combined various systems and drove running of production flow, funds flow, and information flow.

First, it received an order event and analyzed this event; after the process orchestration, it judged which calls had causal relationships and must be serialized, and which calls could be implemented concurrently based on business rules. Next, various services were called according to results of the analysis; after the whole process was implemented, the results were packed and displayed to the foreground end. The schematic diagram of architecture is shown as follows:

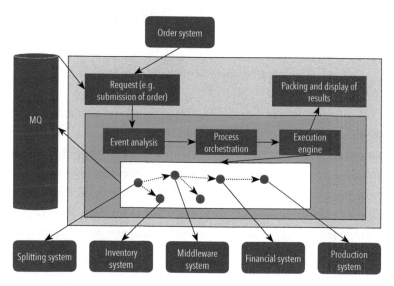

Schematic Diagram of Architecture of the Transaction Engine

The abovementioned diagram shows that an event can activate calls of several services. Conversely, one service would generate several events. The events were transmitted and executed continuously based on the causal relationship and finally formed the business process. A better solution was set up after loose and separate services were combined through events and processes like building blocks. This is the target of SOA.

Moreover, it tackled the problem of cascade reaction. First, it changed calls of service to concurrent execution.

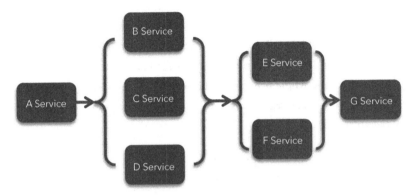

Schematic Diagram of Concurrent Call of Services

The response time of the whole process equaled to the time of service A + the longest time of service BCD + the longer response time of service EF + time of service G. Formerly, it was the total response time of all services. Secondly, the former model of one request with one thread was abandoned. Similar to coroutine, threads and requests were decoupled, thus avoiding a surge of number of network connections due to intensive RPC calls and effectively preventing the impact from service failure spreading throughout the systems, i.e. the "butterfly effect."

In the above sections, only several interludes in the magnificent epic of transformation are explained. There are incalculable thought-provoking stories behind these interludes. However, this is only a prologue for JD. With O2O, big data, and cloud computing in the ascendant, JD is marching toward a new epoch.

Author: Zhao Haifeng

Innovation

Which application innovations does JD have? How does JD inspire innovation?

This chapter will present the exploration of JD's R&D segment in the field of application innovation from the three aspects of mobile innovation, big data application innovation, and innovation incubation management mechanism.

Let's see how JD realizes trying on the glasses or clothes via mobile phones, how big data drives and optimizes JD's core supply chain and supports decision making for the purchase categories, pricing, promotion, inventory, logistic routes, and more.

- Cloud platform
- Mobile innovation
- See into the future through big data
- Wise purchase & sale
- Innovation incubation

CHAPTER 15

Top Gun: The Cloud Platform

Cloud Background of JD

Cloud computing is the third reform, following the personal computer revolution and the internet revolution in the IT industry.

E-commerce takes the IT information system as the core, which makes the support of cloud computing necessary for e-commerce. Internally, cloud computing can reduce the system costs, and improve the reliability and e-commerce operation efficiency at levels of development, operation and maintenance. Externally, SaaS service of cloud computing can provide upstream and downstream vendors with rich e-commerce applications. Rapid development of e-commerce has created a lot of business demands and technical difficulties for cloud computing, which also leads cloud computing to move forward.

JD's Cloud Platform, established in May, 2012, was listed as a tier-one department in the R&D system of JD. In 2011, JD determined its overall strategy driven by technology which aimed at developing four strategic businesses including an e-commerce platform, logistics platform, technical platform, and internet finance, and planned to give full play in cloud computing, with Cloud Platform as the technical platform of these strategic businesses over the next decade.

Meanwhile, JD also drew out a long-term development strategy for the cloud computing, i.e. with the cloud computing as the basis, providing a cloud computing technical platform, and cloud computing services and solutions covering SaaS, PaaS, and IaaS for JD's internal information system, external software development enterprises, and individuals and all enterprises and individuals of the whole society. Major business included construction and maintenance of JD's private internal cloud architecture; JD Open Cloud and JD intelligent hardware cloud business catering for the JD Ecology; and JD's e-commerce cloud, development cloud, industrial cloud, etc. offered to all enterprises and individuals.

The strategic target of JD Cloud was to open all resources and capabilities of JD's e-commerce business and provide JD Cloud services to all links throughout the industrial chain in the form of the cloud by 2015.

JD Cloud evolved by three major steps. The first step was to cloudize various e-commerce resources and capabilities within JD and set up JD's internal Cloud architecture; the second step was to open the clouded e-commerce resources, build JD e-commerce open cloud platform, and foster a JD e-commerce application ecology; the third step was to integrate more external e-commerce resources into the JD e-commerce cloud and provide more valuable external e-commerce cloud services for the entire industry and society. In the future, JD cloud is determined to grow into a cloud service operator and a cloud computing solutions provider to supply comprehensive cloud computing services to all walks of life.

Internal JD Cloud

Cloud architecture is a new generation of technical architecture under construction and its core is to apply the cloud computing technology to various tiers of JD's technical architecture in order to materialize cloud upgrading of the fundamental technical architecture.

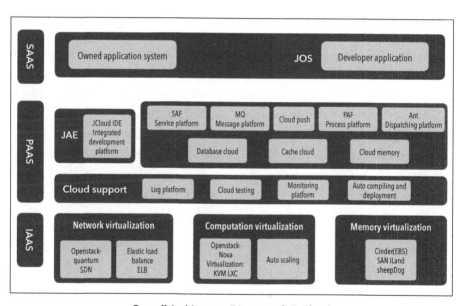

Overall Architecture Diagram of JD Cloud

The overall architecture of JD Cloud marks partial materialization (with emphasis on JD's demands) of cloud computing capability framework, instead of complete materialization. The architecture of JD Cloud is divided into 3 layers: IaaS, PaaS, and SaaS.

Capability of Layer IaaS

JD Cloud utilizes OpenStack, KVM and other technologies to realize network virtualization, computing virtualization, and memory virtualization, and provides functions such as elastic load balance, auto scaling, etc.

Load Balance: it shunts the traffic requested by users to various VMs in a balanced way to avoid downtime due to excessive traffic on one VM. It can provide you with the maximum fault tolerance and seamlessly furnish load balance capability required by the application traffic requests in case of VM breakdown or excessive loads. Load balance can detect an unhealthy VM in the VM pool and then allot the traffic to a healthy VM until the unhealthy VM is recovered. Users who intend to achieve sequentially consistent application program performance can use the load balance in a single zone or multiple zones.

Auto-expansion: conduct auto-expansion or recycle according to the user-defined conditions. If the method of Policy is utilized for a configuration when the system achieves the demand index peak set by users, auto-expansion can achieve a seamless increase of the number of user instances. In case the method of Schedule is applied, users can conduct auto-expansion or recycle on a yearly, monthly, weekly, or daily basis, or according to instances at certain fixed time frame, thus minimizing the cost and saving resources.

Capability of Layer PaaS

At the layer of PaaS, JD Cloud places emphasis on aPaaS, bPaaS, cPaaS, dPaaS and iPaaS. JD Cloud provides the integrated development environment (JAE), automatic compiling and deployment, cloud testing, and Ant to realize aPaaS; PAF process platform is set up to realize bPaaS; cache cloud and cloud push are provided to realize cPaaS; data cloud and memory cloud are equipped to realize dPaaS; and MQ message platform and SAF service platform are used to realize iPaaS.

1. Application Engine Platform

- ANT: provide a uniform platform for deployment, allocation, monitoring, and elastic expansion, and development framework for diversified Worker/Daemon.

- Automatic deployment: the automatic deployment system is designed to help those in charge of operation and maintenance to bring services online. It facilitates batch release, rollback, and application restart, and supports both web-type items and non-web type items. The automatic deployment system has the following features: it standardizes the online processes and project's program package structure, lowers the online complexity, shortens the online waiting time, and reduces the possibility of errors caused by frequent manual modifications to configuration files; less time and energies are consumed by bring the project online and R&D troubleshooting, thus reducing the human cost. This is also the core value of the automatic deployment system.

- Continuous Integration (JCI): continuous integration is a major way to guarantee the quality of iterative development during the evolution of software engineering. The code quality can be guaranteed automatically as early as possible through continuous integration. Continuous integration service provides functions including construction engineering within self-defined time, quick compiling, deployment of code package, development, and testing of servers.

- Automatic Compilation: An automatic compilation system is an important step to compile the source code package to executable files and generate the release package in the process of bringing projects online at JD. It realizes package compilation application, examination & approval, configuration (manual and automatic configuration), compilation & package extraction, testing, release of online package, and feedback of online results.

- Automated Testing: the automated testing platform is a testing tool independently researched and developed by JD. Its core value is to reduce the testing workload and get a quick feed-back on product defects by setting up a regression testing system so that the product quality can be ensured. The test framework Superman, which was also independently researched and developed, is applicable for automated testing of WebUI and compatible with popular testing frameworks; it is an automated testing tool kit with functions such as task scheduling, analysis of cause of errors, data report view, etc.

- Mobile Cloud Testing: The Mobile Cloud Testing Platform is an online application testing platform provided for developers/testers of mobile applications, including compatibility testing, UI adaption, performance, stability testing, and custom script function testing. It can return detailed testing reports with logs and screenshots, thus contributing to the fast iteration of mobile application development. The system background provides true terminal devices based on Android and iOS for testing.

- JD Code Library: the JD Code Library is a Git-based code management system using JD Cloud Platform to store resources, including the social programming functions such as source code version management, online editing, code submission at Git Client End, project information management, project member management or derivation, request consolidation and more.

- Jclipse: Jclipse is the product originated from secondary development of Eclipse 4.3.1 and has functions including JD engineering code generation, provision of static code inspection, code review, fast submission, etc. It improves the quality and standardization of developer codes and unifies JD's development environment.

- Code Review (JRB): it is a set of products developed for Code Review and caters to JD's characteristics. It can submit codes to the review servers via Jclipse plugin or Web-based methods. Multi-person review is also available and every reviewer can put forward his or her own review comments.

2. Business Process Platform

• PAF: Independently deployed and distributed business process management (BPM) service

3. Generic Module Platform

• Cloud Push: The Client End establishes a long connection with the Server End which then actively pushes the real-time message to the Client End. In certain application scenarios, the Server End can push messages to the Mobile End, such as pushing order information related to the users of Android mobile phones.

• Short address: plays a role in changing long addresses to short addresses, real-time data analysis, and analysis of traffic sources. Its application scenarios include overlong URL address, Mobile End, e-mails, messages, and multimedia announcements.

• Mobile Analysis: it focuses on comprehensive, real-time, and professional user behavior analysis services for applications of the Mobile End. Cloud analysis tools help mobile application developers analyze and excavate user attributes and user behavior data so that they can make use of the data to optimize mobile products, adjust operation models, and make decisions for announcements, thus improving the user experience of mobile products and winning more and qualified users. Cloud analysis supports currently leading mobile operating systems including Android, IOS, and Windows phone, and is capable of a log compression ratio of less than 50% and a single log with a file size of less than 0.3k, thus sharply alleviating impact on the terminal user traffic. Moreover, it supports one-key burying point, which only needs a line of code to complete application integration SKD, with easy access and small volume of development.

• Cache Cloud: it provides a high-performance, highly available, and highly expansible open cache platform and supports common cache usage scenarios, such as multi-fragmentation, read-write splitting, persistence, multilevel replication, and switch on failures.

- Log System: it provides services including log collection, forwarding, backup and subscription for various business systems, and whole-network mass log retrieval, early warning, and analysis services. It is a log data bus of various business systems.

4. Data Processing Platform

- UHP: it is PB-level data storage and processing platform with high reliability, expansibility, performance and failure tolerance, and provides elastic MapReduce calculations. The application scenarios include offline and mass data mining, conversion, and storage.

- CEP: it is a Storm-based streaming computing framework which provides a set of abstract and easy-to-use SQL-type syntax and modules, and simplifies the coding process of common streaming computation tasks. Its application scenarios include information flow processing, continuous computation, and complex event handling.

- JProxy: it provides unified access to databases including MariaDB and MySQL and possesses functions of traffic overload protection, automatic data fractionation, configurable routing rules, seamless data migration, etc. Its application scenarios include applications requiring data sub-library, sub-list, and auto dilatation.

- JDS: it provides one-key application, automatic backup, automatic fault migration, recovery of the data deleted by mistake, and cloud services like the highly reliable MySQL, MariaDB, and MongoDB. Its application scenarios include various businesses requiring database services.

- JBUS: it is synchronous with near-real-time isomorphic/isomerous database and supports cross-machine room data backup. Its application scenario is extraction of online data to JDS.

- JFS: it is a highly reliable, available, and consistent storage system designed for the online core data. JFS specially conducts deep optimization for small files and supports duplication of multi-data centers.

- JSS: it is a cloud storage service based on JFS and provides reliable RESTful storage service for various internal businesses (such as mobile and website transactions) and public cloud customers. It has the same application scenarios with those of AWS S3 and Google Cloud Storage.

5. Service Integration Platform

- SAF: it is distributed service middleware with characteristics of failover and high-performance calling, and consists of a RPC framework and service configuration center.
- MSP: it is a distributed message service platform featured by high availability, high performance, good expansibility, and management monitoring.

Capability of Layer SaaS

SaaS of JD Cloud is mainly divided into a self-owned application system and JOS developer application. JOS, i.e. JD Open Service, is a cloud service platform catering to e-commerce. With JOS, we can connect the expert information system with JD's marketing system, supply chain system, logistics system, and service system, and realize seamless linkage of the vendor information system and JD information system. JOS enables the independent third-party software vendor (ISV) to develop independent commercial software systems for vendors and share customer resources, including JD's supply chain and vendors.

Currently, the initial cloudization of IT resources has been accomplished, JD Cloud architecture has basically taken shape and its role in the stabilization of JD's businesses, system optimization, and efficiency improvement begins to be realized. Key modes of e-commerce applications are reusable, the average R&D cycle is reduced by more than 50%, and the business response speed is greatly increased. Elastic scaling of systems is realized to stably cope with the peak of the 618 and Double 11 promotional campaigns. The overall usage ratio of servers has doubled and the average cost of network visitor volume dropped by 60% on a year-by-year basis. The usage amount of cloud storage surpasses 10P, covering e-books, digital music, commodity pictures, historical orders, etc. The usage rate of cloud storage exceeds 80% and the automation rate of operation & maintenance surpasses 80%, accompanied by improvement of system stability and reduction of labor cost for operation & maintenance by 50 %.

JD E-commerce Open Cloud

JD E-commerce Cloud is the cloud information platform of JD e-commerce open ecology. To better satisfy demands in e-commerce applications and IT services of vendors and customers, JD E-commerce Cloud provides cloud services focusing on the full life circle of e-commerce applications and cultivates the e-commerce application ecology together with vendors, users, ISV, and application developers.

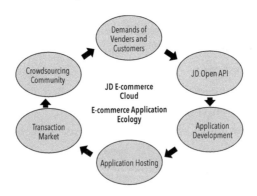

Diagram of JD E-commerce Cloud Ecological Chain

At present, based on JD e-commerce cloud ecological chain, JD Cloud offers five solutions including JD Zeus, JD Cloud Tripod, JD Cloud Engine, JD Cloud Peak, and JD Cloud Convergence to provide open interfaces for JD's systems, service transaction market, cloud hosting platform of e-commerce applications, application development cloud platform, community ecology environment for ISV and individuals, which initially form a complete e-commerce cloud architecture.

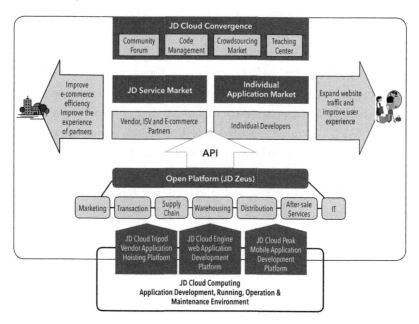

JD E-commerce Cloud Architecture Diagram

It is a transaction market that provides e-commerce applications and IT services for the upstream vendors of JD E-commerce Open Ecology and other e-commerce partners. JD's service market enable ISV, e-commerce IT service providers, and other e-commerce service providers to display and online trade their products and services such as e-commerce applications, e-commerce operation service, e-commerce training service, and shop decoration services. In such case, servers may release products and services online, vendors may order services online, servers may settle accounts with JD online so that quality products and services can be delivered conveniently to the upstream users, IT demands from upstream users are met, and the business efficiency and experience are improved.

1. JD Zeus

Based on JD's e-commerce best practices regarding user experience and self-built logistics and through all-round opening of integrated e-commerce systems of marketing, transaction, data, logistics, and after service, JD Zeus (Jingdong Open Service) service was launched. JD Zeus provides the vendors, suppliers, software developers, and industrial partners with open interfaces and supports them in docking with systems and businesses, sharing JD's achievements made by opening and jointly setting up a qualified e-commerce ecology. Furthermore, it takes an open technical platform as the carrier and combines JD Cloud service to provide the partners with JD's core advantages of "cost and efficiency" and form an integrated and open ecology core competence. At present, JD Open Service (JOS) has linked with over 40,000 vendors, introduced more than 600 third-party e-commerce applications, and over 3,000 shop templates, opened over 500 interfaces of eight categories, comprehensively established a qualified and efficient e-commerce open service ecology, and provided one-stop e-commerce services for the whole industry.

2. JD Cloud Tripod

The cloud hosting platform for e-commerce applications launched by JD Cloud provide vendors, ISVs, and other partners with hoisting operation environment and JD e-commerce data opening services of e-commerce applications. JD Cloud Tripod offers safe, stable, comprehensive, and elastically scaling computation resources and network environment, including complete e-commerce application hosting cloud services such as elastic computing service, cloud database, cloud storage, and cloud monitoring. Above the e-commerce application running environment set up by JD Cloud Tripod, it also provides data push services for orders, commodities, sales returns, inventory, etc. Data push services can be applied for e-commerce applications deployed on the Cloud Tripod to realize real-time and seamless data synchronization of vendors' applications and JD's business data systems to better satisfy vendors' demands for real-time usage of business services and operating data analysis.

3. JD Cloud Engine

It provides convenient application development, deployment, and hosting services for application developers who only need to submit application codes to the code library of JD Cloud Convergence and then Cloud Engine will automatically complete application compiling, deployment, and hosting without complicated operations and maintenance. JD Cloud Engine offers rich application module services to application developers. In terms of those frequently used application function modules, developers can directly activate and call module services, thus greatly reducing their workload of development and application resource demands. The Cloud Engine provides application developers with considerate operation & maintenance services including cloud monitoring, and cloud log, and enables them to accomplish operation management and monitoring analysis over applications via a simple console.

4. JD Cloud Peak

It provides application developers with convenient development services of mobile application Client End and fosters a full-process and close-loop cloud solution catering to the mobile application Client End. Developers are only required to submit application codes to the code library of JD Cloud Convergence and then JD Cloud Peak will automatically complete application compiling and packing to generate application Client Ends that can be downloaded and installed by users. Before the release of the mobile Client End, developers can conduct cloud testing on the Cloud Peak. Currently, JD Cloud Peak has taken cloud tests online for nearly 100 popular mobile terminal devices for testing and provides automatic compatibility testing, UI adaption, performance and stability testing, and custom script function testing. In addition, JD Cloud Peak offers component services of Mobile Client End to application developers. Developers can directly activate and call the module services for those frequently used application function modules, thus greatly reducing their workload of development and application resource demands. At present, JD Cloud Peak has launched cloud push services for mobile message push and short domain name services, for the conversion of domain names and URLs. Finally, for the released mobile applications, JD Cloud Peak also provides a mobile user behavior analysis tool. Cloud analysis of the Cloud Peak can help mobile application developers to analyze and mine user attributes and user behavior data so that they can make use of the data to optimize mobile products, adjust operation models and make decisions for advertisements, thus improving the user experience of mobile products and winning more and qualified users.

5. JD Cloud Convergence

It creates a community interaction platform for all participants in JD's E-commerce Cloud, provides developers with services including exchange learning, trouble shooting, code hosting, crowdsourcing markets, and offers full-process support from "learning"→ "production"→ "sale." The Developer Forum is designed for community exchange, discussion, and problem solving, focusing on the JD E-commerce Cloud, various solutions, and products. The Teaching Center provides all interested parties including developers, vendors, JD E-commerce Cloud users, etc., with rich online teaching materials and development experiences. JD's code libraries realize full-process code management service including subcontract management of development tasks, online and offline code editing, coding assistance, code version management, and so forth. The Crowdsourcing Market provides all interested parties including developers, vendors, JD E-commerce Cloud users, and others with an interactive supply-demand trading platform to stimulate the platform's ability to "create wealth."

By the end of 2013, seven core business systems at JD opened over 500 API interfaces, attracted more than 550 ISV partners, and 30,000 individuals to join JD's e-commerce application ecology. More than 30,000 e-commerce applications were developed, 550 of which were traded on JD Service Market. The third-party e-commerce applications cover over 80% of JD's POP vendors.

E-commerce Cloud Solutions

Advantages of the JD "E-commerce" Solutions

JD's E-commerce Cloud solutions helps centralize and standardize e-commerce resources and brings more value for JD's e-commerce strategies:

1. Improve the productivity, business value, and e-commerce customer service ability: through JD's e-commerce cloud service platform, customers can use much smaller IT inputs to provide the business service of the same and even higher level;

2. Substantially simplify system management: IT running environment constructed by using E-commerce Cloud centralizes and simplifies the IT system, and the potential human errors are reduced by automatic operations provided by JD;

3. Reduce IT costs: the enterprise can reduce the purchase amount of hardware equipment and software licensing to reduce one-off purchase costs and relieve the workload on the personnel in charge of

system management, operation, and maintenance, thus helping the enterprise reduce invested costs, and operational and maintenance costs on the whole;

4. Obtain JD's e-commerce platform resources, including but not limited to thorough ISV outsourcing services from template finishing and system integration, and professional e-commerce consultation services from traffic management to client management.

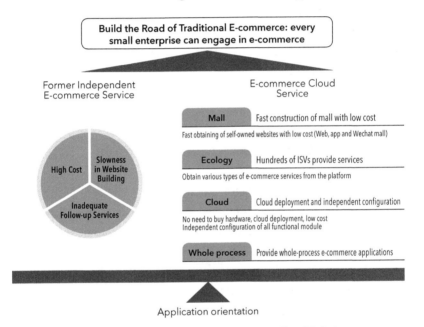

Diagram for Advantages of JD E-commerce Cloud Solution

Application Scenarios of JD "E-commerce Cloud" Solutions

1. Traditional enterprises: establish online transaction platforms;
2. Vendors of JD and Taobao platform: unified platform management;
3. Internet-based enterprises: open the access to mobile sale;
4. Enterprises and life service vendors: formulate e-commerce strategies.

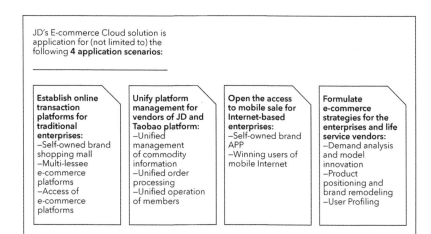

JD's E-commerce Cloud solution is application for (not limited to) the following **4 application scenarios:**

Establish online transaction platforms for traditional enterprises:	Unify platform management for vendors of JD and Taobao platform:	Open the access to mobile sale for Internet-based enterprises:	Formulate e-commerce strategies for the enterprises and life service vendors:
–Self-owned brand shopping mall –Multi-lessee e-commerce platforms –Access of e-commerce platforms	–Unified management of commodity information –Unified order processing –Unified operation of members	–Self-owned brand APP –Winning users of mobile Internet	–Demand analysis and model innovation –Product positioning and brand remodeling –User Profiling

Diagram for Application Scenarios of JD E-commerce Cloud Solution

Composition of JD "E-commerce Cloud" Solutions

E-Commerce

It provides enterprises with complete e-commerce solutions for marketing, building of a transaction platform, multi-channel management, and integration, order processing, storage and distribution, logistics optimization, including B2B and B2C online transaction platforms.

1. Transaction systems, including but not limited to Web transaction system and Wap transaction system (including self-owned brand App and Wechat-based stores);

2. Whole-network marketing system, including but not limited to traffic announcements, socialized media aggregation, sale data analysis, and more;

3. Multi-channel operating system, including but not limited to unified multi-platform background management, integration of supply chain, e-commerce reports, etc.;

4. Consultation services that mainly target customers' special demands and application scenarios, including but not limited to pain point

analysis, e-commerce strategy, model innovation, and operation modes implemented by e-commerce to effectively integrate online businesses with customers' current businesses.

L-Commerce

It provides the local retailing and life service enterprises with mobile Inter-cloud solutions.

1. Wechat-based mall: set up online stores based on the Wechat platform for vendors to realize Wechat traffic;
2. Smart business: provide local marketing programs for vendors based on Jbeacon and Wi-Fi Bao technology independently researched and developed by JD;
3. Big data analysis: accurate marketing, smart recommendations and advertisement injecting based on LBS;
4. Innovative service experience: provide self-help positioning, mobile e-wallet, near-field payments, and location navigation for vendors.

JD Smart Cloud

JD Smart Cloud is a cloud service catering to smart hardware products and aims at fostering a win-win smart hardware ecological chain. Depending on the strong technological accumulation by JD Cloud, we will provide our partners with all-round technical support including the Internet of Things, big data analysis, cloud computing power, open platform, super App, and more, to help hardware manufacturers realize product intellectualization rapidly and conveniently.

1. Technical Support of the Internet of Things

JD Smart Cloud provides a set of open Internet of Things protocols and offers JD's communication chip technology and smart Wi-Fi chip technical support to the partners, which realize hardware networking rapidly and conveniently and easily connects different smart hardware.

2. Big Data Analytical Ability

JD Smart Cloud helps the smart hardware connected to the platform in terms of data collection, transmission, analysis, and presentation, and utilizes JD's big data analytical ability with consideration of JD's user behaviors to conduct deep data analysis.

3. Multifaceted Cloud Service Support

JD Smart Cloud will open its cloud computing capability, which has accumulated for years to partners, provide elastically scaling cloud hosting capability and mass and stable cloud storage capability, offer cloud analysis, cloud testing, and cloud push services to mobile apps, and provide developers with an elastic application engine that supports multiple development languages.

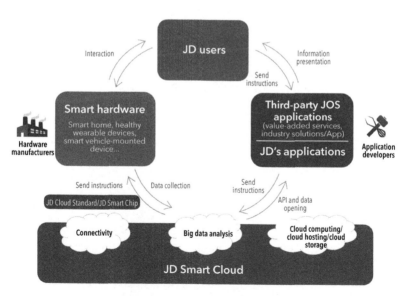

JD Smart Cloud Product Architecture Diagram

4. Construction of Open Platform Ecology

In terms of application, JD Smart Cloud will provide partners with JD information system and data open service, thus helping partners and the third-party ISVs to develop individual value-added applications. In terms of hardware, we devote ourselves to building a hardware opening platform, supporting chips and sensors of partners to connect to JD Smart Cloud and offering them to other hardware partners.

5. Powerful Super App

Depending on the complete JD account system, JD Smart Cloud enables billions of users to use all smart hardware managed by a Super App and enjoy a convenient and rapid one-stop smart life.

Authors: Guo Lijing, Sun Xuebin, and Hou Chao

CHAPTER 16

The Devil Wears Prada: Mobile Innovation

Virtual Try-on Mirror

At the Mobile Department, innovative products emerge in endless streams, such as Photograph Shopping, Color Shopping, "Story" Channel, Mobile Seckill, Shake, etc. However, the most innovative products are the Virtual Fitting Room and Try-on Glasses.

The Try-on Glasses project is to improve the user experience of JD's mobile client end and help users to see the experience of wearing the glasses. With reasonable innovation, it combines the augmented reality technology and operation of try-on programs and makes up for lack of the experience of online shopping.

As to the positioning of the glass try-on products, we hope that all users feel the convenience and interest of using the products. Therefore, technically, we endeavor to provide every user with the best try-on effects through the easiest interaction.

Project Establishment

In 2013, the Department decided to launch Try-on Glasses on the market as the first augmented reality product. Image recognition, augmented reality, and other technologies are important technical reserves of the Mobile Innovation R&D Department. Based on the development status of these technologies, after the initial functions and product form design were formed, to guarantee the quality and effect of products, Manager J, the head of Innovation R&D Department, decided to cooperate with technical experts in this field and make joint efforts in forging competitive products.

Then he invited W, Director of the Image and Graphics Research Institute, Department of Electronic Engineering of Tsinghua University, who led a high-profile team in the industry. In addition, Manager J was also joined by Z, who had years of experience in image processing and once worked at renowned companies such as Sony and Shanda. After discussing the requirements, we basically determined the product's technical indexes and difficulties and conducted a detailed and deep investigation. In this case, we had macroscopic evaluation of the project's workload. With efforts of Manager J, JD signed a cooperative contract for the Try-on Glass Project with Tsinghua University, thus brainstorming among mobile internet engineers and researchers from top universities.

The First Hilltop: PC Demo

"Detection, tracking, projection, and plotting", said with one voice by Lao Z and Professor Z of Tsinghua University responsible for algorithm of the Try-on Glass project. "The expert will prove the truths or reveal falsehoods." Both parties were unanimous in the division of worker modules of the project. After that, Professor Z studied parts of several theses and put forward several technical proposals. Lao Z conducted a feasibility study with years of experience in development of actual projects from the perspective of engineering and maintenance. Those in charge of App development at JD also gave feedback from the perspective of arithmetic transplant. We finally determined the proposal and started with the PC demo.

After less than one month, the first version of PC Demo was worked out. Everyone excitedly tried the 3D glasses before the laptop camera: someone assumed various postures like "scratching ears and heads" which attracted many onlookers, someone "wagged heads" and did exaggerated facial expressions to spy the range that the glasses could track. This Demo caused a great sensation among employees of the Mobile Department and even those outside the Innovation R&D Department also came to experience it. "Interesting" and "Amazing" were the first impressions received by everyone and their acceptance also proved the feasibility of the proposal. Later, Lao Z deeply analyzed the algorithm codes and proposed several recommendations for improvement of detection precision and range. PC Demo was subject to several rounds of optimization and upgrading. At this point, the Try-on Glass project basically came up to expectations and the algorithm was also finally determined.

The Second Hilltop: Mobile iPad

Success in the PC Demo was merely a feasibility test for the whole project and we had to do quite a lot of work to truly enable the Try-on Glasses function for mobile phones. The first problem in front of us was that, the performance of mobile processors was not as good as that of a PC, and the running speed of the algorithm with high computation complexity on mobile phones was much slower than that on PCs. To lower the development risk, Manager J first arranged two women from the iOS Development Team, D and C, to be responsible for transplanting algorithms to iOS devices. Why were these two arranged to lower the development risks? Because in the department of Manager J, most women worked for iOS team and members of Android team were all men. Android mobile phones had varied models, screen sizes, and performance of machines, so we had to verify effects of various models, thus doubling the workload and the time of launch would be doubtlessly delayed. We chose iOS devices also because Xcode (the development environment of iOS devices) supported direct compiling by C language, thus reducing the workload of arithmetic transplant. Accordingly, this decision provided guarantees and lowered the risk of delay for the on-schedule launch of the project.

D had not only rich iOS development experience, but also a working background of image processing and research on OpenGL 3D rendering techniques. She was the right person to take the position as the leader of the App development. She spent around one week running the algorithms on iOS devices and C helped D to test the interactive interface of the app. Then everyone contributed their Apple devices to verify the performance of algorithm. "IPhone 4 is so slow. It is jammed and cannot work!"; "the effect on iPad is good. I've got iPad 2, and who has got iPad 1? What? IPad 1 is not equipped with a camera? Then forget about it -_-!"; "See, how amazing my iPhone 5 is. It is running so smoothly!" Through experiments, we determined that iPhone 4s, iPad 2, and the subsequent models could support the algorithms. Manager J then instructed us to develop an iPad version followed by iPhone version after collection of user feedback on the iPad, with a small user amount and further optimization of products and performance.

Difficulty of Migration

However, colleagues of the Mobile Department faced a brutal reality: they had only several months to release it from scratch, so what should they do? Facial forms, eye locations, and light conditions were different from person to person, then what should they do? During trial, users may hold the mobile phones and iPad to check the effects, and what if the glasses were not worn well? The processing capability of mobile devices was too weak, so what if they failed to operate the complicated wearing algorithms? There was no problem that cannot be solved. Measures would be taken as the situation called for.

Limited time: our team cooperated with the Image and Graphics Research Institute, Department of Electronic Engineering of Tsinghua University, to develop the algorithms and accelerate the progress of development by using long-standing technology accumulated by this famous university.

Difficult algorithms: after repeated analysis and study on various algorithms accumulated by the university and the best products involved in the current industry, our team absorbed and improved different advantages, and finally determined the algorithm for virtual trial of glasses which surpassed the top level in the industry after countless attempts. Our product minimized the differences on the final wearing in users' facial forms, eye locations, and the impact from device shaking during trials, resulting improving various adaptive capacities and continuously comparing with the initial statuses of users. In addition, users only need to click on the screen once to wear the glasses or correct the awry glasses.

Hard optimization: after the algorithm was determined, our team soon transplanted the wearing module to mobile devices. However, at this point, a new problem emerged: it was slow! Quite slow! Due to significant differences in hardware architecture, the processing speed of the algorithm on mobile devices was slower by nearly a hundred times than that on the testing platform! Therefore, our team repeatedly deliberated and optimized from the whole algorithm process to examine every variable, and try to make every single line of code better adapt to the hardware characteristics of mobile devices. All functions and external libraries required by the module were thoroughly analyzed, adjusted, and optimized.

The Second Hilltop was taken

While the algorithm was under transplantation, the teams of the Mobile Department and the Product Department also participated in the Try-on Glasses project to undertake tasks of product design, interactive operation, model making, and graphic designing for iOS devices. L, one of T4-level Product Managers of the Product Department, first took the field. Quietly, he listened to our ideas and observed various competitive products, and then handed a PRD of over thirty pages to the R&D colleagues. Instead of being frightened into submission by his momentum, we read and discussed it. L explained details of the product design patiently and humbly accepted our suggestions. PRD and prototype diagrams were subject to repeated alterations. X, who was in charge of the user research, was assigned to collect opinions from the team trying the Demo so that the product design could be finalized.

D and C conducted the development of Client based on PRD, and the project leaders H and Z further optimized the algorithm, rewrote the core instructions, used Arm Neon technology to improve the speed with special instructions at the bottom layer of codes, and finally increased the speed by almost 30%. W, from the Product Department, made 20 pairs of 3D glasses models, including near-sighted glasses for white-collar workers and students, fashionable sun glasses, as well as retro and cartoon funny glasses to cater to the trial experiences of different users according to the choice of L. Through design, development, and testing, the function of glasses trial for iPad was released by the end of 2013. Users could enter the JD App, click the trial button, and align the camera at them to watch the effects of wearing 3D glasses on the screen.

The Third Hilltop: More than Migration through iPhone ends

Release of the function for iPad inspired the team. After the period of collecting user feedback, the version for iPhone was formally released after the Spring Festival of 2014. This product was added with a function of "Photo Wall," the design of which was led by D, a Product Department intern.

This handsome boy born after 1990 was more clear about the product requirements of young users. He thought that, current users often wanted more product functions. They desired to participate, share, and show off. "Photo Wall" was designed to meet their requirements in sharing and showing photos after they worn the glasses with others. Moreover, the viewers could "like" the photos they favored. In addition, multiple campaigns were held for the Try-on Glasses program, and every campaign had different themes. The user obtaining the most "likes" would obtain real glasses for free.

Over 20,000 phones were unexpectedly shared in the first campaign. It is worth mentioning that, during the development of glasses try-on function for the iPhone, with the previous team running-in, the project leader H thoroughly and effectively implemented the agile development mode: it only took six weeks after the Spring Festival to accomplish development and bring the version online. Two iterations cost three weeks respectively. During the first iteration, database, and port design, false data joint debugging, code framework development for Server and Client were carried out; during the second iteration, we refined the functional logic for Server and jointly debugged the Client's interface, tested and modified bugs, and finally increased the burying points necessary for data statistics. The whole team cooperated and effectively completed the development of the version for iPhone, and accumulated valuable project and development experience for the department and the team.

Looking at the smiling faces on the "Photo Wall," Manager J also gave a satisfied smile. This product was specially designed to enable these users to wear various glasses without going out and such purpose was finally achieved. As one of innovative products representing JD, Try-on Glasses took part in the 7th High-tech Expo held from May 13 to 18, 2014. Leaders of the Beijing Government paid a visit to JD's booth and appreciated the innovative achievements made by JD. Many general visitors also visited JD's booth and gave sincere praise after trying it.

With the relevant marketing activities held by those in charge of the operation, the virtual glass try-on module achieved great success. At the same time, users unexpectedly developed a new playing method: due to strong adaptability of the wearing algorithms, some users even put our virtual glasses on newborn babies, cats, and dogs and shared the photos on various community platforms.

Virtual Fitting Room

User's Vision

One day in January, 2014, JD user Lili opened the JD Client through her iPad as usual. She wanted to buy a good-looking down jacket, but JD Client popped up a striking window which hinted that JD Client released an important new function — JD Virtual Fitting Room for your trial.

JD Fitting Room

In fact, Lili had expected such function from JD for a long time, so she clicked the "Confirm" button to have a try. In a moment, iPad prompted that the new version of JD Client had been downloaded successively and asked whether it should be installed. Lili could not wait to click the "Yes" button. The new version of the JD Client was presented before Lili.

The interface of new Client was roughly the same as that of the former version, but a beautiful icon was added to the middle tool bar. This icon was of cartoon-style clothing and the word "Wear" was put below.

In excitement, Lili quickly clicked the new icon. A few seconds later, a brand-new interface appeared. There was a beautiful model who was wearing only the underwear on the left and various styles of clothes in rows on the right. By reading the simple directions, Lili knew that newly released JD Virtual Fitting Room enabled users to try on the clothes they were interested in using the virtual model and users could iconically see how did those clothes look when the model put on these clothes. By dragging the cursor, Lili cheerfully took the clothes on the right to put them on the virtual model on the left. By dragging-and-dropping, the clothes were quickly put on and all the clothes inside and outside were naturally matched. For example, a shirt was put on outside the underwear and a sweater outside of the shirt. It was easy to use this function. The same type of clothes would be automatically replaced instead of overlapping. For example, if the model had put on a skirt, when Lili dragged another skirt, the skirt on the model would be taken off automatically and the new skirt would be put on. Lili could put various closes on the model to her heart's content without racking her brains. It was more convenient to take the clothes off by dragging the clothes from the model (Of course, the model's underwear could not be taken off).

Model Try-on Picture

Lili spent half an hour on this new function with great interest. She coordinated various clothes for the model and found several to satisfy her. At this moment, a problem crossed her mind: the virtual model on the left was good-looking and had a shapely body, but it wasn't her. The clothes were suitable for that model, but may not be for her. She carefully compared the stature, skin color, and hair style of the model with hers, and found that she was more plump than the model, and their skin colors and hair color and length were different. Lili doubted that there would be great difference in the effects after the clothes were put on the model and her. Lili's doubt was quite necessary and this was the purpose for JD to launch the Virtual Fitting Room: let the user be the model!

Lili thought, this Virtual Fitting Room would not only enable the virtual model recommended by the system and with perfect stature to try on and there must be other functions. She carefully checked the tool bar under the Fitting Room and found a button of "Photo by User." Why did it ask the user to take photos? There must be new functions. Lili pressed the button and a window popped up, whose contents excited Lili so much: you can create a virtual model using your avatar photo and data of height and bust/waist/hip measurements (BWH). I knew it! Lili was so excited and immediately took a photo of her full face. Then cute little Joy designed by JD appeared and hinted that "it" was working hard to create an individual model for her. After a while, the little Joy told her that "it" had successfully identified the head of Lili in the photo and marked the head's edge with red line (if you were satisfied with the accuracy, you can enter the next step; otherwise, you could let Joy try again or take another photo).

As Lili provided a clear photo with sufficient light, Joy easily made an accurate identification. Lili was satisfied and clicked the button "Next." A new interface showed up. The preview of Lili's virtual model was on the left and Lili's head portrait was on the right with a red line marking the edge. There were some small dots on the red line, which could help conduct fine adjustment on the virtual model by moving them so that a more accurate effect could be archived.

JD Fitting Room helped Lili find a virtual body with the same skin color as that of Lili's head and they matched perfectly. After the fine adjustment on the size of the head portrait, Lili entered the next operation. The interface presented a picture of a complete virtual model with head that resembled Lili, but the stature was slightly different, since Lili did not give to the JD Fitting Room the data about her stature in the previous steps. This step was to set the stature of virtual model.

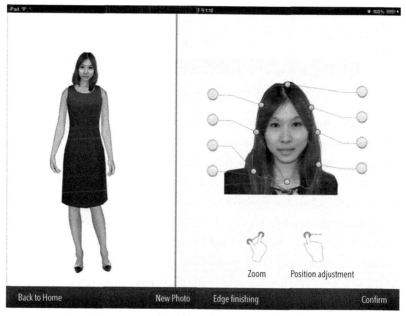

Effect of Face Change

Lili found it was easy. There were several sliders beside the virtual model and when she dragged these sliders, the stature of model would be immediately changed. For example, the slider near the shoulder was dragged and the shoulder breadth would change. There were 12 sliders for overall control of the stature of this virtual model.

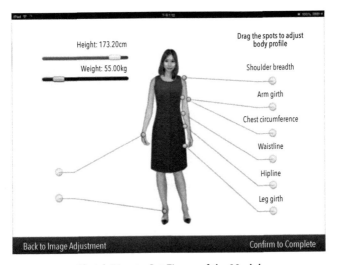

Sketch Map to Set Figure of the Model

Lili typed in her height and weight data and dragged the sliders to change the bust/waist/hip measurement. She felt this virtual model was almost identical to her in terms of appearance, stature and skin color. Now she could use this virtual model identical to Lili (JD Fitting Room referred to it as the individual virtual model) to try on the clothes.

As the model was identical to her, Lili became serious-minded. Just now she felt it was a game, but at this right moment she took it seriously in order to pick out clothes. She saw a purple down jacket. Ordinarily, Lili was often in red or orange and had never tried purple before. Since it was convenient to try on clothes, she decided to try every color and every style. She put the purple down jacket on the model and found the purple color matched her skin color well. She had gotten plump recently. Red and orange clothes made her look plump, but purple seemed to slim her. Lili was very pleased and decided to change a style and buy a purple one.

Wait, don't place the order immediately! Lili found the JD Fitting Room had another function: sharing. In other words, she could share her look with this purple down jacket with her friends and see what they commented. Lili clicked the button to share and the JD Fitting Room reminded her that she could share the pictures through Wechat's Moment, Sina Weibo, and other popular social network sites. Lili had more friends on the Wechat Moment, so she shared the picture and added some words she wanted to say to her friends.

Feedback was provided quickly from Wechat's Moment. Lili's friends found her new clothes and wrote comments or gave "likes." Looking at their compliments and inquiries, Lili was full of pleasure and thought, ha-ha, "You are outdated as you still did not know about the JD Fitting Room." With this introduction by Lili, her friends soon knew about the JD Fitting Room and entered to have a try. The Room became more and more lively and so did Moments.

Establishment of the R&D Scheme

When users were using the JD Fitting Room, its development team was paying close attention to the user data displayed in the servers. With a rapid increase of the background data, the project leader G was quite excited. He had worked for this project for six years. In the first five years, he immersed himself in the research of solutions to virtual try-on of clothes. In fact, the concept had been spread for more than ten years. Scientists from Fraunhofer-Gesellschaft in Germany initially applied 3D scanners to scan the human body to build a 3D virtual model for a real person and this method was proved to be feasible in the laboratory, but not in the commercial field, because the feasibility in commercial field was done on the basis of a cost-benefit analysis. The 3D scanner was too "advanced" for general users because of its high price (currently, a civil 3D scanner is priced over RMB 100,000) and complicated operation. Most users were not engineers and it was impossible for them to operate a 3D scanner at home. The high cost was hardly acceptable for users and merchants.

Six years ago, G was stuck in the difficulty of developing a set of commercially available customized virtual try-on system. Commercial availability required the balance among the try-on effects (the degree of customization), difficulty in operation (ease of use), and operational cost (making of a virtual model and clothes). The 3D approach was costly and G gave up this solution quickly. A 2D approach was also eliminated due to its lag in technology and poor visual effects. The scheme finalized was named Z3D, which displayed the head-on visual effect (or back the lateral effects) on the basis of 3D core technology. Modeling of the virtual model and clothing was only for the front (back and side), thus the cost could be significantly saved. Automatic modeling was achieved based on photos of users and clothes and the light and shadow effect of 3D technology could create a visual stereoscopic impression and sense of reality with effects much greater than that of 2D.

The scheme had been well defined, but there were still a lot of difficulties. First, this scheme should not provide complex operations for users. The idea of G was that the user was only required to take a head-on photo, inform the computer of height and weight, and then the computer should automatically build a virtual model identical to users. To materialize this idea, the computer must be intelligent: first of all, it should be capable of identifying the head of the user in the photo (this was not hard now as the face identification technology developed rapidly); second, it should determine the user's skin color and provide a reasonable average value as the user's head portrait must be perfectly combined with the body of the virtual model and significant mismatch of skin color should be avoided; next, the body of the virtual model should be adjustable freely, like a clay figurine. For this function, a set of bone and skin system like human body must be built, with movable bones and adjustable distance between the bones and skin, thus changing the posture and thinness.

Solutions to Major Problems

Through years of research, G finally found a relatively reasonable skeleton structure which enabled the virtual model to lose or put on weight naturally and freely adjust the skin color or even various actions. Thus, the users only needed to take a photo and move the cursor.

The next puzzle was how to put clothes on the virtual model. If the stature and posture of the virtual model was fixed, this puzzle would be tackled with ease, but obviously, this went against expectations. The same clothing had to be put on the virtual model with different statures and postures and it would appear to be natural and reasonable without the effect of being rigged.

The problem of making different clothes for the virtual model with different statures and postures (i.e., various versions must be modeled for the same clothes) could be solved, but it went against the principle of low cost in the commercial system. A garment needed various versions and there were an enormous number of garments at JD, so it would require an enormous cost in making the garments. So how could we solve this problem? G worked hard on this and vetoed many proposals.

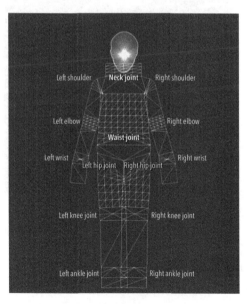

Skeleton Structure Diagram

At his wit's end one day, G was on the Olympic Plaza walking and thinking, and suddenly saw a kite flying like a garment. The kit was made of a thin skeleton and paper. He was enlightened. The kite's structure was the same as a garment. We could set some virtual skeletons for the clothes. The size of skeletons determined the size of clothes and the movement of skeletons could drive that of the clothes, thus the posture of the clothes could be adjusted. The clothes could change accordingly with statures and postures of the virtual model if the skeletons of clothes corresponded to the skeletons of the virtual model. G materialized this idea by using C++ language in the software and after a long period of optimization and improvement, he was finally satisfied with the effect.

Skeleton Diagram of Clothes

Online Launch

In October, 2012, Z3D Virtual Try-on System was born. G applied for a software patent for it and built a virtual try-on project team at JD to start research and development of the JD Fitting Room based on Z3D.

The Windows-based virtual try-on software was soon transplanted to iOS and subject to various improvements. Led by G, within less than one year, the virtual try-on team launched JD Fitting Room 1.0, which transplanted most functions of Z3D and was operable through the iPad. The software was built through the JD Client end and users could experience the JD Fitting Room without downloading other Clients (or Apps).

The market and media gave positive feedback for the JD Fitting Room. A great number of mainstream media began to report on the JD Fitting Room and some amateurs even wrote tips for "having fun in JD Fitting Room." The JD Fitting Room was also displayed in various exhibitions. This cutting-edge technology began to be closely linked with e-commerce platforms.

Authors: Li Songfeng, Zhao Gang, Jin Jianming, Hou Huiman, and Zhang Sicong

CHAPTER 17

Minority Report: See into the Future Through Big Data

Evolution of JD's Big Data Platform

Big data has been one of buzz words arousing heated discussions and it has also attracted more attention in JD.

In early 2013, JD's development plan for the next decade clearly pointed out that big data would be one of the key strategic directions of the company. Since then, big data made the debut on JD's stage as a strategical direction. In fact, before this strategical plan was announced, the application value of big data had been reflected in various aspects of the company's business, such as deep excavation of user consumption behaviors, implementation of EDM targeted marketing strategy, sales forecasts and auto-replenishment, continuing optimization of search referral system, precise injecting of ads, etc. Behind these projects crucial to the company operation were continuous exploration and research for innovative applications of big data. With the adjustment and development of JD's businesses, new breakthroughs have been made in accumulation of highly valued business data, evolution of big data technology, as well as innovative application and productization process of big data at JD. With the establishment of a big data mining platform, real-time big data solutions, referral search system, and e-commerce full-chain enterprise-level data warehouse, big data has shouldered a more important mission on the road of development of JD.

As for the administrative ownership, JD's big data platform is directly affiliated to JD Group and provides data services for JD Mall, paipai. com, JD Finance, and overseas business divisions as a basic data technique platform. It also plays a partial role in providing external data services. The platform is dedicated to research and application of mass e-commerce data processing technology, building of a fundamental platform with high performance, stability and security for data governance, analysis, mining, and provision of whole-process solutions and technical guarantee for JD and e-commerce industry to excavate the value of big data. The enterprise-level data warehouse independently designed, researched, and developed by JD has undergone tests about highly concurrent data production performance from 618 and Double 11 campaigns and supports JD's decision-making data analysis and high value-added data application products.

JD's big data platform has finished a complex evolution within four years. It developed from scratch, and evolved from centralized to distributed type currently and from Oracle data warehouse to JDW2.0. With the development of JD's data warehouse, Tiger, the chief architect of JD's big data platform, had been thinking about two problems: how to build a data warehouse for the complex business of e-commerce and how to reduce the cost for data usage with security guaranteed. Building of a "self-help business intelligence (BI) platform" that "enables everybody to be an expert of big data" seems to be the only way out. Then how to do that?

This could be traced back to one day in December 2009 when Xing and 3 fellows were present at the preparatory meeting for the foundation of the Data Department in the conference room on Suzhou Street. As the

first manager of this new department, he was in a disconsolate mood: how
we could deal with so many data requirements from the purchase and sale
segment?! What is worse, there was no time left for even a sigh. Looking
around, everyone was kept on the go all day long like fighting a battle
as orders were surging. The purchase & sale team would come to us for
"demanding repayment." In the past few months, soar of requirements
about data in various respects made Li, the head of technical R&D system
realize the importance of data and he held that it was necessary to make
plans in the future while supporting the data requirements from business
departments, so preparations were made for establishment of such as
department. Half a year later, Tiger joined JD, the Data Department was
established, and he took the post of Director of the Data Department.

On a sunny morning in August 2014, Xing was invited as a guest lecturer
to give talks to the Special Training Class for E-commerce and President
of Tsinghua University. Although he had gotten rid of the melancholy
mood, he was still excited as he was confident in preaching the knowledge
about e-commerce big data to the dozens of the elite sitting in front of him.
As the senior manager of Data Innovation Department of JD's big data
platform, he had expanded his team by nearly tenfold. Most of the team
members were senior data mining engineers and senior data analysts who
shouldered important duties for innovative applications of big data. The
entire big data platform headed by Tiger was comprised of 200 members
and several departments including the Data Architecture Department, the
Data Product Department, and the Platform Operation and Management
Department, all apart from the Data Innovation Department led by Xing.

The bright future could not be reached without taking tortuous roads.
Today's Data Department also underwent some rough development
processes. In the latter half of 2010, the Data Department was divided into
two departments according to different objects of service functions. Tiger's
team was mainly responsible for providing data support for the Purchasing
and Sales Department and the Marketing Department while the other

team offered services to the Warehousing Department and the Logistics Department.

Tiger's team laid the key emphasis on data analysis and data reports, but in that age without a data warehouse, analysts had to rely on two query machines provided by DBA to queue up for writing SQL data extraction and then take back for analysis. In case that the business demands failed to clearly describe, plenty of time should be spent on communication, surveys, and repeated data extraction. Apart from long elapsed time and great effort, we would be continuously met by demands. The dependent data extraction process caused low efficiency in data analysis and usage. The business personnel, of course, could not understand the difficulty of analysts and once even made one of the analysts Yulan cry due to failure in an extraction of mass detailed data in time. With JD's rapid growth, it was an unforgettable experience for everyone. Sometimes we chatted together and all sighed, "At JD, women should work like men and men should work like cattle." After laughing, we also rejoiced in having an opportunity to grow up rapidly.

Tiger noticed the plight of the lack of freedom in data services and was very anxious. Meanwhile, JD's businesses had undergone rapid development, the volume of orders and transactions had frequently set new records, new warehouses were put into service throughout the country. Besides, the former simple and crude ways of data extraction and analysis would soon become bottlenecks. Consequently, in the long run, building of data warehouses was the only road to achieve independent data services. Moreover, Tiger made a longer plan: data services should be independent and self-help services must be provided for data demanders! While building data warehouses, supporting product system for data scheduling and production, data analysis and extraction, data knowledge management, data report rendering, and data quality monitoring was also developed independently and a corresponding data mart was established for joint promotion and usage. This is today's big data platform of JD.

At the same time, the other data team encountered the same problem. the self-built data warehouse also became the only proper course to take. However, the most significant difference was that, the decision makers from the telecommunication industry held that, it was faster and more secure to purchase commercial products provided by Oracle by using the mature experience in the data warehouses of traditional industries for reference. In the short term, such was the case. Two Oracle RAC minicomputers were arranged and the efficiency of data processing was significantly improved. The costly Oracle BIEE business intelligence platform showed enhanced power in data processing and presentation. The initial version of the data warehouse independently built by Tiger's team was based on the open-source relational database management system MySQL and applied cluster application architecture to support large-scale data storage and computing applications. The open source technology was also adopted for independent R&D of data extraction and report rendering products with the Java program for the background and Ajax framework Extjs for the foreground. Such lightweight data products were inferior to BIEE in terms of stability and service capability, but it supported a fast iteration and unparalleled flexibility which could not be replaced by mature commercial products. Independent R&D, fast iteration, and flexible application which were applicable for Internet-based enterprises enabled a series of products and technical proposals to support data requirements of various scenarios at JD with rapid development, and fostered big data platform at JD today. It provided an important reference significance to other growing internet-based enterprises. The data warehouse solutions of traditional telecommunications or banking enterprises were noted for their stability, provided that the business system of these traditional industries was also fixed and the database and list structure would hardly be changed. However, with frequent changes in the business, the internet-based enterprises needed to not only support horizontal expansion, but also face adjustments every half a year at the layer of the overall business structure. Therefore, as time went on, without regard to the cost, restrictions on usage of matured commercial products became increasingly prominent.

Early in 2012, JD's R&D was adjusted again and the Data Department was integrated. Later, Tiger took full charge of the big data platform. At this point, Tiger's team began to build a distributed data warehouse which evolved into today's enterprise-level data warehouse JDW of JD. At the same time, the blueprint of fostering "self-help business intelligence (BI) platform" which "can enable everyone to be big data expert" gradually came into being. Using the data analysis tools, a data analyst who was poor at the data warehouse can acquire and analyze data based on his requirements to provide decision-making support for the business operation.

Based on Hadoop, the distributed data warehouse with Mapreduce as its computing engine can be regarded as the "standard configuration" for big data processing. In August, 2012, the first version of the cluster which was comprised of 40 machines was taken online. Compared with Oracle minicomputers, the performance was substantively improved and we realized the power of distribution for the first time. In December, 2012, cluster servers were increased to 110. However, the performance suffered a bottleneck due to bandwidth limitations. In such case, 10-gigabit bandwidth was adopted and the number of servers increased to 200 in March 2013. Three months later, the MySQL data warehouse was migrated and was no longer the primary data warehouse of JD. The number of cluster servers reached 310. In November, 2013, the data of entire business line was connected to clusters, with the number of servers reaching 440. In December, 2013, after three months of struggle, Lao Ge and Yanming led a team in charge of BI to finally complete the migration of the Oracle data warehouse and take all relevant tasks offline, marking the withdrawal of Oracle from JD's data warehouse. In March, 2014, the number of cluster servers climbed to 800 and the warehouse was comprehensively upgraded to JDW2.0. The dispatching platform became fully functional and the production model was upgraded from the former single-node dispatching to distributed dispatching. Data development, metadata management, data quality monitoring, data rendering, and unified authority management products were popularized and applied widely. The basic data was provided for open services of various systems after processing in the data warehouse by means of data mart, and the standard system was established for product operation and certification training catering to the mart's users. At this point, the JD big data platform was on the way to maturity.

In the mid-2014, the company adjusted the architecture of overall organizations and incorporated the R&D departments in vertical management of the corresponding business system. The big data platform still belonged to JD Group and provided big data applications and technical services for JD Mall, JD Financial Group, paipai.com, and oversea business units. With a new start and expectations, the department organized a group travel. At the boundless and vast prairie, the team showed the grand momentum and gathered power for higher and further targets.

Group Photo of the Big Data Platform Team

JD's Big Data Products

Data products were not new for JD's big data platform under development. When self-built data warehouse was brought online in 2011, the first data product dispatching platform was also launched and put into service. Under Tiger's guidance, the dispatching platform won a lot of praise in terms of UI, functions, and user experience.

Dispatching Platform

Order transactions, warehousing, logistics, and other systems of JD would produce traffic and the size of logs reached 1TB every day. Then how could mass data be collected and transferred to the data warehouse? This required dispatching products to produce traffic. At that time, JD's dispatching platform had developed into version 3.0 and every upgrading and iteration

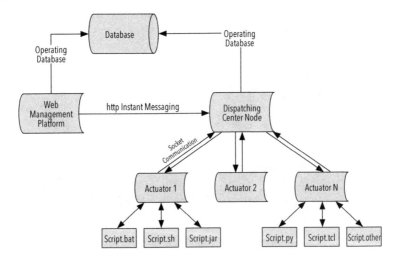

Architecture of Dispatching Platform 1.0

were the result of painstaking efforts of several development engineers working many days and nights as well as the embodiment of our technical breakthroughs and upgrading of functions.

Version 1.0 was taken online in August 2011. One server was arranged as the center node for commanding and dispatching and another three servers were responsible for the related data operation. The tasks were set with dependence relation by means of variable post-positioning to activate the dispatching mechanism. Few tasks were assigned when the data warehouse was just established, so the data size was not enormous and adequate computing resources required by data ETL process could be provided. However, with the increase of data in the warehouse, more and more data production tasks were generated, making the dependency relationship among tasks more complicated. Every BI engineer needed to set the value of post-positioned variables based on his production task to establish the task dependency relationship. With more tasks, the setting process was time-consuming, strenuous, and difficult to manage, and if the tasks should be dealt with again, modification to the pre-positioned variable may impact other tasks.

Version 2.0 was equipped with new dispatching engines to completely solve this problem. The relationship could be established as long as the parent task on which the new task depended. It was an independent process and could avoid disturbance resulting from multiple dependences on the same task. In addition, visual configuration and browsing functions were also applicable for this version. Further functional upgrade was ongoing, and significant function improvement was conducted for virtual nodes. In the process of traffic production, breakdown of some physical nodes may occur despite the low probability of such occurrences and once such a case occurred, it would cause serious impact. In such a case, the function of virtual node was furnished by adding a layer of virtualization to the former physical cluster configuration. In case any time that a production node broke down, the process would automatically switch to another node. Meanwhile, according to the load of different nodes, new tasks were automatically assigned to the nodes with lighter loads to achieve load balance. The materialization of these new functions greatly improved the stability of the platform.

Version 3.0 had more functions and realized a semi-automatic operating mechanism of data production. Semi-automation means that ETL template can be generated and data cleansing is completed after the targeted database and list are configured for the data task and then the dispatching task was created manually to complete the traffic production. In addition, the independently developed data extraction module named Plumber was equipped with this version. Plumber technology enabled fast data exchange between isomerous databases with higher stability and much lower maintenance costs for data import and export. A monitoring system Phenix designed to monitor the running status of servers was also incorporated in dispatching monitoring to collect the data in respect to the running status of severs on a real-time basis and make early warnings for the servers' heartbeat, occupied memory space, consumed CPU resources, etc. As to the historical data supplement problem caused by failure of upstream systems in the former versions, dependent tasks must be checked manually and then click restart after each parameter configuration; the new version was added with the function of one-key restart which BI engineers had long expected. This function supported restart of more than 1,000 tasks in a batch and BI engineers would never have to work until midnight to click one by one.

As the core system of big data platform, the dispatching platform not only shouldered the important mission of data production, but also was responsible for data push, processing of model data, and so forth. More than one third of the staff of the department worked on it, so you could image its importance. Functional upgradation and iteration in the future will lay greater emphasis on characteristics of platform-related products such as automatic service and open operation while the production capacity is improved so that reliable guarantees can be provided for big data management and mining of big data values.

Data Integration Development Platform

Data integration development platform is a milestone product during the development of big data at JD. Its emergence winds up the distressing experience of data analysts and personnel in charge of data requirements from business departments who used to extract data by hands through Client tools, which exerts direct influences on the later generation of data knowledge management platform. Currently the platform users approached nearly 1,000 and the aggregate data subscription tasks exceed 40,000.

The early version of the data integration development platform was named data extraction tool. Data extraction was the greatest hope placed on this product back then. It is believed that the demands of data of every enterprise are "rigid". For JD with rapid development, the data flowing at high speed is indispensable like bloods to human body. Beyond doubt, the task of data extraction should be undertaken by the Data Department. Data analysts were the busiest whether the Data Department was split up or integrated as a whole. At the beginning of every month when the personnel responsible for financial operation analysis needed to extract data, a lot of engineers would joined them. During the last months when the Data Department was still split up, the tasks of data extraction for financial operation analysis were equally distributed to these two departments; while at the beginning of every month, performance of data extraction became the most direct competitive contents. If the business parties were satisfied with the performance, they may send a letter of thanks and the department with poor performance may be embarrassed. In the craziest days after merger of foreground and background data departments, the Data Department required "all staff to extract data". The business parties issued the requests for data extraction via the Company's service management platform, and leaders within the Department would distribute the requirements to different employees. Within a period of time, quantity and difficulty of data extract were even linked up with the performance assessment and data extraction became a very important part of the work.

In such context, data integration development platform 1.0 emerged. This product supported data query and periodic data subscription. Meanwhile, with JD's private cloud service Jbox, it enabled authorized workers to safely and conveniently conduct data query and extraction and was of great help for analysts requiring periodic extraction of mass data (such as fellows in charge of financial operation analysis). Online data query and data subscription through Web end were two major functions. SQL interface supported view of matadata information and could save the codes under edition online. This greatly facilitated the personnel responsible for data extraction. The databases at the bottom layer included SQL Server, MySQL and Hive back then, and SQL was used to select different syntax on the basis of various types of databases and other actuating logic was similar. Product development was mainly in the charge of Yanwei's team, and Tiger also gave a lot of opinions with significant reference value from launch of initial version to functional upgradation. The continuously improved products attracted a great number of users to log in for use.

The front end page adopting Extjs had minor bugs such as malfunction of some scroll bars which exerted certain influences on the user experience. Besides, although the powerful form function of Extjs contributed to the application of the integration development platform equipped with Client end, the restriction on UI style was significant. With rich production lines, newly released products did not use Extjs any longer and turned to Bootstrap front end. In such case, in July 2014, the new front-end technology was employed so that the data integration development platform could be integrated with the data knowledge management and the data quality monitoring products online in the same system.

Data Knowledge Management Platform

The Data Knowledge Management Platform emerged without extra effort. After the specifications for the data warehouse model was determined, a normative classification system was established for the metadata information. This normative classification system conducted classified management over the metadata information and provided content search, Wiki-like edition, maintenance, consultation, and comment functions, thus the Data Knowledge Management Platform was presented before us. It also maintained dimension tables during the upgrading of later versions and greatly facilitated the team in charge of model development and maintenance.

JD Analyst

Apricot, Blueberry, and Cloudberry are the code names of three versions of the report presentation platform as well as the initial character string of product domain names instead of elements of Fruit Matching. The code for current version is Cloudberry and the product is formally named JD Analyst. Doubtlessly, we confer the ability of data analysis apart from the basic data visualization on this product. Users are conquered by the flexible console and incomparable graphic presentation ability of Tableau. What we endeavor to do is trying our best to realize effects of Tableau desktop system in the Web system and laying greater emphasis on the self-help intelligent software analysis platform in terms of product service capability.

As to the technical architecture, JD Analyst conducts independent front-end development of self-defined presentation layout and pack rich graphic presentation modules. Its rear-end report configuration system supports MySQL, SQL Server, Oracle, API, and Hive as data sources as well as online access. In the aspect of interaction, report collection, condition filtration based on graphs, data sorting, and deep drilling are the basic functions. Self-defined report page also provides the function of report push via email which enables the system to regularly send reports for reference by emails. For tables accessible within authorized power, the system can put those tables which are frequently viewed at the top according to browsing records, so as to improve the experience.

Data Mining Platform

Mining of big data is very different from the traditional processing method. JD's data mining platform caters to the construction of a one-stop data mining algorithm platform, and based on a machine learning algorithm, it can develop customized algorithms according to the specific business to meet the algorithm application scenarios. This product mainly depends on the distributed computing and adopts a calculation model applicable for machine learning algorithm for iteration to solve the problem of arithmetic processing of mass data. Basic data mining processes encapsulated in the platform such as Cross Validation and Grid Search provide the data miners with simple and easy-to-use mining tools.

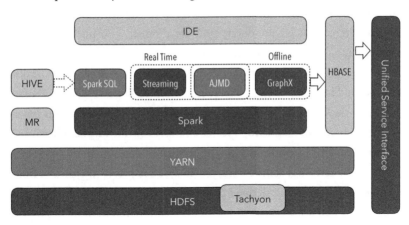

Architecture of the Data Mining Platform

To reduce the expenditures for data substantialization, the mining platform employs a memory-based storage engine, as well as cluster resource scheduling and management based on Hadoop Yarn to guarantee high availability and expandability of the cluster computing performance. The platform was formally launched in the middle of 2014 and has begun to provide individualized data mining algorithm services for the advertisement system, recommendation system, etc.

Data Quality Monitoring Platform

Timeliness, accuracy, and completeness of data concern the outcomes of data application. At the beginning of construction of the big data platform, we did a lot work for data governance, unify data calculation apertures, and set data verification rules to ensure the data quality. After upgrading the data warehouse, great attention was paid to the data quality and then we conducted management at the product level. Viewed from the process of data production, basic functions of the Data Quality Monitoring Platform include quality inspection during data production, quality evaluation after data loading, scanning, filing of all production logs, and generation of data quality analysis reports. Quality monitoring in the process of data production is mainly designed to conduct rule validation for changes in the source list structures and consistency of field information during data production, and carry out quality evaluations based on the validation results, automatically restart the data with quality problems and notify the subsequent dependent tasks. The loaded data will be subject to data check through field granularity. Rule validation can be conducted for the enumerated value, field data check type or maximum, minimum and average values of numeric fields to confirm whether the data is changing within a reasonable range.

Technological Innovation for Big Data

Currently, the industry has nearly formed a set of common technological architectures of technical schemes for big data processing. However, in the face of different industries and varied actual business demands, certain R&D inputs are still necessary for core technologies required by construction of big data platform, to realize directed technological breakthroughs and applications. During construction of JD's big data platform, we kept the general goal in sight while taking hold of daily tasks and conducted customized development and productization based on the common open-source technological architecture to realize micro-innovation and breakthrough innovations at the level of technology and products and lay a solid platform foundation.

Micro technological innovation is mainly reflected in the platform infrastructure. Through in-depth study of Hadoop distributed technology, several innovations were achieved in the process of localized deployment:

1. Directional development to support index creation based on HDFS;
2. Directional transformation to consolidate small files at the Map level and save resources;
3. Support of a dynamic resource allocation queue;
4. Support of control over the task-running duration and writing-reading volume of HDFS through parameters;
5. Independent development of the calculation functions applicable for JD's big data service platform;
6. Optimization and improvement of Hadoop memory property to support more data storage formats;

The breakthrough innovations at the product level are mainly reflected in the big data management and application, including:

1. Independent research and development of mass data production, scheduling, and management platform catering to complicated business models;
2. Independent research and development of the log analysis platform which connects ad clicks and page views and supports real-time cheat blocking and user model research;
3. Front-end presentation platform which can generate reports directly based on the file system without push to relational databases;
4. Stream-oriented computation platform built by multiple open source technologies;
5. Data mining platform with independent algorithms;
6. Mobile applications integrating various product functions;

In terms of the infrastructure, JD's big data platform is a dynamic and elastic platform and can achieve rapid horizontal scaling using Hadoop distributed calculation technology. Materialization of platform computing technology is divided into the offline computation module and the real-time computation module. Offline computation based on mass data query is gradually transitioning to real-time query and the ability of data insight is more prompt and effective.

As to software architecture, the independently developed big data platform based on Hadoop has provided universal services with high performance, guarantee and availability to JD, strongly supports the work of JD Data Scientists, Data Analysts, and Data Mining Engineers and significantly lowers the data's consumption threshold through a friendly interactive design and function customization to make data applications simpler and more efficient.

As to the business model, as the leader in e-commerce industry, JD possesses premium structured e-commerce data covering the entire chain from traffic, warehousing, purchase, sale, distribution to after-sale services, and commodity. In terms of design and development of business models, traditional business topic models were subject to all-round optimization and innovation, which helped achieve clearer e-commerce topic models and more efficient development. The topic models have now stood up to those complicated business of JD, and are playing a more and more important role in today's JD business system which changes frequently.

For personnel allocation and talent training, the complicated businesses in JD raise higher and stricter requirements against its data engineers. Currently, JD owns several data scientists and nearly a hundred of senior data development engineers. Through the project of "Big Data Platform Certification," special skill training on distributed development technology, optimization of HSQL, product usage, and business models to cultivate more employees proficient in non-data sequence while significant improvements are made to technology and products. The Intelligent data analysis platform can assist the business personnel in solving practical business problems more efficiently. At present, the Big Data Certification project has fostered hundreds of qualified data engineers and data analysts.

Technical Architecture for Mass Real-time Data

Quick decision-making necessarily needs rapid data supports. The real-time data is so important for operators of JD and customers visiting the website. The big data platform began research and application of real-time data technologies in the latter half of 2012. Kan was one of the first batches of the staff stepping into this field. Over the past two years, the related technical schemes have been put into use in major promotional campaigns such as the 618 and Double 11 sales for real-time query of PV, UV, and order volume. In May, 2013, when JD's users searched products on the page, they found the search results were added with tags such as "Purchased" or "Viewed." Such individualized display of search results is also an application direction of real time big data computation.

Web Application of Real-Time Data Computation

The real-time computing of JD's big data platform falls into four stages, where different technologies are adopted.

1. Stage of Collection of real-time data: a project named "Yangtze

River" was established to synchronize isomerous data sources to the real-time data warehouse. The "South-to-North Water Diversion" project would synchronize the data to offline data warehouse at the same time.

2. Stage of stream data computing: the project of "Yangtze River" was followed by the project of "Han River" which better encapsulated storm to facilitate calls of real-time computing API.

3. Real-time query service: with the above two steps, the data has been subject to real-time computing and storage. Then the "Three Gorges" project emerged. The "Three Gorges" project applied Spark and Presto DB to deal with a real-time query of mass data. The query results in billions of data within a dozen seconds.

4. Real-time data mining: based on the real-time data of "Yangtze River" project, the project "Donghai Sea" was set up for real-time data mining which can better serve online recommendation and search.

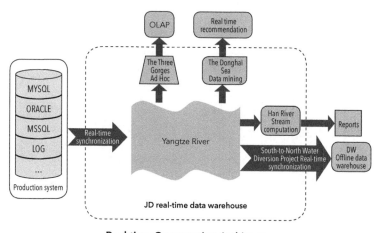

Real-time Computation Architecture

Some of JD's business scenarios require real-time computation of mass streaming data and the Big Data Platform provides a universal platform for the real-time computation of streaming data which is internally called "Han

River." The Han River Platform achieves goals of low delay, high through-put, reusability of results, and simplified computing task development, and employs a compound event model to set up the distributed streaming data computing framework (the bottom layer is on the basis of Storm), with easily extensible functions, partial fault-tolerance, and monitorable data and status. The Han River Platform is capable of processing real-time data streams (the data synchronized by products of the Yangtze River project from multiple heterogeneous data sources in a production environment on a real-time basis), provides the business systems with real time computing results in the form of services and supports the individualized demands of business teams. Currently, the Han River Platform has provided real-time computing data for JD Data Compass, JD Data Navigator, and JD Data Pool.

Combined with JD's business characteristics, the Han River Platform provides two modes for external use: SQL-Like and API programming, and has a lot of built-in reusable functions (such as Distinct, Sum, Avg, Count, Join, etc.) as well as business-oriented functions (such as PV and UV).

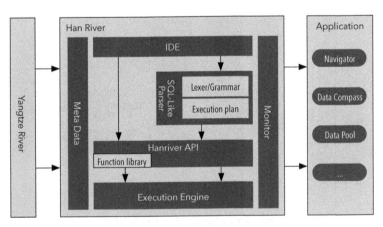

Stream Computing Architecture

Technical Framework for Real-time Query of Mass Data

JD's mass data real-time query product is named "Three Gorges," which provides data query in the form of SQL, responds to billions of pieces of data in seconds and has a low resource occupancy rate.

The entire technical framework is divided into query layers, computing layers and storage layers. First, the query layer will receive SQL statements which are parsed into back-end query language based on the metadata information; and then such query language will be submitted to the computing layer. The computing layer is responsible for decomposing the query request into several Jobs; then the Jobs are distributed to all data computing nodes in the computing clusters; and the data computing nodes will execute the Jobs accompanied by data interaction with the storage layer. Finally, the computing results will be returned and the computing layer merges all results obtained from those data computing nodes and feedback is given to the query layer; and then the entire mass data real time query process is accomplished.

Technologies employed for the entire technical framework include Socket Communication, SQL Grammar Analysis, Cache Cluster, Parallel Computing Cluster, Index, Column Storage, Index, and Meta Data.

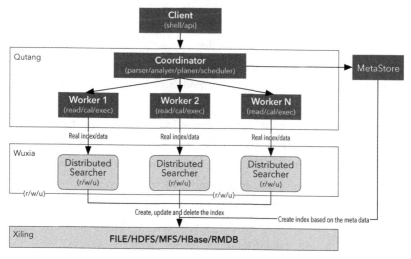

Framework Screenshot for Real Time Query of Mass Data

1. **Client**: it is a window based on command lines and used for reception of user inputs, execution of SQL, view, and return of results and check of the execution status;

2. **Qutang**: it is responsible for SQL parsing, production inquiry plans, computing of execution data, and merging of results;

3. **Wuxia**: it is responsible for creation, query, deletion, and optimization of indexes;

4. **Xiling**: it is responsible for data storage and backup;

5. **MetaStore**: it is responsible for management of metadata.

Online Analytical Processing (OLAP) Based on the Distributed Architecture

Rapid and complicated query processing of large data volume requires the support of OLAP technology, but in the face of enormous data volume at JD, the traditional OLAP technology is obviously for naught. We tried the Hadoop Platform. We used Hive to imitate SQL for data analysis of OLAP and conducted optimization when HiveQL was translated into MapReduce, but the efficiency was still very low. During a multi-dimensional analysis, mapping between the fact tables and dimension tables were still necessary and performance degradation was inevitable in case there were excessive dimensions. In addition to the problem of query performance, the greatest problem of OLAP is that flexible and changeable businesses will necessarily result in frequent changes in business models. Once the business dimensions and measurements change, the technical personnel must re-define and generate the entire cube (multi-dimensional cube) and the business personnel can only conduct multi-dimensional analysis on this cube. This will push them to quickly change the perspective for problem analysis, thus making the BI system into a hidebound daily report system.

We researched and developed our own online analytical processing system based on a distributed architecture through exploration and attempts, as shown in the following diagram:

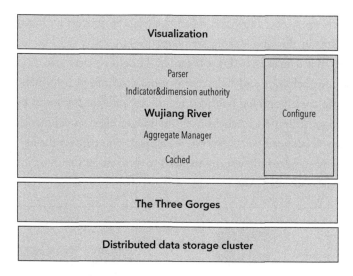

Distribution-based OLAP Architecture

Visualization is a front-end visualization framework suited to JD's usage modes for its businesses. The system, with a code of "Wujiang River," is a service system designed for indicator dimension mapping management, authority management, CUBE creation, and data collection and caches. Parser is an analysis module of logical statements and Configure is responsible for management of indicator dimensions, authority management, and logic cube management. It enables users to adjust flexibly to accommodate flexible and changeable businesses. Aggregate Manager is an aggregate logical processing module. The high performance distributed data query engine, "The Three Gorges," has been introduced above. The distributed data storage cluster at the bottom possesses data storage formats with indicators and dimensions which can be modified and expanded if necessary.

Analytical Processing Technology for Mass Log Data

As an Internet-based company, JD has a sheer volume of online businesses and the user behavior log data can effectively help JD to improve its systems and user experience. However, it is a challenge to process and analyze the mass data. In this application, we adopt JS+HA Proxy+ad hoc log server to meet the demands of log collection. JS-defined data can correspond to the user behavior and help record more customized information. HA Proxy can correspond log writing a request to different log severs by a load balancing distribution mechanism in the case of big data volume. In terms of data collection, ad hoc log servers are employed to convert the log writing requests to standard file writing requests so as to make the most use of the server hardware efficiency.

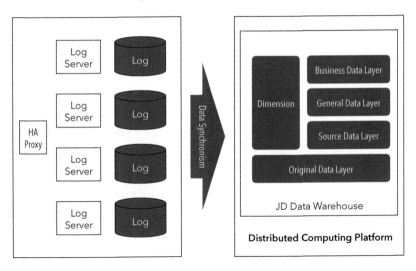

Architecture Screenshot for Mass Log Data Processing

After the collection of the above-mentioned data, we will synchronize these log files to our distributed data processing platform on which we clean and convert the data, load other useful information such as orders and users, and provide normative data (loaded from the files) with paradigmatic definition for customized use of the downstream businesses.

Innovative Application of JD Big Data

Targeted Marketing based on Big Data

Amy became a member of JD recently. With the intention to be a housewife, she would like to learn some cooking skills, so she decides to buy the cooking utensils at JD, but the commodity she fancies is out of stock. Then she finds that JD provides a function of "Arrival Reminding," so she chooses to use this function, fills in her frequently used email address and confirms. Days later, this commodity is available. Amy receives an email which reminds her that the commodity she wanted to buy previously has been in stock and asks her if she still wants to buy. This email also recommends some similar commodities. For many reasons, Amy changes her idea and finds what she has chosen is inferior to the recommendations when she chose to buy the commodity recommended in the email. Amy finishes her first shopping journey at JD via email.

After a period of time, Amy is enamored of photography and wants to buy a DSLR camera. She has searched for a long time, but for a greenhorn photographer, she had no clue. Unexpectedly, she opens the mailbox and finds an email titled "JD tells you how to choose a DSLR Camera." Oh! That's what Amy needs! She reads the email at once and gets to a special page via the email. She finds the camera that she feels satisfied with as expected and places an order immediately in reference to the content on the page.

The birthday of Amy's father is around the corner. She intends to give her father a Samsung mobile phone as a birthday gift. She takes a fancy to one, but the price is rather expensive. With hesitation, Amy adds it to the shopping cart and decides to find a cheaper one. However, on that day she fails to find another mobile phone that is more suitable, and then leaves the page to deal with other things. Three days later, she receives an email titled "The Commodity in Your Shopping Cart is at a Reduced Price!" and she reads the e-mail to find the price of mobile phone she wants to buy has been cut by RMB 500. The price after reduction is acceptable for her, so she buys it at once.

In this way, Amy loses her heart to JD's emails, because they always surprise her, help her to shop, and can guess her intentions of shopping. These special feelings cannot be found through other websites.

There are many more members like Amy who feel the charm of JD's emails, but how could JD's email system do this?

To set out, we know a good email marketing scheme must be able to perfectly solve a 3W problem: What contents should we send, to Whom we send such content and When to do this. To solve this problem, we need to be clear about the user's information, personal preferences and what is needed. This requires the support from big data mining technology and must be on the basis of all user behavior at JD (behind the behavior is a series of data), including the data concerning searches, page views, clicks, consultations, followings, adding to the shopping cart, placing orders, and addresses, and we set up models on the basis of such data to obtain the information of every user, such as gender, age, marital status, with or without children, owning a house or car, and what brands he or she prefers, etc. When we get to know such information, it will be easy to catch the preference of every user. Then we abstract various scenarios and formulate different email strategies based on every scenario. For example, the user adds a product to the shopping cart but doesn't buy or view any product or buys nothing. All these can be counted as scenarios. We prepare different email content based on these scenarios and send to the user at a proper time.

JD sets up targeted marketing architecture as follows based on the big data:

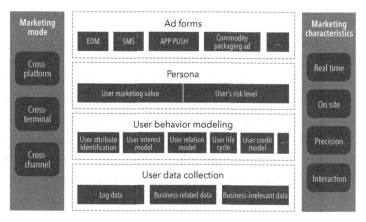

Architecture of Targeted marketing

The detailed data is at the bottom layer, including various log data, user transaction data, and other related data. We conduct modeling for the user behavior based on the user data, such as identification of user attributes, user interests, user relation model, user life cycles, and user credit models. After user modeling, we abstract the personas and supply them as the bottom data to different marketing systems.

Consequently, this architecture provides a solution to problems as to the targeted marketing via emails as well as all targeted marketing problems related to active push, such as message, App Push, and internal mails.

Before introduction of big data to JD's email system, we only sent emails to all users twice a week or made simple partitions based on the user level. Xin, who oversaw email marketing back then, was very upset as many ideas could not come true. With the participation of big data, we abstracted the personas obtained through big data modeling to screening conditions and incorporated such conditions into the email system. In this case, any email operator could screen out targeted users conveniently and the email content became more diversified. More importantly, the user experience was dramatically improved. After automatic trigger email strategies were made for many scenarios based on the big data, JD's emails become smart as well.

E-commerce Big Data for C2B Customization

In March, 2014, when President Xi Jinping and his wife Peng Liyuan were watching a friendly football match between Chinese and German juveniles in Germany, Peng Liyuan used a home-made mobile phone to take photos. A mobile phone used by the first lady would become popular. Then within a period of time, a great upsurge in "First-Lady Phone" was triggered. What kind of mobile phone could be so popular that even our first lady was attracted? The story begins with the JDPhone Plan put forward by JD in 2013.

The JDPhone Plan is a user demand-oriented innovative plan put forward in 2013. It aimed at a deep analysis through JD's mass user data, mining the users' real demand trends and cooperating with branded manufacturers to integrate the industrial resources and jointly foster cost-effective products meeting the user demands and going beyond the user expectations. Such a mode starts with the consumers' demand, and drives the manufacturing industry to design and produce the products is the currently popular reverse e-commerce mode (C2B).

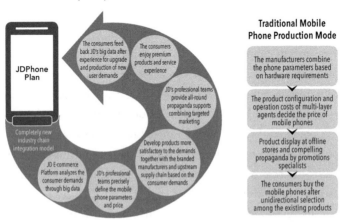

Comparison of JD Phone Plan and Traditional Mobile Phone Production Mode

JD's C2B big data custom analysis system: Huiyan

1. Overall thinking: is the market saturated? Where is the opportunity? What are the consumer demands and the trend? How can we produce products meeting the users' expectations? What is the estimated sales volume if the products are put on production? What is the marketing effect like? Is the anticipated target achieved?

2. Market analysis: analyze the size, saturability, and potential of market and market shares of various brands to inform manufacturers of the present situation of the market and the future development trends.

3. Consumer analysis: analyze the structure, consumption habits, demands, and satisfaction evaluation of consumers to inform manufacturers of the consumer information in all respects, in order to design better products.

4. Commodity analysis: provide the commodity with an attribute tag and classify the commodities into standard and non-standard categories from the dimension of attribute, set up specification portfolios for different people requirements, and assist the manufacturers with profound product customization.

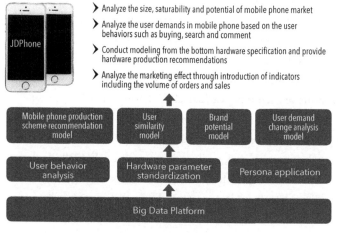

JDPhone Planning Process

Take the mobile phone as an example. Among users who bought two or more mobile phones at JD in the most recent six months, 34% of them tended to choose the mobile phone with bigger screen to replace the old one, but 5.5-inch screen is the limit acceptable to them, probably because Chinese people have relatively smaller hands. It may be hard to hold the bigger screen, so our system will recommend 4.8–5.5 inches as the optimal size. Mobile phones with a price at the range of RMB 500–999 are best sold in Guangzhou and most buyers are migrant workers working at manufacturing and processing plants in Guangzhou, who have limited power of consumption and lower average consumption in terms of mobile phones. They migrate from other places and often make long distance calls to relatives in their hometown, so they are desirous of cheap long-distance communication service. So, the system proposes the mobile phone marketing strategy targeting Guangzhou to focus on middle-end and low-end mobile phones with high cost performance and reduce long-distance calls and roaming charges by combining JD's Virtual Operator service.

JD's Data Innovation Department of the Big Data Platform models from dimensions including price distribution, determinant attributes, traffic, turnover, and consumer's evaluation, excavates functional selling points, mainstream price tier distribution, consumer demands, and value-added selling points to guide manufacturers for R&D, design, and production. Currently, JDPhone Plan has successfully launched Nubia Z9 Max, Nubia Z9 Mini2, Huawei Honor 3C, Nokia X, IUNI U2, and Nubia X6 and the sales volume of each type reached 10,000 every month.

In the traditional C2B mode, interaction, surveys, advance sales, group buying, customization, and matching are all active behaviors which require users to take an active part, while in the process of JD C2B big data analysis, we only need to set up different analysis models for different scenarios and prepare corresponding data sources. Then the system will automatically figure out the answer we want. Users take a passive part in the whole process. We not only focus on the user demand, but also minimize the cost of user participation and this mode will be tend to be the way the future develops.

Persona

Why should we make persona? On the one hand, JD is a large and comprehensive e-commerce company engaging in all categories. Its mass commodities and consumers generate multi-dimensional and full-coverage data system from front-end webpage views, search, comment, transaction to back-end payment, receipt and customer service; on the other hand, increasingly complicated business scenarios and logic make information processing and mining more important. In other words, JD has formed a data gold ore with rich reserves, high grade, and enormous increments, but in a quite long period of time, many business personnel are often unable to benefit from this valuable ore. For example, data analysts and engineers are repeatedly asked by the business personnel, "Why does the user volume fail to grow as estimated since the promotional campaigns have lasted so long and significant discount has been offered?" Viewed from the persona analysis, the answer is most likely to be wrong promotional campaigns are directed at the wrong people at an improper time and place.

Persona is used to provide solutions for converting the data to commercial value and excavate the gold and silver from the mass data. Such high-quality and multi-dimensional data counted in TB can record long-term and a sheer volume of network behavior conducted by users. The persona is developed to restore users' attributive characters, social backgrounds, interests or preferences, and even reveal their inner demands, characteristics of personality, targets of social contact, and other potential attributes. To understand various consumption behaviors and demands of users, precisely depict the crowd characteristics and aggregate user characteristics at different dimensions for specific business scenarios can restore the cold facts to vivid user images, guiding and driving the business scenarios and operations, and identifying and grasping great hidden business opportunities among the mass users.

Logically, it is a learning process which starts with the specific business scenario and is based on the data presentation to sum up benchmark rules or methods followed by conducting repeated iterations for the purpose of generating optimal schemes meeting constraint conditions and widely applying such schemes to similar scenarios. The persona often begins with business scenarios or demands for a specific category. Some business personnel have rich experience in operations, and based on the interviews with them about their experiences and requirements, engineers will abstract business statements and converse with them in common technical language using the data language. Next, they work out the results meeting predictable demands with their miraculous brains and capable big data platform and then through repeated verification by the business personnel, this person is successfully completed. Afterwards, engineers will use their amazing brains again to widely apply the persona to the whole website of JD. Such methods help us develop a great number of high-performance products due to its advantages of quickness, high efficiency, and rapid iteration.

Some essential attributes of the persona are universal for all categories or scenarios, so it is also feasible to skip single-category tests and set up models for users throughout the website.

The persona application service supports all business requirements of JD Group, oriented to varied demands from downstream engineers with technical schemes and using totally different methods, therefore it is necessary to set up a systematic and multi-layered service platform. Within the company, unified data warehouse, data interface service, and productization platform are employed to provide support for different requirements of R&D, purchasing & sales, marketing, customer service, and logistics systems. Employees have varied experiences in diversified business line requirement scenarios. The persona platform enables internal users to operate on the basis of specific business scenarios and service experience: experienced users are provided with deeper comprehensive references and allowed to independently customize or conduct secondary development; less experienced users are not only provided with data, but also trained for the analytic ability; greenhorns are guided to foster the awareness and habits of data-based analysis and operation; it also offers greater supports for external users, such as POP Vendors and their demands are satisfied in individual customization for their own stores and are provided with one-stop service solutions on the basis of various marketing methods.

JD's user behavior logs capture billions of user visits and mass behavior daily. We analyze and excavate the user behavior data to dig out the users' preferences and gradually draw the outline of the persona. Personas are often obtained by combining the business experience and modeling, with a distinction between the primary and secondary ones. Some personas highlight the judgment on business experience, but others emphasize modeling.

The personas delineated using business experiences together with big data analysis lay greater emphasis on describing the users' preference by virtue of the experience provided by the business personnel due to the close relationship with businesses. For example, per the experience of business personnel and based on the customers' contribution to the amount, profit and credit, a multi-layered comprehensive index system is established to grade their value and generate a persona. Our product manager can adopt targeted marketing strategies based on different user values on the one hand, and on the other analyze the proportion of users with different value grades to think how to develop users with low value into high value users.

Furthermore, the business personnel can distinguish users' shopping characters based on what they browsed through before placing an order. Some users check a few number of commodities in a short period before placing an order, and this shows that they have an impulsive-style shopping character; some users always compare a few similar commodities repeatedly and then place orders, then their shopping character belongs to the rational type; some users view a lot of commodities in a long period before placing orders, then their shopping character can be of hesitating type. We may recommend different types of commodities to users with different shopping characters. We may directly recommend the best-selling commodity to impulsive users and the commodity with the best public praise to rational users. For every single user, an individual marketing approach is also customized according to his/her shopping character.

Among people sketched by modeling, we cannot take for granted that users who purchased infant and child commodities before must have children in their family as they possibly buy commodities for others or as a gift. Accordingly, we need to find out whether users buy infant and child commodities for their own use. We can finally figure out if users have any child or children by modeling based on what they browsed through before placing orders, address of receipt and comments on the commodity. Then a child growth model is set up based on the purchased commodity tags, such as the phase number of milk powder, children's books, and other related information to carry out targeted marketing in different growing phases.

JD's own complete categories and conversion of users of different categories is a key business. To excavate potential users of a certain category, the first step is to identify the existing users for this category, and then further divide these users based on the information about their behavior, preferences, and personas to find out their features and finally set up models according to such features and identify potential users for this category.

This phase mainly aims at verifying if the personas are accurate. For example, the persona of a user includes the following information: male, between 36 and 45 years old, with children in his family, unmarried, having a car, and high shopping level. We can quickly find the contradiction between having children in his family and being unmarried. First of all, we can determine that it is a problematic persona. Next, by checking his persona, it seems that only being single is out of tune. Through verification between models, we detect some false cases and analyze the causes, thus improving our model.

The persona provides unified data service interfaces for other products to call to improve communication efficiency and user experience. For instance, it can be called by the function of recommendation and search to display commodities that fit the user's characteristics and preference on the basis of his or her attributive characters, characteristics of personality, or behavioral habits when he or she is searching or clicking so as to provide a friendly and comfortable shopping experience and greatly improve the conversion or re-purchase ratio as well as the user loyalty; the data interface is also furnished to the website's intelligent robot JIMI and enables it to customize the consultation and response strategies on the basis of the persona, such as quickly understanding the user's intention, targeted commodity evaluation or recommendation, individual care, and so forth in order to dramatically improve its level of intelligence and service, and win praise from users.

In the eve of the 618 Anniversary Campaign this year, the interface service of JD products applied the persona model to the products and helped the Business Department to find marketing opportunities and direction, comprehensively improve the product's key influence, and strengthen the user experience. The application model covering the user features such as age, personality, shopping preferences, and purchasing power by sketching the physical features of users at JD and vest certain "fashion styles" to stay closer to users.

During the reign of Emperor Jiajing in the Ming Dynasty, Xu Jie took up the post of cabinet head. There was a plaque above his office space which was as famous as the characters (which reads "Fight! Fight! To be No. 1!") inscribed by Dong on the wall by Suzhou Street. The plaque reads "Return the authority and welfare to the Emperor, allocate the government affairs to the corresponding governmental departments, and empower public opinion to appoint or remove and reward or punish any officer." In my opinion, it means that each performs its own functions and gives play to its own abilities. The persona also serves different service objects and facilitates our users. It can be summarized by JDW+CUBE+BMP.

The result of persona should be first subjected to standard processing and synchronized to the unified JDW platform to solve the data island

and for the convenience of calls by the bottom R&D layer. At the same time, data cubes are established by themes for multi-dimensional analysis directly catering to analysts and engineers. In addition, the related upstream and downstream data and products are further linked up, especially the Big Marketing Platform (BMP), which enables product managers and the front-line purchase & sale personnel to directly call the marketing platform for coupon issuing or EDM after screening out targeted user groups in the cubes, thus reducing a lot of intermediate links, realizing highly efficient operation and targeted marketing and sharply improving labor efficiency. The multi-dimensional cube is one of excellent applications of persona productization. Combining multiple dimensions of personas with orders, commodities, or traffic can quickly achieve intelligent analysis, provide professional and efficient suggestions through data comparison and analysis, and share the data to impart knowledge and aid decisions for everyone.

JD Data Aggregate digs out online shopping interest data through deep analysis on the online shopper behaviors for the current year and analyzes the shopping habits and preferences of online shoppers in different areas based on the persona, users' shopping behavior, and the annual popular hot spots to unfold a grand feast of JD big data and provide vendors and consumers with operational and shopping references. JD Data Aggregate for Year 2012 deeply analyzed the online shopping behavior of users in 2012 through concise pictures and the way of data visualization.

Today, with e-commerce gradually taking up people's daily life, the "e-commerce data" provided by the e-commerce companies is not only a good year-end stocktaking, but also informs future development. The interesting aspect of the data is also an important part of display of big data. For example, on average, 52 of every 100 programmers will buy the book *Cleanse the Soul*. This reflects that programmers enjoy cleansing their souls after busy work to relieve their anxiety.

The Data Aggregate 2013 was unveiled with the theme of "Big Data Explains the Popularity." The players of World of Warcraft (WOW) are potential dads? Fives is not enough to identify the rich? Behind the Chinese Dama is the Chinese Daye? People are most envious and jealous of the men and women from Sichuan Province? A man who is bad at football may lack interest in "sex?" Do you believe these statements accurately depict the Year 2013? Through the hot topics one by one, you can catch a glimpse of things behind the data you are not familiar with.

Store Rating

Throughout the history, every angle of the life is flooded with the concept of ranking, from personal banking credit to the national security level and from the definition of displayers to everyone's wage. Ranking is a product from catering to the people's demands in "standard" and widely applied by the public as a benchmark. In the field of e-commerce, with increasing expansion of business scope and platform size, the number of stores surged by nearly 10,000 per day. In the face of such an enormous group, do we need to set a certain standard to measure the level of stores? And how is such a standard designed?

Information symmetry and fair dealing are two concepts closely related with each other. Information asymmetry is universally present between users and stores and has become the inducement of various unfair deals. When users are lack of the information about a store's service level, the degree of trust on stores will be affected, thus further exerting influences on the user's decisions on "entering and not entering" or "buying and not buying."

Operators at the other end of stores also have rigid demands for information. As the saying goes, "good wine needs no bush," a signboard showing the "attractive in price and quality, and first-rate service" is their crying need for information sharing. Which part in daily operation is well done, which part needs optimization, the users' degree of recognition of various links, and which position they are located at is the information that operators should be informed of promptly and such information has important guiding significance to the operation.

There are a variety of ways to deal with information. Information quantification is the most intuitive and easily understood one, for information storage and exhibition as well as a direct approach for evaluation and assessment. It rapidly provides information users with well-defined and clearly-measured content. Information symmetry and sharing requires more standard and scientific management for large groups, making it necessary to find a method to measure various stores and relay good and bad information about the stores. The store ranking system is a carrier that applies a unified standard to measure the level of different stores and share quantified information of stores in various aspects on such basis.

Multiple important factors should be taken into consideration in the process of establishing the ranking system.

The first factor is the accuracy of the evaluation target. The system regards presentation of the "comprehensive" level of stores as the ultimate goal, but "comprehensive" is an abstract concept covering a wide range. Fortunately, it can be embodied by and described by the concrete behavior. Varied behavior takes place between users and stores, such as shopping, clicks on the webpage, after-sale service, etc. which influence the relationship between stores and users, adjust the impression of users on the stores, and reflect the important quantifiable impact factors on the store's management.

How to start with various behavioral data, accurately identify the attributive characters of evaluation target, and abstract and quantify the key factors and specific indexes are important tasks during the system establishment? After quantification and fitting of the behaviors such as shopping by users using AHP and factor analysis, we find that commodity, service, and timeliness are the most important links impacting the shopping behavior and the feedback of users. The quality of commodities, service attitude, and logistics speed are governing factors of these links. Through a series of analysis and simulation, we obtain clear targets and various detailed factors to be evaluated by the system.

The second factor is comprehensibility. The ranking system is a visual system based on the data and built by abstract thinking to face real business groups. Comprehensibility is an inevitable requirement for wide acceptance, implementation, and advertising, and system incomprehensibility is a catastrophic defect of the system. The relationship between targets of ranking system, system structure, and data basis and the system requires actual business or behavior as the theoretical foundation.

The way of "quantification" is a difficult part to comprehend. It is vitally important to choose an appropriate one. When measuring the level of stores in one aspect, we can adopt a horizontal original value identification, rank the indexes reflecting the store level and then show it to users, or set up horizontal indexing indicators. Considering that some modes may lead to difficulty in comprehension in the process of data standardization and function handling, an easy-to-comprehend way is employed.

The third factor is reasonableness of the system structure. The reasonableness of ranking a system's structure may impact the stable operation of the system. The ranking system can adopt a function structure, multi-layered uncrossed structure, or multi-layered crossed structure. Each structure has unique features, merits, and demerits. After trading off the performance of different structures, we can design a better system structure for the ranking system. Determination of structural layout is followed by further determination of the relation and relevance of structures. On the basis of the data model, functional expressions are obtained as the network vein connecting various structural modules through quantification computing between layers.

The value of the ranking system lies in users receiving help in the process of usage.

After the store ranking system is brought online, both the foreground page and the background system display the content and various results in the store ranking system. Users and operators can quickly and conveniently find the information they need so that both sides can share their information. Users are clear about the performance and level in aspects of service, commodity and timeliness of the store in front of them. Such rich and clear quantified information provides them with efficient and objective data supports. The ranking result is a transcript submitted by operators. This transcript records in detail the level of stores, which helps operators find out their advantages and shortcomings and propels them to work harder. Consequently, the blind angles of operation can be eliminated, more users are attracted and the operation effect is improved by better ranking results, which forms a positive cycle.

The store ranking system, based on the big data research, modeled through abstract and quantified analysis, and finally applied to website operation, has become an important ruler for shopping and store management. Today, information is required to be more transparent and management to be objective and rigorous. The store ranking system has been applied more and more widely and it will make online shopping fairer and more convenient.

Authors: Wang Wei, Chen Yulan, Gao Hui, Liu Pengfei, and Zhang Lijun

CHAPTER 18

Artificial Intelligence: An Intelligent Purchase & Sale System

The Charm of Artificial Intelligence

"We are going to take a trip!" Tian had been very excited since she got up, since her father decided to give her a digital camera as her reward for admission to the university. Tian eagerly entered JD.com and picked one. She placed the order before 11:00 a.m. and the deliveryman delivered the gift to her at 4:30 that afternoon. What makes JD's logistic service so efficient? The answer is its powerful warehousing system, swift logistics, and industrious deliverymen. Behind these, there is an invisible hand driving everything to be efficient and accurate. It is JD's intelligent supply chain.

When a user buys a commodity through JD, the order will be transferred down to storerooms for fulfillment, and then the package will be sent to the delivery terminal for delivery. Commodities in storerooms are purchased from the suppliers in advance or allocated from other warehouses. In case of understock in the storerooms, JD's logistics needs cannot be met. As of June

2014, self-operated commodities of JD have been scattered over more than a hundred storerooms across the country. Controlling the stock of these commodities is so difficult that humans cannot accomplish it. At this point, we noticed the charm of the big data-driven supply chain.

Smart Selection and Pricing

As the saying goes, "A dilettante watches the bustling scene, an expert looks at the way." Today we will explain how JD gets to know what the consumers' preference is and how to set a most reasonable price through its smart supply chain. When it comes to this, the real-time price comparison via a price comparison system must cross your mind at once. As a matter of fact, it is not. JD can not only conduct real-time price comparison, but also carry out big data mining and provide industrial competition data analysis, suggestions on selection of hot-sale products, and intelligent price setting based on the relevant historical data on commodities of other companies. Certainly, these are not realized easily, but fostered gradually by the team through years of experience accumulation.

2010

One day in 2010, JD's seniors passed an important resolution: to launch a price comparison system to improve the user experience. Then a team for development of this system was set up. At that time, JD was still using .Net for development and majority of databases were applied with the SQL Server. The team developed a crawler system (Pachong) based on .Net+SQL Server to fetch the commodity information of other companies and developed Work Synchronization to synchronize JD's commodity information regularly and automatically match Worker. With the data about competitor's commodities, JD's commodities and matching, the price comparison system was released, but it only supported real-time price comparison for self-operated books for the time being.

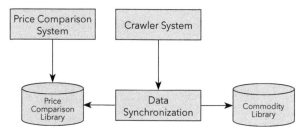

The Initial Architecture of the Price Comparison System

2011 and 2012

From the beginning of 2011 to the end of 2012, JD comprehensively turned to Java platforms and the databases were also migrated to MySQL. Against this backdrop, the team in charge of the price comparison system responded to the Company's strategy and decided to develop the price comparison system by using Java and MySQL. Meanwhile, the price comparison system for self-operated books got a favorable reception from the Department for Book Purchase and sale, and other departments also urged for the price comparison system. Therefore, the team specially set up a project for transformation based on Java+MySQL, introduced the Apache Solr search technique and integrated the IK tokenizer to expand the lexicon tailored for the e-commerce industry. QueryParser of Solr was also self-defined because of the characteristics of the price comparison, enabling it to support auto-match and real-time price search over millions of self-operated SKUs, tens of millions of POP commodities of the same stores and real-time search of commodities at different dimensions.

To support automatic price matching of all self-operated commodities, the team began to develop a platform for automatic price matching. The part of book price matching was separated from the price comparison system. The price matching rules, configuration, and MQ message decoupling based on Web Console was optimized, enabling JD's commodities to match the changed commodity price of competitors on a real-time basis. Upon completion of the platform transformation, the Worker price matching calculation and price adjustment Web console within the system could support horizontal scaling.

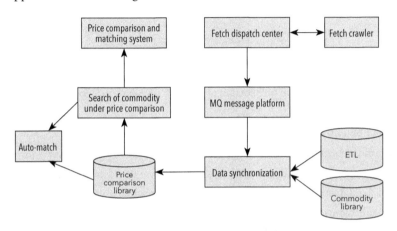

Architecture of Price Comparison System based on Solr and MQ

2013

Early in 2013, the team for price comparison got down to the solution to accuracy rate of automatic matching of the self-operated commodities other than books. We found that the recall rate was high when using the similar computing and sorting built in Solr to automatically match self-operated commodities, but the accuracy could not be guaranteed, in particular articles of daily use. Unlike these commodities that lack uniform matching rules, books could be automatically matched based on ISBN + pricing rules.

Where is the key to make breakthrough for the auto-matching of self-operated commodities other than books? Commodities under a variety of categories differed significantly, and auto-matching had different rules for varied categories. Accordingly, the key to matching was uniform of commodities, commodity attributes and text extraction of JD and its competitors.

The team for price comparison set up a special project for this to separate the duty of commodity matching from the price comparison system for platform transformation. Service-based governance was conducted to decouple on the one hand and visual workstation for auto-matching effect was developed, which enabled us to check the iteration outcome according to the matching indexes observed by virtue of visual tools on the other. Technical cooperation was also developed with the team headed by Liu Sizhe from the Data Department to introduce SVM machine learning algorithm used to unify the automatic sorting of commodities; Solr was upgraded and the distributed deployment was carried out; meanwhile, Hidden Markov Model Tokenizer was independently developed to raise the accuracy rate of attribute extraction through part-of-speech tagging and word order training. The abovementioned technologies worked with the operation workbench to make the recall rate exceed 80% and the accuracy rate surpass 98%, thus fully covering important commodities. By the end of 2013, the transformed system was brought online and put into service successfully. Since then, another important milestone of price comparison system emerged.

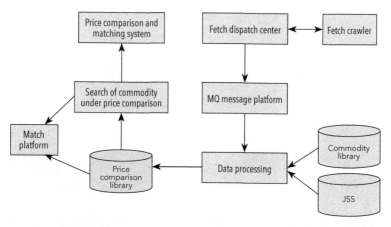

Architecture of the Price Comparison System after Platform Transformation

2014

Early in 2014, the intelligence level of the big data-driven supply chain kept improving and the team for price comparison embraced new challenges and opportunities. In June of the same year, scalable fetch open platform was launched, which was technically based on Sharding+Replica Set of Mongo NOSQL Database and could support dispatching and fetch of tens of millions of commodities per day.

This architecture upgrading materialized flexible and elastic dispatching and distribution of fetch tasks based on the fetch ability of crawler nodes; the fetch nodes can be expanded optionally to support and be deployed at any machine room and site; all modules can scale horizontally, and thus sharply strengthened the scalability of the crawler system. To sum up, no technical problems existed in the scalable fetch open platform for what to fetch and how long it took to complete the fetch process.

In July, 2014, after three years of improvements, the price comparison system had covered JD's and its competitors' commodity data, price history,

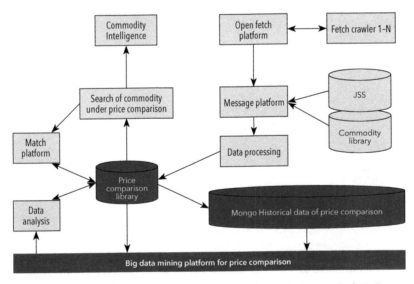

Architecture of the Price Comparison System under the Background of Big Data

sale data, commodity attributes, etc. Based on Mongo+Hadoop+Hive+Spark, and introduction of Scala development language, real time and deep machine learning, industrial competition information analyzer, smart selection and pricing, intelligent products were grandly launched. The team for price comparison made great contribution to the Company's big data strategy as well as the intelligent supply chain!

Forecast on Supply Chain Sales

"There are only supply chains on the market instead of enterprises and the real competition is among supply chains rather than enterprises." This is also applicable for the e-commerce industry and its importance is more obvious for the purchase platform at the front end of the e-commerce supply chain.

With rapid development of social economy and technology and changes of the market environment, production and supplies dramatically surge. The market has changed from production orientation to demand orientation, and demand diversification also emerges gradually. Online consumers have

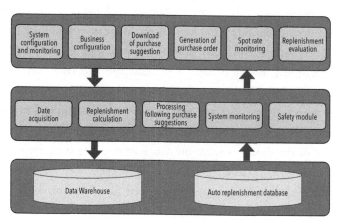

Purchase Management Module System

particularly uncertain and diversified demands. What changes have been made to purchase management in the context of supply chain of JD Mall by fast development of Internet-based technologies? How can we purchase an appropriate number of products with lower price and high quality standard at the right time from qualified suppliers to meet consumers' demands? All these depend on data analysis. The big data drives the entire supply chain system of JD Mall.

The accuracy rate of sales forecast system, as the source of supply chain, will directly affect the downstream automatic replenishment, allocation and internal transfer and inventory health system. The sales forecast model using big data to compute is a gem of the system wisdom, but how can we extract the data needed from the mass data and then forecast the future sales more accurately based on such data? One day in June, 2011, a requirement document was sent to all team members. This document recorded the prototype of the sales forecast system and the automatic replenishment system, and required us to construct a sales forecast model per the historical sales data. After data screening, construction of forecast model, and development and loop test of this forecast model, the system was finally put into service as scheduled.

At the beginning of the system design, we took big data and computing performance into consideration for the sales forecast system. Back then, the open-source Pamirs distributed framework was applied. Two application servers registered module values in the database and read corresponding tasks from the Task Table. This framework was useful as when two application servers were not enough, more servers could be applied to improve the computing performance. However, during the development, we found that most of the time was spent on data reading since there were millions of commodities at JD and the sales data of all dates for every commodity should be recorded. At the outset, we stored data by using major keys of "SKU + distribution center + time" and the data size approached a hundred million soon. The existing MySQL was unable to hold such a big data size.

Later, we re-designed the Task Table of MySQL to provide every SKU with a large field to record historical sales and in this way, the data size dropped to millions.

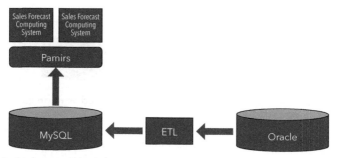

Architecture of the Sales Forecast System based on Pamirs and MySQL

The growth speed of JD in 2012 exceeded everyone's expectations and was embodied in the number of SKU surging from over a million in 2011 to 5 million in 2012. At this point, it was apparently very hard for MySQL to support the sales forecast system. Although developers kept optimizing the system codes, the time taken for computation was still increasing. In June, 2012, it took more than 6 hours every day for computing. The system architecture was pressed into progresses by the environment. In July of the same year, developers decided to transfer the sales forecast system to the Company's Private Cloud. The data in Oracle was synchronized to HDFS every day and the incremental data was incorporated into full data text (every line of data contained a SKU and its complete historical sales, avoiding frequent reading and writing of MySQL) and MapReduce call forecast model was used to complete the calculation. The outcome of such migration was good and the daily forecast computing time was shortened to an hour. Over the past year, the Book Department continuously offered the improvement recommendations to us. Liu's data team made a lot of optimization to the forecast model which was added with promotional types and inventory status, filtration of large orders, smooth extremum and short-term promotion filtration.

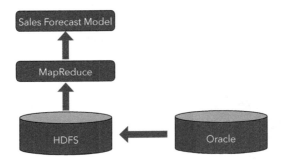

Architecture of the Sales Forecast System based on Hadoop

In 2013, the R&D team for sales forecast system undertook the research on data and model. The sales forecast system in this year received good news: JD's Data Mart came into service. The R&D team re-developed the historical data process for sales forecast and obtained more accurate and stable historical data. More importantly, the team started to prepare for the new forecast model. The R&D team welcomed many new members who were all proficient in sales forecast modeling. In the latter half of the year, the emphasis for the sales forecast system was placed on reconstruction of the historical data and forecast model. The R&D Department set up the Autopo project for the purpose of supporting the replenishment automation. The works for data and model were tangled and no failure was allowed (we planned to bring Oracle offline back then), so the project posed great challenges.

At every regular meeting, the project' pressure made the team members in a low mood. After four months of darkness, we embraced bright days finally. In late November, 2013, Autopo project was successfully accomplished. A complete historical data system was established in the data mart and Arima model with unstable forecast results was replaced by more accurate price model, seasonal model and decision-making tree model. Within half a year, the accuracy rate of sales forecast was improved by 20%, and since then, the R&D team possessed the right of control over the accuracy rate of sales forecast.

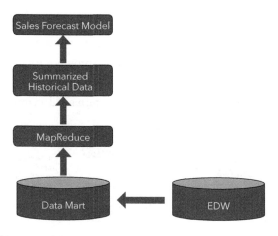

Architecture of the Sales Forecast System based on the Data Mart

In 2014, the work focus of the sales forecast was transferred from the optimization of big data performance in the past to the big data-driven business production. The modeling work shaped up well and the R&D personnel were increasingly enthusiastic about modeling. Every fellow was expressing a strong will to take an active part in modeling. In March, 2014, the experimental platform for forecast model was set up, on which various models would be tested to verify the impact on accuracy rate. The former model optimization and system improvements were incapable of confirming the results in advance. It was common that a modification was made or a model parameter was subject to fine adjustment according to certain requirement, and the replenished quantity of the automatic replenishment system would be multiplied several times the next day.

The forecast simulation platform is a milestone as it turns the sales forecast model into visible wisdom and the accuracy rate of the sales forecast system improved continually with the help of big data. New models are still under development for sales forecast. The promotion model set up in June of the same year could figure out the relationship between price and sales of a commodity and change the promotion plan made by the purchase & sale personnel into predicted sales. On the one hand, the sales forecast system will provide more accurate predicted sales during promotional campaigns, and help the Company to work out more efficient promotion plans through the promotion model on the other so that intelligence can be widely applied to the field of promotional decision making and turn big data into true wisdom.

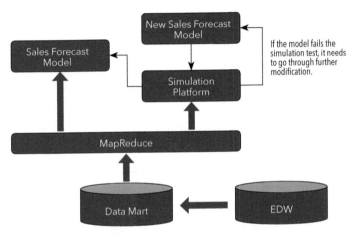

Sales Forecast Architecture with the Simulation Platform

JD's sales forecast system will sow more seeds of intelligence in the future to create a brighter future for the intelligent supply chain.

Basic Logic for Sales Forecast

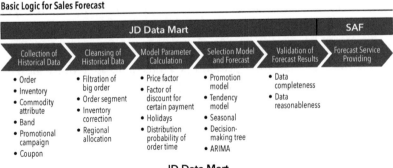

JD Data Mart

The great events of JD Mall Purchase Platform are listed as below:

1. In October, 2010, the DOC system was established and mainly applicable for accessories and hardware products in 3C purchase activities;

Purchase Suggestion System – Auto Replenishment System

Brief Introduction to the Sales Forecast Auto Replenishment & Inventory Health System

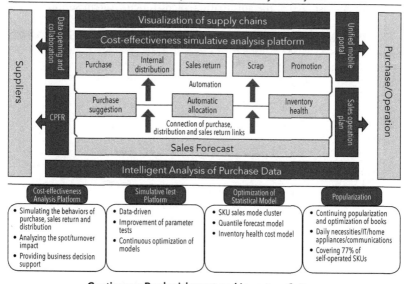

Continuous Replenishment and Inventory System

2. In September, 2011, the sales forecast system and the automatic replenishment system were set up to support the purchase work of the Book Department;

3. In August, 2012, the EPT-BIP project was determined. The BIP (Purchase Integration Platform) was developed to support EPT (Export) overseas sales business, transform the system and purchase the commodities sold overseas (customized/non-customized);

4. In September, 2012, the BIP system was taken online and the first phase enabled purchasers to generate and manage purchase orders;

5. In November, 2012, the function of the one-key creation of purchase orders can create purchase orders by one click based on the purchase suggestions calculated by the system, and this function marked another solid step toward the automation of purchase processing;

6. In May, 2013, the purchase settlement business mode for imported commodities was realized and this project expanded the business line of overseas commodity purchase;

7. In August, 2013, the automatic replenishment system supported the

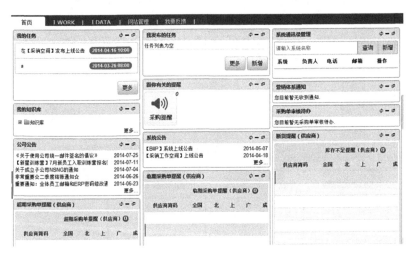

Schematic Diagram of the Purchase Space

automatic generation of purchase orders in case of none in stock. This project supported JD's non-stock sale operation;

8. In September, 2013, the automatic replenishment system enabled the function of full-automatic generation of purchase orders and meanwhile, to better examine and approve the purchase orders and improve the stringency and usability; and the examination and approval process of purchase system was transformed to raise overall practicability, safety and flexibility of the system;

9. In March, 2014, uniform product portal "Purchase Space" of the Retail Platform was launched;

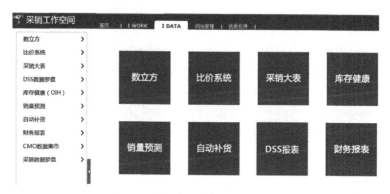

Purchase Space

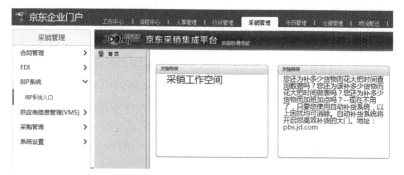

BIP System

10. In July, 2014, the automatic replenishment and sale forecast system had been applied to the whole self-operated purchase application platform and at the same time, "BIP system" (support creation of purchase orders), a most frequently used production system during purchase activities, had operated for three and a half years.

––––––––––

Automatic Replenishment

The automatic replenishment system and the sales forecast system are established in the same period. As the twin brother of the sales forecast system, the automatic replenishment system is expected by the business parties to help them purchase and replenish and the final results of sales forecast and auto replenishment system are reflected in the automatic replenishment. Consequently, compared with the mystery and the high-end sales forecast system, the automatic replenishment system stays pragmatic in business operation.

The complete concept of the automatic replenishment consists of purchase plans and purchase execution. Greater emphasis is placed on the purchase plans here, and purchase execution is put in the purchase order system (BIP). What is a purchase plan? To understand this concept, we can change the thought pattern. Purchase order is a digestible and concrete business document which mainly includes SKU to be purchased, the quantity of each SKU and the supplier's information. Now just imagine, how to obtain the data on purchase orders? Captain's call won't work. There must be a process of computation and various factors should be taken into consideration to finalize the data of purchase orders. This process is called a purchase plan. Simply defined, the purchase plan serves to determine when (purchase timing), how many (purchase quantity) and where (supplier) to purchase. The execution system is responsible for examination and approval of purchase orders, downward transfer to storerooms and suppliers, and cargo receipt.

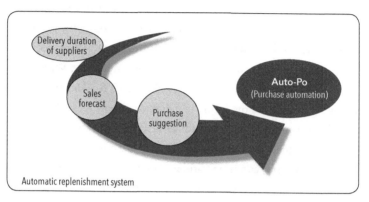

Members of the Auto Replenishment System

Preparation and Survey

In the first half of 2011, the Book Department was with the greatest demand in the automatic replenishment system since its number of SKU had surpassed 1 million back then and it was impossible to replenish manually. In this context, the automatic replenishment system was put into service.

Then the automatic replenishment team led by Developer Manager Shangqiang comprised the architect Jianqi, the Developers Chen, Yang and Yuanyuan and the Product Manger Wei. Project preparation and survey were conducted by these team members and Zhang Yuan and Fan from the Book Department at the same time.

Both Amazon and Wal-Mart, two leaders of the retail network and the overlord of physical retail in America respectively, possess matured automatic replenishment application cases. The degree of intelligence and automation has been particularly high in Amazon and most purchase behaviors are driven by systems. Therefore, the automatic replenishment system of Amazon should be the object we should learn from and refer to. However, because it is one of core systems in Amazon without any information disclosed and R&D personnel were in America, it was almost impossible to directly communicate with and consult them. Our R&D personnel and business departments fully displayed the spirit of JD. Jianqi, who kept working on Java architecture design and code development, picked up the dust-laden Probability Theory and mathematical statistics in college days and began to study probability distribution and modeling. Why should we study probability for the automatic replenishment? Replenishment is made for satisfying the sales in the future which were uncertain, which is the same case for the time that suppliers spend delivering the goods to us. Probability is the most suitable for describing and dealing with uncertainties.

Through multiple communications and discussions with the business departments and based on the theoretical models and practical accomplishments in the field of supply chain, Shangqiang and Jianqi finally completed the requirement document. Unlike ordinary requirement documents, it contained many mathematical formulas, probabilities, charts, parameters and data and specified the computing and using methods for the sales forecast, supplier delivery time and safety inventory apart from the description of requirements for system functions. The subsequent fellows had to comprehend this document to truly know the basis of the automatic replenishment in learning the logic of the automatic replenishment system.

Design & Development

A lot of time was spent on the requirement survey, and construction and validation of the probability distribution model for processing and computing of the data from sales forecast, supplier delivery time and safety inventory, so very limited time was left for design and development. The number of book SKUs exceeded one million and there were 6 book warehouses respectively in Beijing, Shanghai, Guangzhou, Chengdu, Wuhan and Shenyang. The size of data from one purchase suggestion would reach ten million and the middle data from sales forecast and the supplier delivery time also mounted to ten million. The computing and storage architecture must take the data size into consideration.

In face of the data size reaching ten million every day, distributed type, and sharding must be the inevitable choice. As for the distributed architecture, a distributed dispatching structure based on Pamirs middleware was selected for sales forecast, and the automatic replenishment system adopted a simpler method — scattering the data over multiple computing nodes based on SKU ID (many problems exist here and explanations will be given in the following part). In terms of data storage, considering that the replenishment suggestion had higher frequency of utilization and smaller data size than the non-replenishment suggestion, we employed a storage scheme with sharding of replenishment and non-replenishment suggestions. It was proved later that this scheme was simple, but it satisfied the requirement of the Book Department for query performance. The middle data from sales forecast and the supplier delivery time was stored using MySQL big field as such data was only used for troubleshooting.

These design schemes seem to be primary today. The Internet-based companies highlight speed and the outcome is far more important than idle theorizing. As it turns out, the technology that meets the business requirements deserves to be good.

Launch & Popularization

After the automatic replenishment project was taken online, it greatly facilitated the purchase and replenishment work of the Book Department. With the increasing number of SKUs exceeding millions, employees of the Book Department specially assigned to the purchase work reduced. More people were transferred to the work with high added value such as marketing, developing high-quality suppliers and contract/supplier negotiations.

Apart from the Book Department, in the first half of 2012, the automatic replenishment system was gradually applied to various categories such as car accessories and mobile phone spare parts. By the end of 2012, some categories of daily necessities and hardware home decorations of small household appliances division were also accessible to the automatic replenishment system.

With expansion of the application scope, various departments put forward many specific requirements and optimization based on respective business characteristics. For example, the type of the replenishment business model was increased; the replenishment parameters had increased from structure and band dimension to category, supplier, brand dimension and SKU grit.

By the end of 2013, the CMO Office proposed application of the automatic replenishment system within the whole self-operated scope. Full-category popularization of this system was unveiled.

For a long time after the automatic replenishment system was launched, the purchase business parties placed purchase orders based on the suggested data through the automatic replenishment system, reviewed and adjusted necessary data, and then uploaded to the purchase order system (BIP) to form real purchase orders. In other words, services provided by the automatic replenishment system were not automatic placement of purchase orders. It mainly served to provide purchase suggestions and help the business personnel to make prompt and reasonable purchase decisions.

At the same time, the automatic replenishment system, a big and comprehensive name, daunted a lot of business personnel indeed. They thought that this system could automatically place purchase orders at the very beginning. "I need to conduct promotions next week and more goods should be stocked up; I have set a lower purchase price with the suppliers; this commodity should be purchased in bulk; suppliers have fixed production scheduling arrangement …" Various doubts made the business parties worry when they heard of the concept of "automatic replenishment". This also created certain difficulties for system popularization.

System popularization didn't mean that all SKUs were subject to automatic replenishment at once. After all, various replenishment parameters couldn't be determined at the beginning. We need to optimize such parameters in business production per the actual effect.

Given this, in the middle of 2012, the Developer Manager Liu Shu renamed the system as Purchase Suggestion. What we offered to the business departments was suggested purchase order at the beginning, so Purchase Suggestion was relatively reasonable. Since then, the system had another name, Purchase Suggestion.

Automatic Placement of Purchase Orders

As mentioned above, we were not eager to realize automatic placement of purchase orders when the automatic replenishment system was just launched. In the latter half of 2012, we began to implement the automatic ordering. Automatic order also proceeded in two steps.

The first step was to realize one-key ordering, which enabled purchasers to click on a button in the automatic replenishment system to upload relevant suggested purchase data to the Purchase Order System (BIP) for generation of real purchase orders and execute the subsequent purchase order-related processes. The business personnel should click on the button to review the data of the automatic replenishment system. This intermediate step is also called "One-key Ordering".

By July 2013, the completely automatic ordering function was realized for EDI purchase order of books. After calculation of the purchase data, without any manual intervention, the automatic replenishment system can directly enter the purchase order system to generate purchase orders, automatically send to suppliers and execute the follow-up processes.

Architecture Upgrading

Starting from the first half of 2012, the automatic replenishment system was applied to more categories including IT, communications, daily necessities and home appliances. The system was also added with a lot of requirements and optimization for different categories. In this process, the original system architecture became more and more struggling in dealing with new requirements. In the meantime, with expansion of the application scope, the requirements with respect to system performances and stability were stricter and the drawbacks of original system architecture were gradually revealed. Viewed from various aspects, upgrading of the system's technical architecture was extremely urgent.

Firstly, the business models must be transformed. Our Development Manager Shangqiang put forward the concept of business-oriented purchase plan to divide SKUs into groups per the purchase plan. Each group was provided with different replenishment parameters so that the system could meet requirements from different departments and business personnel in charge of different commodity categories. With the purchase plan, it was easier to carry out authority control. The Product Manager Wu further improved this proposal. Dou, Yuanyuan and Yang developed and released the version of the automatic replenishment purchase plan in 2012. This improved version won favorable feedback from the business departments.

Problems also emerged in the initial distributed dispatching framework which divided tasks per the number of machines with expansion of the application scope. For example, if a machine broke down, all tasks under its charge would disappear, resulting in incomplete final data. With the concept of the purchase plan, we regarded every purchase plan as a task scheduling particle. To avoid the task loss caused by failure of any machine, task scheduling was added with the optimistic locking mechanism and accompanied by monitoring retrial. Later, to increase the concurrency, we doubled the instances of every computing node, but no modification was made to the codes.

In the process of the design of the new architecture, Yang subtly found that the data sizes of different purchase plans were significantly unbalanced.

For example, one purchase plan for books would involve more than one million SKUs, but the purchase plans for other categories often contained 5000 to 20000 SKUs. Significant imbalance of the SKU distribution would lead the scheduling architecture based on the purchase plans to degrade into a linear sequential model, thus resulting loss of concurrency and time-consuming computation process. To avoid unbalanced data distribution, Yang came up with the virtualization technology, which was employed by consistent hashing. Hence, the concept of virtual purchase plan was put forward to divide the purchase plans with enormous number of SKUs into smaller virtual purchase plans which were regarded as the basic task scheduling parcel in distributed scheduling.

At this point, the MySQL Database also failed to bear the pressure from increase of more than 50G of data size every day, so DBA requested us to clean up the database at a higher frequency, from once half a year to once three months and then to once a week. The duration for keeping the online historical data was also shortened to one week in the end. However, as a data-driven system, it is necessary to analyze the historical data with great size to adjust and optimize the replenishment effect. This required us to save as much historical data as possible. Considering that a replenishment simulation platform was to be set up, we transfer the historical data into Hbase instead of the data warehouse. In this way, the historical data could be stored in Hbase automatically and the recent data would be kept in MySQL. Simultaneously, the former sharding based on replenishment and non-replenishment suggestions was replaced by sharding based on the computing date and purchase plans to meet the requirements from departments such as daily necessities, IT and home appliances in query of replenishment suggestions. For the business departments, non-replenishment suggestions were also valuable data.

Establishment of the Replenishment Simulation Platform

Spot rate and turnover are core indexes of the supply chain. To improve spot rate and reduce the days of turnover are the targets of the automatic replenishment system. Excessive, insufficient, early and delayed replenishment will exert adverse influences on the spot rate and turnover. How can we evaluate the reasonableness of the automatic system data and its impact on the spot rate and turnover? If all automatic replenishment data is utilized, we can evaluate the reasonableness and effect of auto replenishment data based on the subsequent sport rate and turnover. However, before the reasonableness and effect of system data are proved, the business parties will not adopt the replenishment data provided by the system without careful consideration. This will expose the popularization of system to a controversial issue: which came first, the chicken or the egg?

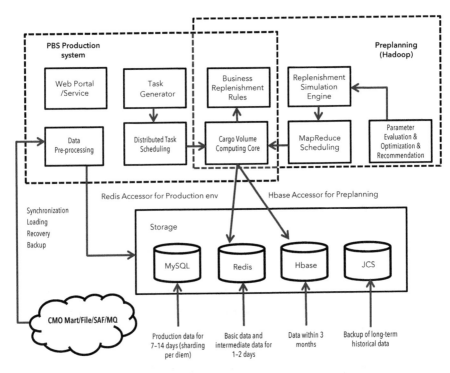

Auto Replenishment Architecture Based on the Cloud Computing

The replenishment parameters need to be adjusted and optimized. It will be inefficient to put the entire process of the adjustment and optimization in the actual production, and with the impact of various interference factors, the expected effects will be hardly achieved.

Our supply chain is driven by the data and these problems must be solved based on big data.

In the first half of 2014, the Replenishment Simulation Platform based on big data technology was launched. This platform was operating in Hadoop clusters and made use of the historical data within half a year to one year, including the data concerning inventory, incoming/outgoing quantity, sales and purchase. It simulated the purchase production according to the data from the purchase suggestions, formed simulative inventory on the basis of daily inventory change and circularly calculated new suggested purchase amount according to such simulative inventory, thus comparing the spot rate and days of turnover calculated on the basis of the simulative inventory with the actual spot rate and days of turnover to quantificationally evaluate the reasonableness of suggested data and the optimization degree of business operation.

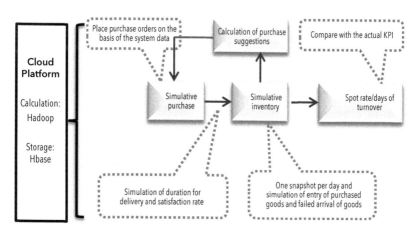

Schematic Diagram of Simulative Replenishment Process

The outcome of simulation was exciting. If the system's data was accepted, hundreds of millions in inventory costs could be saved without reduction of the spot rate.

The changes of inventory in the simulation also fully proved that the system-suggested data could optimize the business operation. Inventory changes for a commodity during the simulation are shown in the following diagram and the simulation result (the lower line) indicated that half of the actual inventory level (the upper line) can help reach the same spot rate.

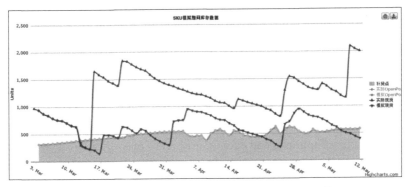

Schematic Diagram of the Simulative Replenishment Effect

Nowadays, the Replenishment Simulation Platform is playing a key role in the system popularization and the optimization of replenishment parameters. The simulation platform for whole-inventory control activities is under construction. Since the inventory optimization behavior, inventory control behavior and changes of new business are uncovered prior to implementation, we can conduct quantitative evaluation on the potential effect and value. This is the charm of the big-data-driven supply chain.

Data Compass

It is getting hotter and hotter in June. The refrigerator suppliers are particularly excited and more prudent in these days because they must catch the purchase peak caused by high temperature and guarantee the inventory as well as goods preparation. At 9:00 a.m. on June 16, 2014, Guo sat before his office table as usual and turned on the computer. He clicked on "JD Compass" to review the inventory. Fortunately, there was no early warning and we had sufficient goods to face the upcoming purchase peak. He checked the recent sales and traffic and found that the sales which should have gone up dropped, especially the popular "Haier" products.

Fundamental Analysis of the Data Compass

Guo immediately opened the industrial analysis module and reviewed the market changes of the air-conditioning industry. The sales volume of this industry didn't significantly drop, but was still rising stably instead.

Through hot sale analysis, he found that the "Haier" commodity numbered 1032689 fell by 3 places in the ranking. Why is that?

Subsequently, Guo decided to get to know the market shares, brand awareness and consumer characteristics of "Haier" at the current stage. In the market analysis module, we can see the whole refrigerator market and know which models and which price tier are among the best sellers, and which regions have the best sales volume and greater potential. Through cross-comparison at multiple dimensions such as attentions, search share and sales volume, Guo found that, compared with "Midea", "TCL" and "Gree", "Haier" was best sold in "Guangdong" and had the greatest market potential in "Zhejiang" (high in search frequency and attention, but low in sales volume), and "Zhejiang" would be the potential market.

As to "Haier" commodity numbered1032689 which should have been sold well, but was low in the ranking. Guo clicked on the traffic analysis and found that the commodity numbered 1077304 and 480730 shared the most traffic from the commodity with the number of 1032689.

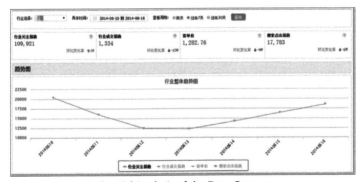

Industrial Analysis of the Data Compass

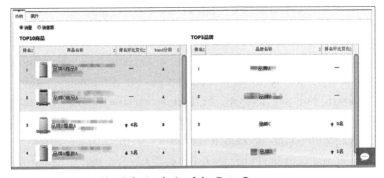

Hot Sale Analysis of the Data Compass

Through analysis over advantages and disadvantages of competitive commodities, he found the commodity numbered1032689 had an inferior position in the aspect of user attention and those paying attentions to the competitive commodities would be potential users.

Considering the abovementioned information, Guo systematically and deeply compared and analyzed the data in various modules and made a marketing plan based on the analysis results to improve brand influence and user viscosity and increase the sales. Firstly, he decided to participate in the 618 Anniversary Campaign from June 17 to 19, 2014 and injected targeted advertisements after knowing the source of page views; secondly, he should

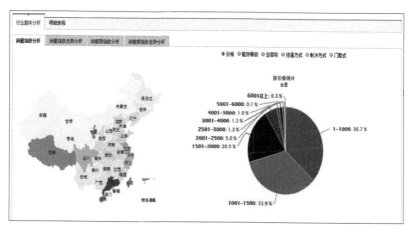

Region Analysis of the Data Compass

Traffic Analysis of the Data Compass

intensify online and offline advertising in regions with great potential such as Zhejiang to exploit potential users.

At the same time, Guo also compiled a product performance report, which mainly set out the attributive characters of commodities with high user interest, attentions and sales, covering price range, gross capacity, energy efficiency grade, temperature control mode and refrigerating method. Moreover, this report could predict the market opportunities, seize user preferences and provide decision-making supports for the R&D direction and design of products based on the negative comments and the trend analysis.

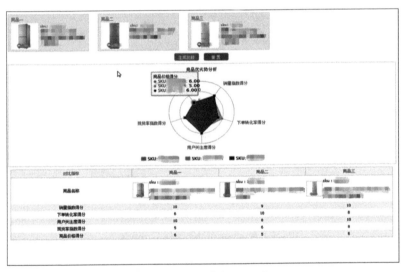

Competitive Analysis of the Data Compass

During the promotional campaign, which continued for three days, Guo tracked and viewed the data information every day. He tailed after the promotional effect on a real-time basis by analyzing the promotional effects, advertisement effects, commodity sales status, etc. During the promotion campaign, the sales of commodities surged significantly and the user attention also went up.

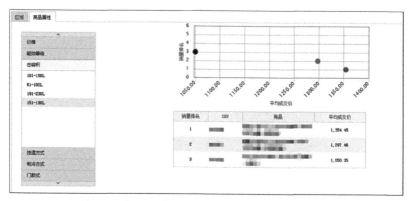

Commodity Attribute Analysis of the Data Compass

After the promotional campaign, Guo found that, as of July 18, 2014, through the promotion and targeted propaganda activities, the brand awareness in potential regions such as Zhejiang was improved and the sales went up as well.

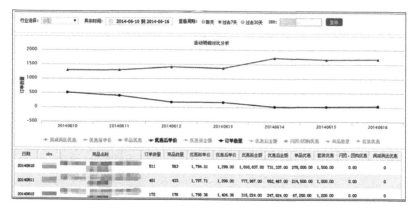

Promotional Analysis of the Data Compass

In face of the constantly changing market pattern and customer demands, JD Compass can better help suppliers like Guo to be familiar with the industrial development tendency quickly, understand the market competition and have an insight into the customer behavior so that they can adopt prompt and effective measures. The data makes it simpler to make business-related decisions.

Authors: Hu Hao, Xie Wei, Ma Dou, Zhang Guoli, Guo Jianhua, Dong Hao, Li Shuai, and Zhang Qiang

CHAPTER 19

The Butterfly Effect: Innovation Incubation

Innovation is a Sense of Values

JD has advocated the concept of innovation for a long time. The journey of innovation dates to the period when Mr. Liu started the business. He originated the e-commerce Dutch Auction but JD did not develop the auction and buy-now price of JD Treasure Snatch Island then. With this micro-product innovation, Liu drew a lot of attention and traffic for JD. Since then, innovation became a gene and has appeared in everyone working at JD.

Early in 2013, JD's senior executives gathered in the Beichen 533 Conference Room of the Group Headquarters and decided to completely revise the core values. The new version of JD values came out in a few days and "Innovation" was included. This day also marked JD's perfect preparation for its sustainable development.

JD has been in the field of e-commerce since 2004 and our business advanced at a full speed, with an annual growth rate reaching 200%. In this process, JD's technologies have been playing a supporting role in guaranteeing effective development of the upstream businesses and supporting an annual sales volume with more than RMB ten billion. By 2013, JD's technologies had developed for nine years and the enormous traffic from the 618 Anniversary Campaign had no longer been the greatest challenge against the systems. Then what is the future of JD technology? What is the role of it in the development of JD?

Before long after the concept of "Innovation" was incorporated into JD's core values, Donny formulated a "Three-step" strategy for JD's technologies: Follow-Lead-Drive. The core of this strategy was technical innovation. Only by innovation can JD's technologies provide stronger support for various businesses and only by innovation could the vision of driving business to move forward by technologies come true. JD's road of technical innovation started here.

Innovation is not strange to technicians. Their routine work is to continuously optimize and improve the systems and products. The work, in a sense, is innovations. We should consider whether the technical team can create greater innovations or even change the world. How to arouse the enthusiasm of technicians to make them passionately work on innovations is truly a practical problem. After several rounds of thinking and discussion, JD Product Forum came on the scene.

"Imagination on JD's Website in the Coming Five Years"

When the idea of the JD Product Forum was put forward, the first phase of activity entered the preparatory stage. Zoey's team undertook all organizational work. Since it was the first time for them to organize such an activity, they were nervous but excited. Through several rounds of discussions, the leaders decided to start with the revision of JD's website and the theme was "Imagination for JD's Website in the Coming Five Years."

This theme aroused the interest of all Product Managers in JD and everyone was excited. First, it was the first time to hold a product innovation activity with such a large scale; second, this innovation activity would provide the Product Managers with a stage to show their capability and imagination. Moreover, these Product Managers do not have to think about too many technological realization problems and only have to give the reins to their thoughts.

This activity kicked off in early April 2013 and lasted for one month. As planned, the innovative website products developed by various teams would be officially released on May 4, 2013 for a PK-based competition. The champion of this activity would be conferred with the opportunity to make its idea come true and the website of JD Mall would be designed according to its proposals. Most Product Managers formed teams by departments and some R&D personnel also joined in. 14 teams including over sixty members participated in the activity in the end. During the competition, the teams gave full play to the imagination of all members. According to the competition rules, the teams participating in the game needed to submit ideas and Demos for a final demonstration. The teams discussed in the spare time and tried their best to design a perfect and amazing works.

Time flies. One month for design flashed and the deadline, May 4, 2013, was around the corner. We would determine the quality of products designed by all participating teams on the field. The finals were the most critical for organizers and we must make sure that nothing would go wrong. Zoey attended to every aspect of activity deployment. First, he specified the staff room at the first floor as the finals site. This was a large and bright place full of the atmosphere of innovations with multicolored chairs, which made people feel comfortable; as to judges, we invited several senior executives in the technical team and the Director of JD Strategy Department to form the jury, and Mr. Liu Shuang, the founder of NOP, was also invited to be the special guest.

On May 4, 2013, the competition went ahead as planned. Even though it was Saturday, the staff room at the first floor was filled with people. Word of the competition had been spread throughout the entire group. All people looked expectantly toward it. Mr. Liu was no exception. He should have attended meetings all the day long, but specially came to watch the competition between meetings. He was not recognized by most people as he stood at the back. Coincidently, the work which Liu watched finally won the first prize and the presenter Hanqing was also praised by Liu.

JD is a Life Style presented by Han Qing

Every team participating in this competition had its own merits. *JD is a Life Style* presented by UED team turned JD into an assistant in the customers' life; *Imagination on JD's Logistics Products from the Warehousing and Logistics Team* perfectly combined the delivery AIO, Community Mart and After-sale Customer Service Platform and sharply improved customers' shopping experience; furthermore, the *Distance between Me and Ego* and *3D Shopping* also received favorable reviews from judges.

The first activity of JD Product Forum not only generated a lot of excellent innovative works, but also transferred strong signals of innovation to all technicians and aroused the enthusiasm of Product Managers on innovation.

In the third month after the first activity ended, JD "Youth" was brought online. The prototype of this product was the first-prize work *JD is a Life Style*.

The idea of innovation blossoms and yields, providing innovative talents with the greatest inspiration. This is a bold attempt and leap in the field of technologies no matter what the market repercussion is. "Imagination for JD's Website in the Coming Five Years" is also deemed as the first milestone in the history of technological innovation in JD.

Group Photo of the First Batch of Participants of the JD Product Forum

The Birth of the Incubator

Founded in September 2009 in Beijing, Innovation Workshop is an investment organization providing entrepreneurs with all-round enterprise training. It offers a package of service including capital, business, technology, market, labor, law and training for the startups to help venture companies at the early stage smoothly start up and develop quickly. Up to now, it has helped a lot of young people with entrepreneurial dreams to succeed.

Many young people born after 1980s or 1990s have no longer taken things as they are like the elder generation. They hope to do things they are interest in and create their own future. Thus, some of them give up stable jobs and turn to start-ups.

As a young enterprise, JD has staff with an average age under 30. Here, numerous young people long to get rid of boundaries and show their talent. This may be the case for JD's technical team. They are well educated and most of them are postgraduates. Through several years of working, they have made achievements in the field of technology and some of them intend to start a business. If these young people leave JD, JD will doubtlessly suffer a great loss. By citing a line from Uncle Li in the film *A World Without Thieves*, "What is the most expensive in the 21ˢᵗ century? Talents." Therefore, how to retain these passionate young people is a key issue.

Moreover, Liu has defined JD as a technology-driven enterprise. The only answer to the problem on how to drive JD's businesses to move forward by technologies is innovation. We need innovations for technology and business and solve practical problems of consumers by technological means. Only in this way can businesses be truly expanded.

After the Double 11 Campaign in 2013, Donny met Liu in America to plot out the future of JD's technology. After Donny returned to China, the first thing he wanted to do was preparing for JD Incubator and Clement, a member of the innovation team was assigned to undertake the specific work. After taking this task, Clement was tingled with excitement. He once founded a company with his friends and was full of enthusiasm about entrepreneurship, but the external cruelty made him to realize the importance of environment. Now with more resources and guidance, the probability of venture success would greatly increase.

Clement could only communicate with Donny and consult the relevant data to obtain more information on what kind of an organization JD Incubator was and how it operated. The data indicated that Cisco was the earlier one to have an attempt on internal entrepreneurship mechanism among the global top IT-based enterprises. According to *On Top of Tides* describing Cisco's internal entrepreneurship mechanism, "If someone in the company would like to start a business and the company thinks the business they want to engage in is promising, then the company could allow them to start a business in the company instead of leaving. Cisco will treat these people in the capacity of an investor rather than a manager. Once this small company succeed, Cisco has a right of priority to acquire them, thus expanding Cisco's scale. Founders and employees of these independent small companies can receive high returns. In this way, the people who want to leave Cisco and start a business at first needn't to leave and could continue to do what they want to do." Is this mode applicable for JD? With questions, Clement communicated with leaders of relevant departments. Through the communication, he found two problems that could not be ignored. The first was the cultural difference between China and US. Domestic enterprises and employees were relatively conservative, so most people were not optimistic about the entrepreneurship; the second one was concerning the miscellaneous rules and regulations in the enterprise which would limit the establishment of related systems.

Only by establishing a targeted innovation system based on JD's status quo could effective operation of the Incubator be guaranteed. There were two critical points: personnel placement and project management. In terms of personnel placement, employees who entered the Incubator would be paid with the same salary as before and the performance was evaluated and determined by project leaders so that more employees could be encouraged to enter the Incubator without worry about making a living. As to the project management, the Incubator used a project CEO system which empowered the project CEO to be in full charge of the whole project and control the personnel, funds and materials, which was identical to the entrepreneur team. Such mechanism would confer more decision-making power on the team and enable project initiators to do things in their own way. All mechanisms of the Incubator were designed to evoke the enthusiasm of employees, guarantee the rights and interests of entrepreneur teams and eliminate their worries behind.

Through two weeks of advice collection and continuous modifications, the *JD R&D Incubator Plan* was finally released. This Plan included all rules from generation of ideas to project closing. It resembled a role to the future and the entrepreneur teams were composed by those travelling on this road. Whether they could successfully reach the destination or not depended on their driving skill. The Incubator was the gas station along the road to offer as many suppliers as possible.

Within one month after the plan was released, the innovation team received more than twenty business plans from employees of the R&D system of JD. These business plans covered wide fields such as O2O, public benefit and game. It was necessary for us to think about how to screen these business plans and which teams could be the first lucky ones to enter the Incubator. Everything was unknown. Clement and the entrepreneur teams were all filled with expectations.

Four "Eggs"

After collection of the first batch of business plans, per regulations relating to the Incubator, every project needed a leader from the tier-one departments to take the position of the project mentor before the project entered the review stage. The mentoring system aimed at helping entrepreneurs to refine their business plans. Without a supporter, the plan would fail the final review.

Six projects were selected for the review stage. At the review meeting, the Investment Commission comprising JD R&D senior executives determined whether the projects were adopted or not by the vote system. As Clement often communicated with these senior executives, he was quite clear about the project focuses they concerned about. Prior to the review meeting, he had targeted communications with the entrepreneur teams and expected them to perform well. The gap of projects was insignificant sometimes and all projects would have certain risks, and the key was project display and team performance.

The projects attending the review meeting included the Maternal and Child Care, Automobiles and Medicines and every project placed its emphasis on different aspects. The performance of these entrepreneur teams differed greatly. Shi Tao was nervous when presenting his project on Automobiles and failed to concentrate on crucial points. The presenter for the Medicine project was seasoned and was well prepared for questions that may be raised by senior executives. Finally, four out of six projects were approved through discussions by the judges.

When Clement told the entrepreneur teams that their projects were approved, they were all mad with joy. The next step was to work like real entrepreneur teams. A tough entrepreneurship journey was awaiting ahead.

Every team was confronted with various tests. After the project was approved, Mutao Team suffered the loss of a founding member. It had two members at the beginning, but now only one stayed. What was the next move? To give up or carry on? The founder Zhongliang told Clement that he would carry on even if only he stayed. Then the next task was to find the developers. Through discussions with Donny, Chengdu Research Institute was appointed to undertake the development work. However, another problem emerged, that was, to assure the quality of products, Chengdu team expected more than the role of the developer. They wanted to deeply participate in the product design. Its original intention was in good faith, but some contradictions were made. Would the entrepreneur allow others to interfere with his product? The product was filled with so many emotions like his own child. However, if not, another team must be set up for the development. Clement took a very firm line on this. He would rather suspend the project than adopt the advice of Chengdu team as it may stifle the passion of entrepreneurs for whom independent product design was more important than the returns. Consequently, Zhongliang had to find another team. At the beginning, he invited two part-time colleagues, but the progress was slow because they were not familiar with the development language. Two months later, when we reviewed his product, Donny decided to set up a special team to support Zhongliang. With twists and turns, Mutao team finally became a small team with 7 members.

Apart from the Mutao team, three other teams also suffered difficulties. However, when they were confronted with difficulties, the top management often tried in every way to give them support. In this process, the Incubator was an utterly inadequate measure since there were so many business problems that should be solved by their own. On the road of starting a business, everyone had to work day and night and what they wanted to achieve was — success.

What is the role of Incubator? Does entering the Incubator mean a destined success? The Incubator should be deemed as playing a significant role if it could help the startup projects improve the success rate by sever percent points. To succeed depended on favorable climate and geographical position and support of the people as well.

JD Incubator Plan provided internal entrepreneurs with a platform on which they engage in larger innovation programs, but also were exposed to greater risks. Entrepreneurship is a game for the brave.

"Micro Innovation Prize"

Members of innovation team have always been exploring the innovative management methods for JD's technologies and learning advanced experiences from those famous Internet-based companies at home and abroad.

In May, the temperature in Shenzhen had exceeded 30°C. Clement took the occasion of integration with ECC to visit the headquarters of Tencent. It was a rare opportunity to learn to discuss with the fellows of Tencent Internal Lectures Collection. JD needs to learn a lot from three tycoons in the field of Internet, Baidu, Alibaba and Tencent (BAT).

In the process of further communication, Clement specially observed that Tencent Internal Lectures Collection held a contest for micro innovation prize every month. The product winning this prize might be very small, or even a function point, but such incentive method could greatly arouse the innovation enthusiasm of Tencent's employees. You do not have to create any great innovative products, and had chances to apply for the prize as long as you achieved any progresses in your work even it was just a slightest improvement to the user experience. It was an encouragement as well as recognition.

When Clement returned to the Company and reported to the superiors, the Director, Bill, also noticed this and thought that this measure could be carried out in JD immediately. It would help the culture of technological innovation in JD to make it better. Bill reported to Donny soon. Donny instructed him to make a scheme firstly and this measure could be executed after being of approved by the management meeting.

Clement was so excited that the bosses accepted this idea quickly. After two days, the proposal for JD Micro Innovation Prize was sent to Bill's mail box. Through discussions and modifications, the management meeting finally approved this proposal. The Minor Innovation Prize would be granted starting from June for once a quarter and the total bonus was RMB 50,000.

It took 3 weeks to propagandize and collect works for the first Micro Innovation Prize. During the process of application, we found that the applicants were not so clear about the definition of micro innovations. A lot of works submitted were large and wasted great manpower and long time. Strictly speaking, these products didn't fall within the scope of micro innovations. To inspire more people to take an active part, we didn't set strict limits. The awards would be granted if the works were accepted by reviews.

Award of the Micro Innovation Prize

We deemed spiritual incentives more important than material awards. What kind of spiritual incentives could make fellows who won the prize feel greatly honored? We made JD "Micro Innovation Wall," which referred to Nanyang Technological University. In a college of Nanyang Technological University, there is a wall displaying names of students who took the first place in scholastic attainments and it is a supreme honor for the students. The "Micro Innovation Wall" will become a history book of JD's technological innovations, recording heroes who have made remarkable contributions to JD's technological innovations.

Micro Innovation Prize is a small part for JD but with great significance. It drives all-involvement innovation and makes the employees feel the contributions they made to the Company no matter what improvements they have achieved. It is an expectation and the topic of conversations at leisure. We hope it can sow a seed of innovation in the hearts of all technicians in JD.

Innovation is a Sense of Culture

Clement still remembered what Donny said when they had a lunch together in early 2013. He said, "Now there is no person in charge of JD's technological innovations. You find a solution and try your best to develop it." Clement had no idea back then since "Innovation" was a nominal word. There was no clear evaluation criterion either. Clement thought that he could start from pasting banners. Later, with sponsoring of innovation activities, establishment of Incubator and introduction of the Micro Innovation Prize, the map of technological map was slowly unfolded.

Innovation management is complete closed loop from cultivation, acquisition, selection, implementation, benefit to motivation. Only when this closed loop is formed can the innovations come into being continuously.

The technological innovation in JD is carried out following this train of thought. JD Product Forum is an effective means to acquire innovative ideas and can cultivate an atmosphere; the Incubator is an independent innovation institution with free space for innovations; the Micro Innovation Prize is the driver for all-involvement innovation. With minor innovations, great innovations will increase.

Creation of an innovation-related atmosphere inside the enterprise is of great importance and it is identical to the culture of seedlings. JD incorporated the concept of Innovation into its core values and regarded it as the focus of the enterprise culture in 2013. Our architecture is also developing toward a mode of small teams which are more flexible and can make quicker response. The systems and processes are the greatest setbacks for innovations sometimes, and JD's technical teams are endeavoring to remove all processes that may comprise the efficiency and achieve a balance between efficiency and quality, and efficiency and safety.

JD's technical team invested several million in another key link for innovation, motivation, every year. JD encourages any kind of valuable innovation. More importantly, all technicians can acquire a sense of satisfaction, accomplishment and acceptance in the process of innovation. Names of these innovators will be recorded on JD's history annals.

In the future, JD will keep a global foothold for its technical innovation and seek for super talents worldwide. The direction of innovations in the future is to make life carefree and joyful, which is also JD's vision. All these elements will be displayed on JD's platforms. Innovation will finally go out of JD's technology system and go to every corner in JD to form a great culture of innovation.

Author: Fan Chen

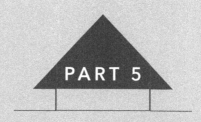

PART 5

Genius

Great minds always appreciate each other. Behind so many products, technologies and innovations, who are leading and practicing the values? In this chapter, we will introduce these backroom boys to you and they are creators of this e-commerce world.

Come on! Follow these talents to learn how to change the world!

– JD's Technical Talents

CHAPTER 20

S.H.I.E.L.D.: JD's Technical Talents

Pioneer: Deng Zhengping

Expert in the Mobile Business, Intelligent Hardware, and the Intelligent Cloud

#Gold will glitter one day, and persistence makes success! #

There are several legendary figures at JD's R and D system and Deng Zhengping is one of them.

In early 2014, CEO of JD, Liu Qiangdong held a press conference during which JD's five major strategies for the future were announced, including a strategy for the mobile business. Then a journalist asked, "Is it late for JD to start its mobile business and has it lost the first steamer ticket? However, insiders knew that JD had begun to develop the Mobile Client as early as in 2010, and the first head of JD's mobile business was Deng Zhengping.

In 2010, Zhengping set up JD's mobile team from scratch. Within two years, he led the team to research and develop mobile clients and websites based on Android, iOS, Symbian, Kjava, Wp, Win8, and TV, thus realizing transactions for most physical and virtual businesses through JD Mall.

As we lacked information on the mobile business back then, someone even doubted that, "Who would like to buy goods through mobile phones with such a small screen?" That was a hard time for the development of mobile business. Nevertheless, by 2013, end users of mobiles had exceeded tens of millions and took up 10% of the total orders. Zhengping headed his team to develop and expand JD's mobile business and laid a solid foundation for JD's mobile strategy.

By the end of 2013, the company started to deploy the intelligent hardware. For this new field, which started from scratch, Zhengping was selected by the company again. He was assigned to be the person in charge of JD Intelligent Cloud and lead R&D of the technologies for JD's intelligent businesses. In June, 2014, Zhengping directed the team successfully to pioneer the Intelligent Cloud Platform and JD Super App. This business aimed at cooperating with JD's partners, including various hardware manufacturers, chip solution providers, application service providers, and third-party developers to create platforms to enter the field of intelligent hardware, and all-win intelligent hardware ecological chains. Currently, dozens of enterprises including the industry magnates such as Haier, Hisense, Midea, TCL, Chigo, Huawei and Hikvision have accessed to this platform, making it become the most influential intelligent Internet of Things-based platform in China.

Recalling those days of exploration, Zhengping said, "I had been at JD for 4 years, and witnessed the development from simple .Net+SQLServer-based systems to the large-scale distributed systems mainly basing on Java, saw the increase of members at JD's R&D Department go from a hundred to several thousand now, saw JD's growth from a 3C vertical e-commerce company to an Internet magnate engaging in B2C e-commerce, C2C, finance, logistics, overseas business divisions, and JD's development from a small company located by Suzhou Street to a listed company with a market value exceeding USD 30 billion. It is just the beginning. JD's objective is to become the largest e-commerce company with a sum of business transactions exceeding trillions. The technological challenges we are facing will be unprecedented and I expect more technical geniuses to join JD."

As a pioneer, Zhengping has rich experience in not only the software development and design of system architecture, but also in team management and business expansion. Before joining JD, he worked at Souhu and ChinaSoft. His rich working experience and keen sense endow him with strategic insight and height unattainable by average people and he has the expansive spirit of being brave enough to be the first and continuing to innovate, which is also the spirit of "innovation" emphasized by JD's values!

Currently, Zhengping is continuing to accomplish his mission of opening new territories for JD's intelligent Internet of Things-based business.

Ever-changing Fairy Dragon: Yang Siyong

Expert in POP platform, mobile business,
e-book, front-end web

#Fight and fight to be the top#

Yang Siyong is called an Ever-changing Fairy Dragon because of his adaptive capacity and achievements made from the constantly changing work. Reading his resume at JD, you would believe that it is the case. After joining JD, Siyong assumed the first task to transfer the systems to Java. He said, "When I was assigned with this task, I knew little about it, and luckily there were others who were proficient. We learnt and worked together to finally make it." Behind his humor hides hardships and efforts we cannot imagine.

When he just joined JD, we had backward R & D technology and primitive tools. To turn to Java, the team had to split up to learn advanced technologies and then share internally. Since then, a tradition of sharing took shape. Later, some valuable information and practices shared were also compiled and incorporated into the textbook about best practices for the developers in the JD University.

In 2010, Masong led Siyong to develop the POP Open Platform. At the beginning of establishment of this platform, they needed to link up all systems of JD and provide the third-party talents with the access to these systems. Then the SOA solution prevailed, so they communicated with colleagues in charge of orders, commodities, and after-sale system and requested these colleagues to write the interface so that the interfaces of the old systems could be directly called to display the data. It turned out that the performance was unacceptable. It took 3 seconds to present each page, and thus they had to employ the scheme of heterogeneous database which is popular today. Through repeated attempts, the POP Platform was finally set up. The Platform laid a Java platform foundation for JD and defined various code planning and MVC frameworks, which also had far-reaching impacts on JD's current architecture.

In October of the same year, Siyong began to work with Deng Zhengping and some other colleagues to develop the Mobile App. With the Company's strategic adjustment, the project of e-books kicked off in 2011 and was shouldered by Siyong again. Siyong, who knew nothing about e-books then, cooperated with another Senior Manager, Li Songfeng, to build a team quickly. They spent only 3 months completing the background management program which enabled purchasers to type the books in; after 5 months, the first version of E-book Client was formally released.

Currently, Siyong oversees the web foreground, which is one of the segments with enormous traffic as well as the most requirements from business parties, so its technological work is of great importance.

"After joining JD, I often worked overtime. I have few hobbies. In the past, I liked playing computer games, but now I have stopped; I am also fond of independent travel, mountain climbing, watching movies, and delicious food. As I get older, I rarely listen to music and spend less time on roller skating, which I loved very much in the past," said Siyong.

He can always bring happiness and continuously says something interesting. We often hear his hearty laughter far away. He is popular among girls at the R&D Department. He always positively adapts to the surroundings, embraces changes, keeps learning, introduces new technologies, and maintains an optimistic attitude to work. I think that's why this "Every-changing Fairy Dragon" is so charming.

Coding Maniac: Zhao Gang

Expert in possession of completely proprietary intellectual property rights and proficient in the world-class Z3D individual virtual try-on technology

#to build the most influential technical team #

Zhao Gang has never stopped writing code for 16 years and has totaled over 1 million lines of codes. He deeply studied the assembly language, C/C++ language, and advanced dynamic language. Codes written by Zhao Gang can even revolve around the earth for countless times. He has obtained a doctoral degree in communication and information systems from Beijing University of Aeronautics and Astronautics, and is Chairman of the CTO Club Special Committee sponsored by CSDN, as well as a senior member of iTechClub. After joining JD, he devoted himself to research and development of intelligent mobile ends in the era of cloud computing and oversees the JD Virtual Try-on Project.

The virtual try-on project for iPad is a major innovation project which the Mobile Department is proud of. As the inventor of this core technology, Zhao Gang led the innovation team to develop JD's individual online fitting room based on cutting-edge computer intelligence and simulation technology, and the tool for quick generation of costume elements for the third-party vendors to solve difficulties of individual try-on, low-cost simulation, multi-layered costume matching, low entry threshold for users, and high fluency which have baffled the e-commerce industry for a long time. Six relevant patents for invention have been reviewed by the company and submitted to the Patent Office for review.

Through analysis on the usage data from online users of iPad version, Zhao Gang's team optimized the product's developing route and puts forward a product design thought on the basis of the path of "Look→Try→Do." This train of thought was also applied to design and develop the version for iPhone.

The background costume data making and management tool is one of the keys to the success in the virtual try-on project. Only when the costumes could be made and launched quickly and the costs were acceptable to vendors, the technical difficulty in operation was low, the users and vendors could be attracted. Consequently, Zhao Gang led the design of a costume making and management background system (CMS system) which was another pioneering work and enabled vendors to take part in custom making and launch in person for the first time, thus solving key technical problems such as slowness in costume making and high cost.

The advanced JD individual online fitting room plays an important role in raising the sales of the self-operated and POP Platform's garments and creates huge value for the company, and also plays an active part in the improvement of JD's user liveness and traffic.

Zhao Gang is stuck on studying in the spare time and has a keen interest in new technologies. He often sits in front of the computer all day long to optimize an algorithm, losing sleep and weight. He conducts long-range research on computer graphic images and intelligent technology and has obtained several technical patents and software works. Apart from hiking with his family, he only likes writing codes and has stayed at the front line of development for 16 years.

Speaking of the feelings after joining JD, Zhao Gang said, "As the leader of the e-commerce industry, JD did not achieve its success by accident. Except for the business mode and commercial opportunity, its favorable environment for technology R&D, mechanism encouraging innovations, no fear of failures, and the company's great input for the technology R&D and innovation and care for the technicians really create a broad development space for technical talent. Mass transactions, highly efficient warehousing, and good user experience need the support of technologies. JD has done well, but it can do better in many aspects. This is a place where technical talent can give full play to their professional skills and JD welcomes any capable talent who has lofty ideals."

Father of the Azure Dragon System: Li Dong

Expert in the logistics supply chain system

#Architecture work is a process of continuously reconstructing my thought and pursuing perfect user experience#

There are several systems of the JD R&D Department that we should mention, such as the Transaction System, POP System, and Azure Dragon System. The Azure Dragon System is one of core systems for JD logistics and has more than 30,000 users per day. It needs to deal with all orders to be distributed by JD's logistics department. The leader for the overall architecture of this system is Li Dong.

In 2011, the Azure Dragon team, which was comprised of over 30 members, began to design and develop the Azure Dragon System. Through six months of development and testing, the system was finally put into trial operation in regions of Central China in April 2012. In October, 2012, the Azure Dragon System started to run formally across the country. On the anniversary celebration day on June 18, 2014, this system could deal with over four million orders.

In 2011 when the Azure Dragon System was still at the design stage, the Company lacked SAF support, so Li Dong developed a simple framework himself for the Azure Dragon System. Since then, he continued to summarize and think about the architecture of this system, and extracted a Clover Distributed Task System. Through two years of development in spare time, this system now can support integration of multiple protocols such as Hessian, REStful, Dubbo, and Soap, distributed scheduling and asynchronous call of various protocol services, JMS protocol conversion as well as multi-cluster deployment. Clover replaces the former Work in many systems and strengthens the availability, expansibility, and stability. There are two clusters and another 200 services are running in Cover, covering systems such as warehousing, logistics, and CRM.

The Azure Dragon System is highly complicated, consists of a lot sub-systems, involves forward and reverse processes and must dock with the automation equipment. To make these systems efficiently operate in a cooperative manner and help the field staff make an effective use of the Azure Dragon System, Li Dong and his team made great innovative efforts in the architecture.

1. SOA architecture was completely adopted and a dozen sub-systems were divided by layers to reduce the case of system coupling;

2. The production system is completely separated from the monitoring and query systems;

3. The sorting center is added with the design of caches and offline production to improve the efficiency of production;

4. The business is basically subject to asynchronous processing and the process design which places the physical objects in the first place and information in the secondary place so that the systems enjoy a good fault-tolerant ability;

5. The Azure Dragon System is equipped with many servers and uses highly efficient tools such as automatic deployment and uniform log to facilitate the launch of systems and troubleshooting;

6. The Azure Dragon System is completely subject to automatic testing to guarantee the quality of systems.

These forward-looking designs help JD's R&D Department "win the first place for many times." The Azure Dragon System is designed to process

2 million orders per day. Thanks to its good scalability, the system's current processing capacity has far exceeded its original capacity.

Li Dong is a good man who loves his family, and is obsessed with the NBA and writing code. His six-year-old daughter is going to attend primary school this year. As to the achievements he made in JD, he said, "JD is a stage that makes my dream come true. I grow into an excellent architect here and now I am leading my architect team to meet greater challenges. Trust JD, trust the team and trust ourselves."

A Man Controlling the Cloud: Liu Haifeng

Expert in the distributed system and
architecture of cloud platforms

*#Embrace the changes, meet the
challenges and believe in the power of
technology#*

The distributed file system, distributed cache, and high speed key-value independently developed by JD.com have become the cornerstones of its e-commerce business. As the largest self-supporting e-commerce enterprise, JD spent 10 years absorbing more than 474 million activated users. In 2013, the volume of orders reached up to 323.3 million and the gross merchandise volume (GMV) exceeded RMB 100 billion. Now JD is a member of the global PB-class data management club. To effectively store and manage the PB-class data, a robust and highly efficient large-scale distributed system is crucial.

Liu Haifeng is the man who controls the system and adds the skeleton to the Cloud.

Liu Haifeng, the Director of JD Architecture Committee, the Chief Architect of Cloud Platforms, and the leader of System Technology Department, has obtained a bachelor's degree and a master's degree in computer science from the University of Science and Technology of China. He once worked in Baidu and has expertise in the R&D of Internet infrastructure.

Since 2013, Haifeng led his team to independently research and develop the distributed file system JFS (i.e. Jingdong File System). JFS has been provided with functions such as storage of mass small files, block storage, and a new picture system. Structured storage of meta data and integration with Hadoop are under research and development. He also led the R&D of distributed cache and high-speed NoSQL service which supports more than a hundred businesses and a thousand machines. His spirit of innovation has helped him make continuous breakthroughs in the business, which can be evidenced by design of new message queue, construction of the new service framework, R&D of the new picture system, and realization of CDN upgrading in seconds. Haifeng has had to meet some challenges while making brilliant achievements.

"JD's storeroom system is facing a billion records and billions of pictures of commodities every day. These files are basically stored in KBs. The relational database is poor at processing these small files in a large number as it is difficult to expand and regular deletion is required. In case of open-source storage systems, we must undertake the heavy maintenance workload and carry out customized development," said Liu Haifeng.

After repeated investigation, Haifeng proposed to turn the direction from open-source customized development to independent R&D and expected to realize flexibility and controllability of the systems and obtain long-term and sustainable technical returns. JFS 1.0 which is operating currently possesses strong consistency similar to the Paxos algorithm and features such as no single-point failure, no memory index and transparent compression. It supports operation of over three hundred business applications.

With respect to the key-value storage based on memory, Redis was first used by JD. When the number of independent Redis instances reached several thousand, the difficulty in management of these decentralized systems emerged. "Excessive memory, slowness in startup and difficulty in scaling drive us to innovate based on the former Redis Platform," said Haifeng. At present, JD's memory-based key-vale storage system JimDB has been able to satisfy the demand in e-commerce businesses in the accurate fault monitoring, automatic failover, two-level memory, online vertical expansion and online horizontal scaling. The protocol and the data type of this system are perfectly compatible with Redis — Haifeng's foresight is admirable.

Haifeng spent one year creating a qualitative leap for JD's cloud technology. Currently he is in full charge of basic cloud services for storage, middleware, and elasticity computing. He is Liu Haifeng, who embraces changes, meets challenges, and believes in the power of technology.

Lighthouse: Peng Qing

Expert in the R&D management/
architecture of highly concurrent systems/
machine learning and natural language
processing

**#JD always strives for the best; details
determine success or failure. #**

"E-commerce industry emphasizes both 'electronic' and 'commerce.' As an e-commerce enterprise deeply involved in many retailing links, JD needs large amounts of technical experts to optimize the retail business by technological means. We will build a swift supply chain driven by big data. The shape of 'future retail' will be taken by our hands."

When Peng Qing said this with smile and confidence, the Order Production System under his charge is delivering orders to the warehousing system at a speed of several thousand orders per minute. At the same time, the marketing and price comparison team he leads is continuously providing data references for fellows of JD's Purchase and Sale Department to set prices and promotions.

Before joining JD, he once worked at Internet-based companies such as Kingsoft and Storm and engaged in technical architecture. In Ambow Education, he acted as the leader to set up a complete set of R&D processes and documents meeting the listing specification and cultivate a batch of excellent architects. The first version of prototype for JD's Java Code Specification was compiled by him.

Since 2012, Peng Qing's team began to upgrade the architecture of the Order Fulfillment System. The major target for this task was to build an order fulfillment process system with centralized control that was easy to operate and could support high concurrency and high performance. JD's businesses determined that the order fulfillment processes were complicated with numerous branches. There were more than thirty systems that should be transformed. To catch up with the 618 Anniversary Celebration, they only had one month to accomplish the task. With limited time for an arduous task, all members of the team threw themselves into the project with 200% enthusiasm. Everyone tried hard to fill the gaps of the proposal and we often saw some of them up to their ears in heated arguments for a process branch at the resting area, but after a while, they ran back to their positions for encoding. Within one month, all team members had to work until midnight every day, but no one complained. One day, the overtime working ended, and when they prepared to go home, a handsome guy stopped everyone and asked them to take a group photo as the evidence that he had really worked overtime in the company to show to his wife. Then Peng Qing felt guilty, but was also proud of such an excellent, united, and positive team.

In 2013 when Peng Qing took over the price comparison team, this team was at a loss as the price comparison system could be seemingly used for providing reports after fetching the prices. It was a limbic system with a lot of trivial details. The confused atmosphere was followed by the dismissal and job transfer of many members. After taking over the price comparison team, Peng Qing found a direction for the team through communications with the team and business parties. He set two goals: the first one was architecture upgrading, i.e. greatly improving various indexes of the entire system, in particular the capture rate of the crawler, matching accuracy rate and recall rate through optimization of the crawler algorithm and matching algorithms so as to guarantee the system's data quality and sharply strengthen the confidence in the team; secondly, the train of thought with "pricing" and "selection" as the product direction was determined and an innovative product "Commodity Wisdom" was developed. The historical data was utilized for data mining and machine learning, and constructing the price model and selection model, and the data from external competitors was applied to provide those in charge of purchasing and sales with reasonable pricing and selection suggestions. "Commodity Wisdom" was praised by the business parties and laid a solid foundation for the future development of the team.

An architect should act as a lighthouse to set goals for the team and be responsible for architecture upgrading and setting up more convenient and quick systems, and meanwhile lead the team to fight hard. Such architect can be described as "talented!"

It is worth mentioning that Peng Qing's wife is a doctor of natural language processing. Under her influence, Peng Qing also conducted some researches relating to the natural language processing in the spare time and the major direction is the identification of named entities. "Every successful man has a great woman behind him."

OCD Patient: Zhang Kefang

Expert in infrastructure management and
network operation and maintenance

#Innovations are fruits of OCD#

Behind the success in every technical innovation, there are countless failures. Work needs "OCD." Forcing himself to be better and perfect — that has been the experience of Zhang Kefang since he joined JD. In his view, there are no unsolvable tough issues.

After Kefang joined JD in March 2010, he was mainly responsible for the architecture design and operation and maintenance management of JD's data center network, self-established CDN service, domain name resolution service, and load balancing service, and the works relating to the infrastructures of system operation and maintenance and server resource management. He is the direct participant of early construction and development of JD's operation and maintenance system, and laid the foundation for multiple technical frameworks and operation and maintenance modes which are currently applied by the Operation and Maintenance Department.

Under the leadership of Kefang, JD's self-established CDN service has been expanded from 3 nodes in early 2010 to dozens of nodes throughout the country now, and the capacity of the band width has increased from several G to several hundred G, with earthshaking changes both in scale and architecture. In the latter half of 2012, the commercial hardware load balancing and the Squid structure for CDN architecture were replaced by the open-source HAProxy used for seven-layer loading and ATS (Apache Traffic Server) as the cache software. Kefang empowered operation and maintenance of CDN to Jianxing and served as an architect to take a part in this project. In this period, Sixing worked to optimize the performance of HAProxy, such as using network cards with multiple queues to raise the performance of open core protocol stacks under a mutli-core CUP, thus avoiding locked overheads caused by multiple process of HAProxy scrambling for users in the kernel mode; and amending HAProxy source codes to reduce the CPU usage rate under the user mode; modifying Linux Kernel to solve the problem of large protocol stack overheads caused by too many VIPs in a single machine. "These known problems which have been solved are far from meeting the demands from the rapid development of JD, and we should continue to work for development and optimization," said Kefang, who is ready for the coming challenges with great passion.

In 2012, various bottlenecks and problems of scaling emerged due to huge traffic into JD in the aspect of the performance of stability of commercial hardware load balance. Kefang then started to organize upgrading of the online hardware load balance. Through secondary development and optimization within half a year, the architecture of the load balance and the performance optimization of the loading software had taken shape. The open source software LVS+HAProxy+Nginx was used to replace the commercial hardware load balance. Starting from the end of 2013, smooth transfer of the online hardware load began. So far, 90% of JD's business is operating in this system, which has stably lived up to the traffic impacts from Double 11 in 2013 and the 618 Promotional Campaign in 2014. "Load balance is the service entry of all business systems and we are still refining and optimizing it. In the future, it will support all business systems of JD to pass through the 618 Anniversary Celebration and Double 11 one after another," said Kefang with full confidence. A man who foretells things, nips in the bud, and forces himself to be the best can be called a talent in JD!

"JD is a platform witnessing the rapid development of technologies. After joining JD, my personal technical skill has improved quickly; I fall into the pits I've never fell into before and use the technologies and equipment which I've never tried before. The innovations are created by forces and fruits of 'OCD.' I force myself to find solutions to all problems and try my best to do the work. If there are no problems or bottlenecks and everyone is confident in his system, no one will take the initiative to come up with better and more efficient solutions. JD has numerous innovations awaiting us and countless pits to be buried. Looking into the future, I expect 'OCD' to infect everyone in the team," said Kefang.

The Soul of Databases: Fan Jian'gang

Expert in the distributed database and
operation and maintenance

#Build a No.1 database technology team#

Fang Jian'gang joined JD in 2007 and took charge of the operations and maintenance of databases and management of the DBA team. Up to now, he has managed more than 2,000 database servers and accumulated rich management experience in large scale, high concurrency, mass data access and big data application; moreover, he has also researched and developed the "Blue Dolphin" distributed database system with proprietary intellectual property rights, and submitted a dozen applications for database technology patents.

Fan Jian'gang has worked in JD for seven years and this period sees continuous development and refinement of JD's databases.

Fan Jian'gang first took part in the management of the SQL Server, which was also the earliest and most widely applied database. More than one hundred servers applied the replica technique and replicated over eight billion commands a day, and this figure was among the top three of the OLTP system. The DBA team led by Jian'gang has conducted multiple innovations for replica technologies, some of which are absorbed by the International Data Bank of Microsoft. DBA, with the courage to bring forth new ideas and continuing researches, replicated various advanced technologies such as clustering, log shipping, and mirroring to the latest Always On and memory databases and integrated them into JD's business system, achieving good results. It is still stably running in much of the core business now and supporting various business links from commodities, orders, storage, and distribution.

With upgrading of JD's overall technical architecture, the databases were gradually transferred to MySQL, and wide application of sharding exerted great challenges against the efficiency of R & D and management of operation and maintenance. In face of the challenges, Fang Jian'gang led the database team to research and develop a distributed database system with proprietary intellectual property rights, called Blue Dolphin. The Blue Dolphin could automatically split up and horizontally expand the database system, support writing-reading abruption and load balance, which played an important role in improving the system performance. The Blue Dolphin was formally released on March 28, 2013 and used for the Order Track System; the Blue Dolphin 2.0 was released on April 8, 2014 and has been applied to partially important systems. A dozen patents have been awarded.

The success in Blue Dolphin and the successful application of the SQL Server advanced technology dramatically improved the performance of JD's database, raised the development efficiency and significantly reduced the cost for database operation and maintenance, indicating that JD's technology level has reached a new high in the industry.

Facing such remarkable achievements, Fan Jian'gang believes in the famous "Inverted Triangle" theory: brand, KPI, supply chain, or user experience are all based on the "team."

"The most generous salaries are offered to top performers and top performers can create the greatest values. We welcome all excellent talents to join JD and you will obtain greater room for self-improvement and bring your talent into play. Come and join us, and we will respect and treat each other frankly and take advice with open minds to work together to build the #1 database technical team and create a bright future."

Data Expert: Liu Sizhe

Expert in optimization of algorithms for the recommendation system and big data

#To be passionate makes us positive#

A graduate from the School of Statistics of People's University of China in 2005, he once worked at Asiainfo-Linkage BOC and Digital China Sitech DSS and was mainly responsible for providing telecom operators with services such as data mining and business consultation.

When he set foot in JD with full confidence in 2012, he was still surprised by JD's data. Only the Internet could generate various detailed data with ease and he could not help being attracted by the sea of data.

"I was still working at the National Convention Center then, and I clearly remembered that I got off work and took Subway No. 8 that day. When I thought that I could use so much data and worked on various models the next day, I could not help laughing." For him, a data expert, JD is doubtlessly the main wave of data science and heaven for a data scientist. Such good conditions, certainly, can drive him to struggle hard.

With JD's recommendations system moving from 1.0 to 2.0, the time arrived in late 2013. The architecture of the new recommendations system had been basically stable, but there was still certain gap between the actual values it created for the company and the anticipated values. How to improve the efficiency of the system and convoy JD's rapid development became the problem he was most concerned about. Through deliberation, he employed the following methods to improve the recommendation effect.

1. Take data analysis as the tool to strengthen the understanding of data and business;
2. Integrate different types and dimensions of data sources based on the user feedback data;
3. Test the effects of different algorithms (even parameters) at different data sources.

To validate the above-mentioned methods and gradually figure out the optimal strategy, he led the team to conduct over a hundred experiments which covered almost all recommendation positions. In the process of optimization, indexes such as the click rate, click conversion rate, and coverage rate were all greatly improved and good effects were achieved as expected.

Someone said, if you put the confidence in yourself, you will be powerful forever. He has kept creating brilliant achievements again and again with his full energy.

As one of the leaders for algorithms in the recommendations team, he headed the team to increase the proportion of orders brought by the recommendation system for PC to all the orders by 100% and the amount of sales by 67%.

He led the offline recommendation algorithm team to improve the proportion of orders brought by the recommendation system for the Mobile End from 0.5% to more than 6%.

In the spare time, because of his interests, he initiated the Data Science Salon and took part in holding China R Language Conference.

He is Liu Sizhe, a real data expert.

Thinker: Sui Jianfeng

Expert in the website transaction and architecture

#Embrace the changes! JD's business, technology and management are all developing and changing quickly, and we need to positively embrace the changes instead of waiting the advent of changes.#

"I have a house and a car, and obtained a registered permanent residence of Xicheng for my child, whose school is also determined. It seems that there is almost no life pressure for me and I can do anything I am interested in. I am very satisfied with the current working status," said Jianfeng with a smile.

Sui Jianfeng, as JD's architect, is mainly in charge of research and upgrading of the architecture and core technologies relating to the transaction platform, including major entry pages such as JD Mall's homepage, commodity pages, list pages, and channel pages. Before joining JD, he once worked at Sina and Sohu for six years, and engaged in work on Internet technology, accumulating rich experience.

With this rich industry experience, he gave his talents into full play at JD, a broader stage. One project which he is proud of is the real-time price realization and this project enabled the display of upgraded prices in seconds.

At the beginning, JD's prices were displayed by pictures and used CDN caches where serious problems existed.

1. Excessive resources were occupied;

2. High frequency of price upgrading resulted in a high penetration rate of CDN and very low hit rate;

3. Many commodity prices may exist in one page and every price should occupy a separate request, thus creating a great volume of request resources.

In face of these problems, Sui Jianfeng calmly analyzed the situation, and changed the price display by pictures to real-time price realization. He adopted Nginx+Lua+Redis and reduced the number of servers from a hundred to ten, achieving the real-time performance in seconds. Requests for a combination of multiple prices were also available, thus sharply driving the volume of request resources.

Another important project was separation of the pre-sale second killing system from the primary transaction process. This project significantly reduced the number of orders for hot commodities maliciously placed by dealers and users and lowered the system overhead and risks caused by robot refreshing.

Then Huawei Honor 3C products gained greater popularity, many dealers continuously made panic purchases of these products by continuously refreshing JD's transaction system. In particular, when the promotional campaigns were held, the visitor volume of the transaction system may increase by 100 to 1000 times, thus bringing very heavy pressure to the system. Dealers made panic purchases by machines, so normal users were unable to make a successful purchase. The original intention of these campaigns was to surrender part of the profit to users of JD, but these products were grabbed by dealers who then raised the price and sold them to the final users.

In face of such severe status quo, Sui Jianfeng considered that the complexity of transaction systems made this problem hard to solve. He then originally separated this special business from the primary transaction process, and drove all future sales promotion modes accessible to new pre-sale second-killing process.

The facts proved that the separation of the pre-sale second-killing system from the primary business processes reduced the proportion of orders placed by dealers from 99% to 10%; partial business processes were changed to control the frequency of system refreshing by robots and protect the systems, thus more resources of the systems could be used for more complicated risk control logic and to accurately identify the users. This remarkable achievement won him the first prize for technical innovations in the second quarter of 2014.

Sui Jianfeng, who is pragmatic and is good at innovations, cooperation, and thinking, brings the architecture of JD's transaction systems to new heights. Sui Jianfeng not only has first-class skill, but also is pleased to share the experience he gained through hard work.

He has often said, we should combine the business to develop technologies and apply core technologies to core businesses. Think while acting and think while practicing. For example, some problems could not be solved well. Traffic shunt could be employed and data comparison or online data mirroring pressure measurement could guarantee the reliability of the systems. Furthermore, the technologies took the priority and many systems had a lot of historical problems. Technically, solutions must be provided prior to the appearance of bottles and problems, and then we should choose a good opportunity to apply new technologies to the online business systems. However, this required at least three months or half a year of technical reserves.

"Think while practicing," and it is a common feeling of many talents who join JD. JD is developing so fast, so most of the time the technologies are developed to meet the business demands. That's why we need thinkers and practitioners like Jianfeng. Only repeated attempts can lead us to a road.

Problem Solver: Wang Chunming

Expert in the data processing and site search

#Build a team with the strongest force of execution#

"JD's technical team may not be the team most capable of R &D, but it must be a team with the strongest force of execution," said Wang Chunming, who is proud of the team and has confidence in the future of JD.

When Wang Chunming just joined in August, 2011, he was a Development Manager of site research and responsible for site research of commodities, background of list pages, and vertical search. Since then, he organized and participated in the upgrading of search architecture for many times, but what impressed him most was the first project for upgrading. That was the first large project after he joined JD.

Back then JD adopted Lucene to search and encountered many problems about user experience that could not be solved. The target of this project was independent R&D of a search engine to replace Lucene. The major challenge was that for the cut-over, it was necessary to guarantee the system stability and support the old business in the system and the new business added during development of new system version; and it had to be assured that the user experience of new systems was better than that of old systems. However, the search team had less than 10 members, 1/3 of who were interns. The difficult situation did not stop their enthusiasm for challenges. Wang Chunming quickly organized personnel to split the tasks and everyone was assigned with a content segment. In case of any problems, everyone gathered near the office table for discussions. If no conclusion was drawn after discussions, they would try to find various solutions from technical forums. Many existing problems relating to performance and high memory occupancy in new systems were solved in this way. Later, when the new version sorting encountered Bad Case, they adjusted the parameters repeatedly, found new models, and then conducted regression testing again and again. Finally, new architecture replaced Lucene and was mainly applied to many scenarios such as main search and list page.

This upgrading improved the system stability and scalability. While the business demands were met, the pressure caused by increasing data size and page views on the search system were eliminated. The system withstood multiple tests from the 618 Anniversary Celebration and Double 11, and operated stably.

The real-time indexing project also impressed Wang Chunming. As the quantity of commodities on JD's platform surged, the function realization based on the timestamp increment became slower and slower and failed to meet the business demands. Therefore, Wang Chunming led the team to engage in the real-time indexing project, which would amend the increment indexing to message realization and the difficulty mainly lied in the reduction of system performance caused by real-time indexing. When the indexing instantaneity was improved, they needed to lower the impact on the performance. Consequently, Wang Chunming optimized the index structure and query flow, and finally controlled the delay of commodity presentation at the search pages within 10 seconds after the system was launched, thus successfully solving the problem of long delay and reducing the performance loss, but the cost of online servers did not increase dramatically.

Three years ago, Wang Chunming left a chip design company and joined JD, but he never expected that he would make such great achievements in a completely new industry and company. Now he is the leader of site search and takes charge of the important applications including site search, mobile search background, Wechat commodity search background, Jshop search/ list background and PC/mobile list page background. These pages embrace more than 100 million views and create over 70% of JD's GMV.

"After I joined JD, our platforms expanded quickly and raised problems one after another against our R&D process. Majority of these problems only existed in JD and lacked good solutions. It is painful to solve such problems, and sometimes I think I can hold them. However, our team provides me with firm support and we finally solved these problems." These experiences made Wang Chunming grow. "JD's platforms are still expanding and challenging problems are increasing. I expect more talents to join our team and we can solve these problems together. We will become stronger and stronger in the process of problem solving," said Wang Chunming, who is looking forward to more challenges.

Wheel of the Four-in-hand: Chen Chenggang

Expert in the basic operation and
maintenance

*#We don't lack the way to do things,
but the resolution and boldness to press
forward.#*

In 2013, JD announced its grand strategy of four-in-hand in the future. For Chen Chenggang, one of the founders of JD's Operation and Maintenance Department, this meant that he and his operation and maintenance team — the wheel of this four-in-hand must withstand the pressure caused by rapidly running four horses. This was a great challenge, and every link of construction of core networks, CDN system, DNS system, load balance system, and infrastructure was the key to guarantee stability and availability of websites and various businesses.

Facing this situation, Chen Chenggang, who had worked in Beijing for 14 years, just said indifferently, "I have experienced panic, anxiety, and indifference, and I am capable of devising strategies within a command tent."

Chen Chenggang joined JD in 2007 as a developer. JD began to establish the Operation and Maintenance Department in 2008 to independently manage the application operation and maintenance and the network environment. Then he switched to the operation and maintenance and started to establish the Operation and Maintenance Department as one of the founders.

Back then, the Operation and Maintenance Department only had the capability of server management and network management. In 2008, JD's website was subject to comprehensive revision from the technical architecture to front-end display and the difficulty of operation and maintenance was improved by several classes. Chenggang had to undertake almost all system launches and handling failures alone. With seven years of R&D experience, he could quickly locate and solve problems and failures of various systems. However, .Net+SQL Server technology was employed to all systems at JD then, resulting in complicated maintenance and impossibility to maintain in batch. Sometimes he even directly modified the developers' codes and SQL statements to solve online failures. He experienced extreme pains and rapid growth in 2008.

After the website revision, JD needed the planning and deployment of CDN. At the very beginning, he didn't want to build independently and attempted to use third-party services because his lacked enough technical strength. However, a failure completely changed his idea: an accident occurring in the machine room caused the website to be inaccessible for an hour. Since then, the idea of self-establishment of CDN kept hovering over his mind.

In early 2009, the first self-built CDN node was born in Tianjin. It was a hard step as technical selection, network planning, software development, testing, deployment, launch, and troubleshooting were all completed independently bit by bit. From this CDN node, JD gradually refined its CDN system. Now, CDN nodes have spread throughout the country. The bearing capacity of the single node increased from 1-2G to 10 gigabits, and the nodes could bear more than 20G. Customers across the nation could visit the nearby system based on regions they are in, then the user experience was comprehensively improved. With the effort made by Chenggang and his team, JD successfully set up a unique CDN system with JD's characteristics!

It may beyond your imagination that at a website with an annual turnover reaching hundreds of million RMB yuan, the core equipment for the production environment network where it was operating was merely a Tplink switch, and it was actually the case. To remove this mine buried in the heart and avoid such mines in the future, a long-range network planning was essential. JD's business developed at a rate exceeding 200% per year and since 2009, the number of servers, switches and equipment cabinets increased substantially. After the mine was just cleared, the network development failed to keep pace with the Company's growth rate. The Company's business developed too quickly, bringing a continuous increase of system pressure, and the only solution was transformation. Despite of a sea of troubles, thistles, and thorns, Chenggang believed that nothing was unsolvable. Expansion of bandwidth, change of architecture, network switchover, transfer of application system, and several rounds of equipment and system migration were conducted to cut over smoothly, without interruption of data transmission and influence on the front-end client access. Over the years, the bearing capacity of data centers developed from less than 200 servers and 100M core equipment to 10-gigabit network environment now. The capacity of servers and network throughput had increased by thousands of times. Great wars came one after another from "timed panic buying" to "second kill," "8.15" price war and annual "618" and "Double 11." Every large promotional campaign was a test for colleagues of the Operation and Maintenance Department, including Chenggang.

"Persistence is what I uphold these years when I work for operations and maintenance. Operations and maintenance is to be continuously optimized, and do and refine this without stop." This northeasterner is straightforward, indomitable, and tenacious, so he can shoulder the heavy burden of the wheel of four-in-hand. As the saying goes, how fast and far a carriage can run depends on not only the velocity of horses, but also the quality of wheels.

JD can move forward so fast because there are numerous colleagues working at the Operation and Maintenance Department like Chenggang who drive this carriage.

Intimate Lover: Liu Shangkun

Expert in the data search referral

#You needn't to be afraid of making mistakes and have chances of trial and error here. The only thing you need to worry is that you may lag behind the growth rate of the platform.#

After joining JD in 2011, Shangkun was assigned to undertake the R&D work as to search referrals and held the post of the head of JD's search engine. The search engine independently researched and developed by the team he led was taken online in early 2012. In the latter half of 2012, Shangkun led the optimization of JD's advertisement algorithm and became the founder of JD's advertising system. The advertisement platform was launched in 2013. Since 2014, Shangkun undertook the task for the R&D of architecture, algorithms, and product operations of search referral in the Data Department.

Three years later, with his own effort, he was promoted from a supervisor to Deputy Director and the search referral team grew into a large team with 70 members. He and his team had made indelible contributions to mining and application of big data at JD.

In 2011, open-source systems were used for search at JD. Under his leadership, in early 2012, JD launched a self-developed search engine Jsearch 1.0, which, dramatically improved the performance and helped engineers to develop algorithms with facility. After a series of algorithms were launched, the conversion rate of the search referral was doubled. Since then, Jsearch 2.0 was worked out, and currently supports the search and category services at JD's Web End, mobile platform, Wechat/Mobile QQ. Its daily search volume had exceeded one hundred million and JD's search engine was then the fifth largest in China. In middle 2014, Shangkun led the team to make persistent efforts and launched Jsearch 3.0, a distributed search engine that could bear mass SKUs. Separation of sorting and architecture was realized and this rock-solid search engine enabled business to develop better and faster.

In 2012, Shangkun took charge of the advertising algorithm team and became the founder of JD's advertising system. The advertisement system was brought online in early 2013, and created a large amount of net income for the Company. In this process, CTR prediction algorithm and ad sorting algorithm of which R&D was led by him played a crucial role in the improvement of click rate and income.

With their effort, RPM (GMV generated per 1,000 requests) of the referral engine was doubled. GMV generated by the referral was improved by 300%. Meanwhile, they also completed development of distributed search. Currently, the proportion of orders contributed by PC and the Mobile End reached about 50%, taking a leading position in the industry.

From complete dependence on the external search to the construction of JD's search referral engine and platform, people working in JD represented by Shangkun explored a unique road growing out of nothing. "After joining JD, I grew together with this platform." Recalling the past, Shangkun considered that his greatest harvest was to see the team developing rapidly under his leadership. For example, many new colleagues who were not specialized in the referral search became experts in this field within six to twelve months.

Shield of 618: Wang Xiaozhong

Expert in the architecture of transaction systems

#everything can be achieved through technologies#

In speaking of Wang Xiaozhong, we must mention two major promotional campaigns every year: the 618 and the Double 11. These two sale promotions were tightly bound to his road of becoming a technical talent in JD.

As an R&D worker, he was most afraid of and expected challenges caused by high traffic and high concurrency from the two promotional campaigns. Within less than 1 month after Xiaozhong joined JD, he took a part in the preparatory works for the Double 11 Campaign that year, but this experience made him feel bad.

Back then, the systems architecture was backward, and the systems broke down continuously on Double 11. The technical seniors were to blame and there was a rumor that servers must be doubled. As an architect of transaction systems, Xiaozhong thought that it was a crying shame and swore to bring about an upswing. However, the transaction systems were facing two difficulties: all systems had versions based on Java and C#; and servitization was incomplete and a lot of key systems could not be horizontally expanded.

Fortunately, the whole transaction team had high morale. Technically, they set up a complete monitoring system for the transaction systems to define bottlenecks of current systems; secondly, they pragmatically analyzed the transaction systems based on C#, treated different cases differently, and designed all key systems to support horizontal scaling; lastly, they worked together with the others to complete architecture planning, and worked out the first version of Java-based transaction system. In the 618 Anniversary Celebration the next year, the transaction systems operated stably and made Xiaozhong and his team relieved. The systems also passed through the Double 11 smoothly, proving the reasonableness of system architecture again.

Since then, Xiaozhong was rated as the expert in dealing with 618 and Double 11 and he led the team for transaction systems to continuously be upgraded and embrace another greater challenge.

In the 618 Anniversary Celebration this year, i.e. the first 618 after the company's listing, everyone was under mountainous pressure. It was worth celebrating that the transaction system was normal and operated stably. In other words, the transaction system was the most important for JD's website. With the stable transaction system, we felt relieved.

For JD, Xiaozhong said, "If you like challenges, please join JD, we are the perfect stage for you. Both the infrastructure and the system architecture calls for talent. If you are pragmatic, please join JD because there are many practical system problems to be solved here. You can find the sense of achievement brought by completion of impossible missions within a limited time here. Join JD, and you will not fight alone. Fighting with the team members with the same values may be of great pleasure in your life."

Innovation Pioneer: Yang Kai

Expert in the e-commerce business architecture

#we are ordinary people, and can succeed by wisdom, perspiration and making greater efforts than others. #

Before joining JD's R&D Department in March 2010, Yang Kai was engaged in the technical work relating to the Internet and e-commerce. When he worked at JD, he designed products, wrote codes, managed projects, led teams, and took charge of dozens of successful projects, so he had rich experience in the e-commerce business and technologies. In March, 2011, through a struggle, he obtained the chance to attend the First Rotation Training for Managerial Staff. Within over one month of work at different business positions, he learned about all company business, and the work at the front line helped him better understand users' demands and problems. This chance also made him find the favorite work orientation: e-commerce business architecture.

The first project he took charge of was construction of POP platform vendor and commodity system. He finally designed a world-leading data structure for commodities and categories, which took the vendors' mass commodities and changeable category structures into full consideration, introduced the concept of vendor and shop into JD's system for the first time and laid a foundation for overall development of POP business.

With the POP platform vendor and commodity system maturing, a new market favorite emerged, namely group buying. In late November, 2010, he was assigned with the task, and was required to complete R&D and launch of the group buying system before December 15 the same year. Back then, there were only 3 R&D persons, including him. He was very clear that at this point, the company was pursuing business expansion as early as possible, instead of a perfect system. Through analysis, he purchased a PHP-based group buying system and transformed this system to connect with JD's systems for users, commodities, payments, and orders. After 3 weeks of R&D and testing, the group buying system was surprisingly put into service on December 14, 2010 and saved time for JD to occupy a place in the group buying market.

Yang Kai is always passionate about the innovative products. By the end of 2011, he started to lead the whole product line of JSHOP (JSHOP system is a platform for decoration and display of special events for PC and mobile end, and vendor's shops). The product was mainly comprised by the special events and vendor shops. The Special Event System became the only entry to launch promotional campaigns, special shopping, and main venue for 618 and Double 11; the Vendor Shop System was the facade of all vendors at JD and the major entry for vendors to obtain orders. With implementation of the company's strategy for mobilization, the event and shop platform for mobile end were also put into operation this year. He firmly believed that JSHOP project would create values for users, vendors, and JD with its wider service scope and more product innovations.

"During these years in JD, I have made significant progress in all aspects of the technologies and management. The most important harvest is that I become a person who keeps promises, pursues cooperation and mutual benefits and thinks about problems from the perspective of users. Based on this, I have had a chance to work at core positions to improve my capacity and do well at various positions. JD is a stage that can make dreams come true and have countless chances for you. You can also embrace challenges and witness how great the values created by technologies are," said Yang Kairu.

Author: Liu Jiarui